Michael Roskin (handwritten signature)

PRENTICE-HALL
CONTEMPORARY COMPARATIVE POLITICS SERIES
JOSEPH LaPALOMBARA, Editor

published

COMPARATIVE LEGISLATURES • *J. Blondel*

COMPARATIVE LEGAL CULTURES • *Henry W. Ehrmann*

LIMITED GOVERNMENT: A COMPARISON • *Carl J. Friedrich*

COMPARATIVE REVOLUTIONARY MOVEMENTS • *Thomas H. Greene*

POLITICS WITHIN NATIONS • *Joseph LaPalombara*

SOLDIERS IN POLITICS:
MILITARY COUPS AND GOVERNMENTS • *Eric A. Nordlinger*

THE COMPARATIVE STUDY OF POLITICAL ELITES • *Robert D. Putnam*

OTHER GOVERNMENTS OF EUROPE:
SWEDEN, SPAIN, ITALY, YUGOSLAVIA, AND EAST GERMANY • *Michael Roskin*

COMPARATIVE POLITICAL CORRUPTION • *James C. Scott*

THE CRAFT OF POLITICAL RESEARCH: A PRIMER • *W. Phillips Shively*

COMPARATIVE POLITICAL VIOLENCE • *Fred R. von der Mehden*

forthcoming

COMPARATIVE URBAN POLITICS • *Robert Fried and Francine Rabinovitz*

COMPARATIVE POLITICAL IDEOLOGIES • *Peter Gourevitch*

COMPARATIVE BUREAUCRACY • *Martin Landau*

COMPARATIVE ELECTIONS AND
POLITICAL DEMOCRACY • *Douglas W. Rae and Michael Taylor*

ERIC A. NORDLINGER

Brown University
Written under the auspices of the
Center for International Affairs,
Harvard University

Prentice-Hall, Inc.
Englewood Cliffs, N. J. 07632

SOLDIERS IN POLITICS

MILITARY COUPS AND GOVERNMENTS

Library of Congress Cataloging in Publication Data
Nordlinger, Eric A.
    Soldiers in politics.

    Bibliography: p.
    Includes index.
    1. Military government. 2. Civil supremacy
over the military. 3. Underdeveloped areas—
Politics and government. I. title.
JF1820.N67   322'.5   76-40016
ISBN 0-13-822163-4

SOLDIERS IN POLITICS:
MILITARY COUPS AND GOVERNMENTS
Eric A. Nordlinger

© 1977 by Prentice-Hall, Inc., Englewood Cliffs, New Jersey

Printed in the United States of America

10 9 8 7 6 5 4 3 2 1

PRENTICE-HALL INTERNATIONAL, INC., London
PRENTICE-HALL OF AUSTRALIA PTY. LIMITED, Sydney
PRENTICE-HALL OF CANADA, LTD., Toronto
PRENTICE-HALL OF INDIA PRIVATE LIMITED, New Delhi
PRENTICE-HALL OF JAPAN, INC., Tokyo
PRENTICE-HALL OF SOUTHEAST ASIA PTE. LTD., Singapore
WHITEHALL BOOKS, LIMITED, Wellington, New Zealand

for Joseph Mayer

CONTENTS

FOREWORD ix

PREFACE xi

1 THE STUDY OF PRAETORIANISM 1

2 A POLITICAL SOCIOLOGY OF THE OFFICER CORPS 30

3 THE COUP D'ETAT 63

4 OFFICERS AS GOVERNORS 107

5 NATIONAL INTEGRATION AND ECONOMIC CHANGE 147

6 AN ASSESSMENT OF PRAETORIANISM AND ITS AFTERMATH 189

BIBLIOGRAPHY 211

INDEX 221

FOREWORD

The series in Contemporary Comparative Politics is unabashedly committed to several goals. We assume that the undergraduate student is by and large not interested in becoming a political scientist but is planning to follow other pursuits. This being so, we aim to expose these students to aspects of politics that will be salient to them throughout their lives. In order to make this point stick though, we believe it is necessary to avoid using the so-called "grand theories" of political science as organizing frameworks. Such "theories" are subtle forms of misinformation; they mislead students—and sometimes others —into believing that we know more about political systems and processes than is actually the case.

It is also our assumption that only the rare undergraduate wishes to master the workings of any single political system. Even where such interest may be present, the study of single countries rarely leads to anything resembling systematic comparative analysis. Therefore, we have sought to focus on a wide range of interesting and important aspects of politics that individual volumes in this series treat comparatively.

We also believe that those aspects of politics included in this series should be treated from both an institutional and a behavioral perspective. Political science will remain a hobbled discipline as long as those who write or consume it elect one of these orientations or the other. Political science will become or remain an arid discipline if we neglect to treat the normative side of politics. The authors of this series are neither bare-facts empiricists nor "cloud-ninety" political moralists. They are prepared to use whatever forms of comparative analysis are available to permit us better to understand the relationships between political institutions, behavior, values, and man's condition. The range of understanding we seek to achieve is reflected in the core of the series (Joseph LaPalombara, *Politics within Nations*) and in the titles of individual series volumes.

Because no series can encompass all areas of politics, we have had to make choices. Some of these choices introduce the reader to aspects of politics not often treated on a comparative basis. Our published volumes on political violence, political corruption, and legal culture, and this book on the military and politics, fall into this category. Other choices expose the reader to more traditional aspects of government and politics treated in a fresh comparative perspective. Series volumes on national legislatures, bureaucracies, and elections fall into this category.

Eric Nordlinger in this volume gives us an unusual perspective on military elites as they intervene in those aspects of the political process considered to be the jurisdiction of civilians. Nordlinger has put together a number of provocative theoretical ideas that help us to understand—the when, how, and why—the emergence and characteristic modes of governance of the praetorian state. These ideas are developed with extensive illustrations from the actual experiences of about a dozen countries, including Brazil, Peru, Nigeria, Ghana, Egypt, Pakistan, Burma, and South Korea, and references to some two dozen others. Anyone who wants a better understanding of the causes and consequences of military political intervention will be rewarded by reading this book.

This volume does not contain statistical information on a global scale. It does not pretend to "explain" the military's intervention in politics wherever it may have occurred in time and space. But it does deepen our knowledge about a method of seizing or transferring political power—and of governance—that is endemic among contemporary non-Western nations. Military coups are now so frequent and widespread they must be considered as significant as elections. Comparative political analysis is enriched by Nordlinger's sophisticated treatment of this important but neglected subject.

JOSEPH LAPALOMBARA

New Haven

PREFACE

More than two-thirds of the countries of Latin America, Asia, Africa, and the Middle East have experienced varying levels of military intervention since 1945. The frequency with which non-Western officers have entered the political arena has provided me with the very real challenge of analyzing military intervention in a general fashion without losing sight of particular cases. I have consequently written about both the theory *and* practice of soldiers in politics. The book is theoretical insofar as it offers descriptive and explanatory generalizations that are applicable to the great majority of military coups, governments, and regimes. The book is about the practice of military intervention in that these generalizations do not rely upon abstract or vague concepts. They remain close to the political "ground," to the attitudes, motives, goals, and behavior of the so-called praetorian soldiers, using numerous examples to illustrate and to give meaning and empirical support to the generalizations.

In accounting for the patterns of military intervention I have combined two kinds of explanatory factors that are too often kept separate. There are the internal features of the military, which include its hierarchical structure, level of professionalism, and corporate interests, as well as the officers' class backgrounds, communal identities, self-image, and political attitudes. The external or "environmental" variables include the actions of civilian chief executives, the performance and legitimacy of civilian governments, the politicization of workers and peasants, the severity of communal conflicts, the extent of socioeconomic modernization, and the rate of economic growth. These two kinds of variables are brought together in order to understand the officers' behavior patterns from the vantage point of the soldiers themselves, for the soldiers' political options and decisions are limited and shaped by both types of variables.

Several writers have pointed out that far greater attention has been accorded the overthrow of civilian governments, the coup itself and the events leading up to it, than to the praetorians after they have seized power. Most coups have marked political and economic consequences, but what the soldiers do after taking control of the government—how a society is governed—is usually of greater consequence than the identity of the governors and the manner in which they have attained their positions. This book therefore gives somewhat greater emphasis to the officers as governors than as coup makers. It deals with the structure of military regimes, their duration, the officers' governing style, and the performance of military governments in legitimizing themselves, governing in a noncoercive manner, promoting modernizing and progressive economic changes, and averting communal and class-based violence. Indeed, the final chapter takes us beyond the period of military government to examine its impact upon the structure and performance of the civilian regimes that are installed after the soldiers return to the barracks.

Despite their well-intentioned efforts to be as objective as possible, social scientists often "find" exactly what they were looking for at the beginning of their inquiries. The working assumptions with which they began turn out to be confirmed, at least so it is argued. Such claims are sometimes warranted, which is also to say that sometimes they are not. I would therefore alert the reader to the possibility that yet another social scientist may have inadvertently fallen into this easily sprung trap. For I began analyzing the phenomenon of military intervention with two working assumptions that have, I will suggest, been borne out by a reading of the literature, the available cross-national data, and the reasoning that was used to answer the questions I posed for myself. At the outset I tentatively assumed that it is possible to make general statements about military intervention as both a characteristic and a distinctive phenomenon. It is a characteristic phenomenon in that most military officers, governments, and regimes exhibit a good number of common features. It is a distinctive phenomenon insofar as there are notable differences between military and civilian elites, governments, and regimes.

Judging from past experience, it is nearly impossible to identify the specific "origins" of an article or book. That is not, however, true in this instance. During the 1968–1969 academic year I wrote a paper in which I tested various hypotheses about governmental performance in a quantitative fashion with a set of cross-national data. Only four of the one hundred and twenty pages dealt with military governments. Yet Amos Perlmutter, who was then also a research associate at Harvard University's Center for International Affairs, waxed sufficiently enthusiastic about these few pages to encourage me to develop them. That effort resulted in an article entitled "Soldiers in Mufti: The Impact of Military Rule upon Economic and Social Change in the Non-Western States," which appeared in the December 1970 issue of the *American Political Science Review*. Parts of that article are found in chapters 2 and 5. That my attempt to discern and understand the patterns of military intervention culminated in this book, one written for two audiences of scholars and students, is due to Joseph LaPalombara's invitation to contribute to his Contemporary Comparative Politics Series. He has been a most patient editor in getting me to complete the book only two years later than originally planned, and a helpful one in suggesting how I could increase the reader's understanding by decreasing the number of words (but not ideas) in the final manuscript.

I have been especially fortunate in receiving advice, criticism, and encouragement from several friends and colleagues. I am indebted to Maury Feld, Samuel P. Huntington, Morris Janowitz, Alfred Stepan, and Claude Welch for the time they gave to me and even more for their own contributions to the study of soldiers in politics. In fact, considering the scholarly reputations of those who commented on the draft manuscript, I will immediately offer the necessary disclaimer that the final version's shortcomings are my responsibility alone. As in the past, my closest friend, Donald Hindley, has also been my severest critic and an exceptionally well-informed source of information about the politics of dozens of non-Western countries.

At both the beginning and the later stages of this book's writing I benefited from the intellectually and socially congenial setting offered by the Center for International Affairs at Harvard University. Many thanks are also due to Kenje Gleason, Martha Fielding, and Nancy Kaplan for their typing efforts.

My seven-year-old-daughter, Alexandra, is deserving of thanks for her gracious acceptance, if not understanding, of the reasons why I shall be dedicating my *next* book to her.

This book is for Joseph Mayer, who was of absolutely no help in the writing of it, but to whom I shall always be grateful for other, considerably more important "contributions."

ERIC A. NORDLINGER

THE
STUDY
OF
PRAETORIANISM

1

This book is about military coups and governments in Latin America, Asia, Africa, and the Middle East since 1945.[1] The military officers who have intervened in the political sphere have been called "men on horseback" in reference to the traditional mounted position of army officers; "soldiers in mufti" because they often substitute civilian titles and clothing (mufti) for their military insignia and khaki uniforms; "iron surgeons" in recognition of the public justification for their intervention, namely, the need for decisive action in regenerating the polity and economy; and "armed bureaucrats" because their political attitudes and governing style approximate those of the higher civil servants.

We will refer to interventionist officers as praetorian soldiers. Praetorianism refers to a situation in which military officers are major or predominant political actors by virtue of their actual or threatened use of force.[2] This term is taken from one of the earliest and most famous instances

[1] Unfortunately, no single term adequately describes and embodies all these countries. The term *developing countries*, for example, implies constant movement toward the model of the developed countries, simultaneously suggesting an invidious comparison between them. We shall use the term *non-Western states* even though Latin America, with its Roman law tradition and influential Catholic church, does not quite fit the label. Our focus upon the non-Western countries is due to the basic fact that almost all cases of military coups and governments are to be found there, rather than in Europe and North America, as noted on page 6.

[2] This book is limited to officers alone. There are several reasons for not dealing with sergeants, corporals, and enlisted men. These soldiers almost invariably accept the orders of their officers. There have only been a handful of mutinies led by sergeants. And even in these instances they do not attempt to seize the government or influence its policies. Mutinies are intended to achieve better pay and living conditions for the noncommissioned officers and enlisted men. One of the rare instances in which enlisted men overthrew a government in

of military intervention. The Praetorian Guards of the Roman Empire were established as a special military unit for the protection of the emperor. They ended up using their military power to overthrow emperors and to control the Roman senate's "election" of successive emperors. The adoption of the term *praetorianism* is meant to convey a message—one that is summarized in the concluding chapter of this book, but that can be foreshadowed by a statement from Gibbon's classic study, *The Decline and Fall of the Roman Empire.* Here we read that the intervention of the Praetorian Guards "was the first *symptom* and *cause* of the decline of the Roman Empire" (Gibbon, Vol. I, p. 91, italics added).

The armed forces of all countries exert considerable political influence. They are symbols of state sovereignty and the primary defenders against possible external or internal attack against the government. Given their prestige, responsibilities, and the material resources needed to fulfill these responsibilities, all military establishments exercise a significant degree of political influence, even in such countries as Mexico and India where civilian governments are clearly in control. Military officers become praetorian soldiers when they threaten or use force in order to enter or dominate the political arena. They intervene in politics when relying upon their control over the enlisted men who actually wield the guns, tanks, and planes in order to influence governmental decisions or occupy the seat of government themselves.

Thus praetorianism (or military intervention) occurs when officers more or less overtly threaten to carry out a coup d'etat unless certain demands are met, when they stage an unsuccessful coup, when a coup brings about or prevents the replacement of the government by another group of civilians, and, most important, when the officers themselves take control of the government. In the last case, civilian regimes are transformed into military regimes, even though certain civilian individuals and groups often enjoy a good measure of political influence.

In delimiting the subject of praetorianism it is also necessary to ask whether a military regime is considered to be just that ten or twenty years after the coup, even if it is "civilianized," with the leaders shedding their military uniforms and taking on the title of president or prime minister. The answer is yes if the following conditions are satisfied: the military took power by means of a coup, the highest governmental officials have served (or continue to serve) in the armed forces, and the governors are primarily dependent upon the support of the officer corps for the retention of power. For example, the current Egyptian regime continues to be identified as a

---

order to realize material benefits occurred in Sierra Leone. In fact, the "privates' coup" of 1968 replaced a military government with a civilian one. (Cox, pp. 196–203).

military one even though the original takeover occurred in 1952, its two leaders (Nasser and now Sadat) both took the presidential title, and a majority of cabinet ministers are civilians. For Egypt's two presidents were formerly army officers, military officers continue to head the major departments, such as the Defense Ministry and the Foreign Office, and "the regime of Sadat is completely dependent on the military" (Perlmutter, 1974, pp. 112, 116).[3]

This book centers around two sets of questions. The first deals with the attainment of political power. Why is it that some officer corps accept the principle of civilian control over the military while others engage in varying levels of intervention? How do the internal characteristics of the military establishment affect the likelihood of intervention? What factors motivate the overthrow of civilian governments? What aspects within the civilian sphere encourage praetorian actions and provide the opportunity to put them into effect?

The second set of questions deals with the exercise of governmental power. What are the varying levels or degrees of intervention? In what specific ways do the officers restructure the regime and the polity? To what extent do the praetorians adopt a fairly common governing style? How successful are they in legitimizing their power? How do the praetorians regularly handle the crises of national integration? Do military governments usually preserve the socioeconomic status quo or are they more likely to bring about modernizing, progressive changes? What factors affect the duration of military regimes? What kind of legacy do the praetorians leave for their civilian successors?

As indicated by these questions, this study is theoretical insofar as attempts are made to describe and explain *general* patterns of military coups and governments. Yet these generalizations do not utilize abstract concepts. And they stay quite close to the political "ground," to the actual practice of military intervention, using numerous instances to illustrate, refine, and support the hypotheses. This book is thus about both the theory and the practice of military intervention.

The book's broadest "thesis" may be summarized as follows. Various political attitudes, interests, and behaviors are shared by a greater or lesser majority of military officers. In conjunction with certain political factors external to the armed forces, they have a decided impact upon the decision to intervene, the structure of military regimes, the praetorians' governing style, the duration of military regimes, and the policies and performance of military governments. There are civilian politicians, governments, and regimes that share certain features with their military counterparts. Yet the

---

[3] See the last section of this chapter for a further clarification of the distinction between civilian and military regimes.

differences among civilian politicians, governments, and regimes are significantly greater than those found among their military equivalents.

It is therefore possible to generalize about praetorianism as both a characteristic and a distinctive phenomenon. It is a characteristic phenomenon because many statements can be made that apply to most military officers, governments, and regimes. It is distinctive phenomenon because there are numerous differences between civilian and military governments and regimes.

There are marked variations in the confidence that can be assigned to the generalizations found throughout the book. All of them are thought to be valid, but their plausibility differs according to the persuasiveness of the underlying reasoning as well as the amount and reliability of the supporting evidence. Unfortunately the relatively little systematic research that has been done on praetorianism leaves most of our descriptive and explanatory generalizations with far from sufficient evidence. They are thus to be read as more or less plausible hypotheses, rather than as well-tested valid propositions.

WHY STUDY PRAETORIANISM? Why study praetorianism? For one thing, it is an inherently interesting, even a fascinating, subject. An inherent interest in praetorianism may, for better or worse, derive from a commonly experienced attraction to force and violence. Soldiers have guns. Although guns are only fired in a small proportion of coups, there is always the possibility that they may be, and they are always in the foreground as forceful threats.

Military coups may also generate considerable interest because rapidly occurring events are usually more compelling than those that are drawn out over months or years. Coups are executed suddenly and quickly. They surprise, titillate, and often come within a hair's-breadth of succeeding.

Then, too, the powerful often provoke more curiosity than the powerless. Chairman Mao was certainly correct when he stated that "power grows out of the barrel of a gun." The ultimate power of the state, as of those who might hope to overthrow it, lies with the men who possess rifles, machine guns, tanks, and planes. Since these weapons are usually in the near-monopolistic hands of the soldiers, they have enormous potential or actual coercive power. A united officer corps is virtually always capable of maintaining a civilian government in office, or taking control itself.

Reasons that are more intellectually respectable, though not necessarily more salient, can readily be given for the study of military intervention. Praetorianism may or may not be inherently interesting; praetorianism in Latin America, Asia, Africa, and the Middle East is undeniably important. The importance of a particular political phenomenon partly depends upon the frequency with which it occurs. The study of military intervention in non-Western countries from 1945 to the present is then eminently warranted. In fact, given its frequent occurrence in the past, present, and presumptive future of most of these countries, military intervention constitutes one of the major characteristics of non-Western politics, particularly when contrasted with its near absence among Western countries during the same period.[4]

Among the twenty Latin American countries it is only in Costa Rica and Mexico that the soldiers have not acted as praetorians since 1945. There is a popular saying in Latin America that the highest *military* rank is the presidency—a comment that is borne out by the fact that more than half of the 121 men who served as presidents of their countries between 1940 and 1955 were military officers. Between 1945 and 1976, soldiers carried out successful coups in half of the eighteen Asian states. By 1976 the soldiers had made at least one successful or unsuccessful attempt to seize power in two-thirds of the Middle Eastern and North African states. They established military regimes in Egypt, Syria, Iraq, the Sudan, Libya, and Algeria. Officers did not intervene in the tropical African countries prior to 1963, since almost all of these states were under colonial control until then. But already by 1966, civilian governments had been overthrown in Togo, Congo/Brazzaville, Zaire, Ghana, Dahomey, the Central African Republic, Upper Volta, and Nigeria. By 1976 coups had occurred in more than half of the African countries, and in that year the military occupied the seat of government in half of them.

Bringing together these and other data, it turns out that the military have intervened in approximately two-thirds of the more than one hundred non-Western states since 1945. In any single recent year they controlled the government in about one-third of these countries, while acting as praetorians behind a façade of civilian control in the other third. It is exaggerating only somewhat to say that "the intervention of the military in the domestic politics [of non-Western states] is the norm; persistent patterns of civil supremacy are the deviant cases that require special explanation" (Janowitz, 1971, p. 306). Clearly, then, this book deals with one of the most common, and thus characteristic, aspects of non-Western politics.

In and of itself, the coup is an important political event. The first military coup has a major impact upon the "rules of the game." Through it the military clearly signals and sharply asserts its "rights" as a political player; the political arena is expanded to include the military as an im-

---

[4] Only three Western countries have experienced military intervention since 1945: France in 1958, Greece in 1967, and Portugal in 1974, and only in the latter two did the soldiers succeed in taking power. This is why the present study deals solely with the non-Western countries.

portant power contender. Future civilian governments are put on warning that the views of the officer corps must be included in their decision-making calculations if other coups are to be averted.

Successful coups involve the replacement of one group of governors by another. They are a method of succession. Non-Western governments have far more often succeeded each other through coups than through elections and other regularized procedures. And while some coups—those that have been pejoratively labeled "palace revolutions"—involve virtually no changes other than the identities of the governmental incumbents, others have a decisive impact upon the outcome of major civilian conflicts. They provide a large part of the answer to the question of who wins and who loses, who has power and who does not. When the armed forces prevent the winner of a presidential election from taking office, when they remove a government whose economic policies favor one class at the expense of another, or when they stage a coup to preserve the dominance of a racial, religious, tribal, or linguistic group in a communally divided society, their actions clearly help determine which societal groups will gain or lose some of their most important values. Even those coups that are unrelated to group conflicts, primarily involving the defense of corporate military interests, are likely to affect political and economic outcomes. For once in power the officers cannot maintain a neutral posture, despite oftentimes strongly felt preferences to stand above the political fray of conflicting group interests.

Many coups entail immediate and fundamental changes in regime structure. At the outset, the praetorians establish an authoritarian regime that is closed to popular participation and competition. In doing so, they destroy or alter those structural features of the previous regime that do not accord with their own preferences. Thus participatory and competitive structures, as well as those that allow for mobilization and penetration from above, are eliminated.[5]

In studying praetorianism, questions about governmental performance are especially important. Performance refers to the extent to which governments attain those goals and exhibit those operating features that are much desired by the population themselves and seen as intrinsically desirable by outside observers. We can thus ask, What beneficial or adverse impact do military governments have upon the lives of individual citizens? How well or poorly do these governments do those things that all governments should be doing? What factors account for differences in the performance of military and civilian governments? Supplying some persuasive answers to these obviously important questions is perhaps the single most important

---

[5] See pp. 110–17 for an explication of these terms and an analysis of regime structure.

rationale for this study. Comparing the performance of military and civilian governments is also appropriate since the praetorians themselves justify their coups by heavily underscoring the performance failures of civilian governments, concomitantly claiming that they will regenerate the country politically and economically.

Our explicit concern with the performance characteristics of military governments speaks to certain normative issues. How successful are the praetorians in legitimizing their power? Are they generally effective in averting massive violence in societies that are deeply divided along class or communal lines? Do they further economic growth and promote progressive socioeconomic changes? The answers to these and other questions should allow us to estimate the frequency with which military governments are responsive to popular expectations, the extent to which the citizens of military regimes are satisfied with their governments.

The study of military intervention also raises issues about what "ought" to be—normative questions are posed in a forthright manner—because praetorianism runs up squarely against liberalism's unqualified preference for democratic rule and civilian supremacy. According to any variant of the liberal philosophy, military intervention is hardly desirable. The values of political equality, liberty, freedom of opposition, and constitutionalism are thought to be realizable only where civilian supremacy is respected and civilian control is implemented.

Yet certain arguments could be made on behalf of military intervention.[6] What should we make of the practorians' commonly stated theme that their ultimate objective is not only a return to the barracks but the installation of a stable, effective, popularly elected government? How react to the claim that under certain conditions democratic rules and structures can best (or only) be strengthened by a military government that is forced to suspend them temporarily? And what if a civilian government is unable to prevent widespread violence, or defeat a movement intent upon the destruction of existing democratic institutions? Do not the armed forces' responsibility to country and constitution then dictate their intervention? There are also those instances in which popularly elected governments are themselves acting arbitrarily and illegally as they move toward the abrogation of democratic constitutions. Under such circumstances, if the officer corps is the only group with the power to remove the civilian governors, should it not force its way into the political arena? At a minimum, liberalism's abiding and indiscriminate preference for civilian control is a debatable issue. Praetorianism may turn out to be preferable, at least under certain conditions.

Lastly, the study of military coups and governments takes on addi-

---

[6] For an evaluation of these arguments, see the concluding chapter.

tional significance due to its policy implications. Because American policy-makers subscribe to the democratic, egalitarian, libertarian, constitutional tenets of liberalism, they generally prefer open, competitive regimes headed by civilians to authoritarian military regimes. American military assistance to non-Western countries has been undertaken partly to ward off military intervention. With modern weapons, military advisers, and training, non-Western officers were to become more professional, and as will be discussed in the next chapter, professionalization is thought to help prevent the intervention of the armed forces. In reacting to the immediate possibilities and actualities of praetorianism, the United States has utilized subtle pressures on the part of American personnel stationed abroad, faster or slower diplomatic recognition of newly formed governments, increases or decreases in foreign aid, and the dispatch of American marines and warships. When the Peruvian military took power in 1962, for example, President Kennedy took unusually strong measures in suspending diplomatic relations, cutting off military and economic aid, and threatening to suspend Peru's sugar quota. At a news conference, Kennedy stated: "We are anxious to see a return to constitutional forms in Peru. . . . We feel that this hemisphere can only be secure and free with democratic governments." The American reaction may have played some part in getting the Peruvian military to announce that it would hold elections within a year—a promise that it kept (Packenham, pp. 70–75; Stepan, 1973, p. 49).

However, the preference for democratic, civilian regimes is decidedly overshadowed by the goal of preventing the rise of left-wing movements—a policy that redounds to the benefit of anti-Communist praetorians. Given a choice between a freely elected civilian government with distinctly leftist leanings and an authoritarian anti-leftist military government, American leaders have consistently preferred the latter. For example, in the case of the 1964 Brazilian coup that toppled President Goulart's democratically structured government, the United States moved from a position of mild support to one of opposition as the government became increasingly radicalized. Attempts were made to weaken the Goulart government economically by limiting foreign aid, followed by support of the new military government, President Johnson even congratulating the coup makers before Goulart had fled the country (Stepan, 1971, pp. 123–26). On the other hand, the Johnson administration paid hardly any attention to the 1965 military takeover in Indonesia, since it was immediately followed by the slaughter of as many as five hundred thousand so-called Communists.[7] And under the

---

[7] In South Vietnam, the United States actively supported President Diem's authoritarian government, and then encouraged the officers who overthrew him in 1962 in the belief that a military government would be more successful in meeting the Communist threat (Hoadley, pp. 71–76, 160).

Nixon administration the Central Intelligence Agency encouraged and materially supported the 1973 overthrow of Allende's freely elected Socialist government in Chile. In short, American policymakers have evidenced some preference for governments of a democratic, constitutional, civilian variety, but they have been far from displeased with praetorian efforts where these were thought to avoid the installation or continuation of governments with leftist, Socialist, or Communist leanings.

Despite President Ford's stated intention to abide by the relatively low foreign profile of the Nixon Doctrine, the president, the State Department, the Defense Department, and the Central Intellignce Agency are still very much concerned with and involved in the domestic politics of non-Western countries. The likelihood of a coup, the replacement of a civilian government by a military one, and vice versa, are among the most important aspects of domestic politics with which the United States continues to be concerned. The present study offers generalizations about military coups and governments that should be considered in deciding whether to react, and if so, in which manner and direction. For instance, is it advisable for the United States to continue to provide substantially greater economic assistance to countries with military governments? The motivations behind the coups, the structure and durability of military regimes, the praetorians' policies as they favor one social group or another, and the performance of military governments in legitimizing themselves, promoting economic change, and avoiding coercive rule and widespread violence—these aspects of praetorianism should be relevant to an American foreign policy that continues to evidence some interest in the civilian or military makeup of non-Western governments.

THREE MODELS OF CIVILIAN CONTROL

It is sometimes advantageous to begin the analysis of a subject indirectly by discussing what it is not, rather than immediately launching into a delineation of its characteristics. Praetorianism finds its opposite in the principle of civilian control. The officer corps accepts a distinctly subordinate position to the civilian chief executive, be he president, prime minister, party chairman, or monarch. To begin our analysis in this manner not only underscores the differences between civilian control and praetorianism, it also raises questions about the strengths, weaknesses, and limitations of various types of civilian control.

The major point to be made in this section is part of the explanation of military intervention: there are three basic models of civilian control, none of which can be applied in all types of polities *and* securely relied upon to ensure civilian supremacy. The generalization that none of them is widely applicable *and* exceptionally effective in promoting civilian control—that the latter is a problematic undertaking—can then help explain the overall frequency with which non-Western armies have become prae-torian armies.[8]

Military intervention presupposes a conflict between soldiers and civilian governors; and conflict in turn requires some differentiation between the two groups. This statement is so straightforward that its major implication may go unnoticed: in the absence of significant differences between civilians and soldiers, the civilians may quite easily retain control because the military has no reason (i.e., opposing beliefs or conflicting interests) to challenge them. The first model of civilian control is squarely premised upon the absence of civilian-military differences, without which there cannot be any serious conflict between them, and thus no military intervention.

This traditional model of civilian control was most highly developed in the seventeenth- and eighteenth-century monarchies, where the European aristocracy simultaneously constituted the civilian and military elite —a carry-over from the feudal period in which nobles served as armed knights and lords of the realm. The same men wore both hat and helmet. And even as the two elites became somewhat distinctive, with different men serving primarily in one role or another, their interests and outlooks were not dissimilar. Military officers and civilian leaders came from aristocratic backgrounds, they were imbued with similar values, and they maintained familial bonds through blood and marriage. Noble families with several sons often sent one into the army, another into governmental service, and a third into the church.

Moreover, on those rare occasions when strains did appear between civilians and soldiers, the aristocrats were civilians first and soldiers second. They were primarily interested in their power, wealth, and status as civilians. "The aristocrat was an amateur at officership; it was not for him a vocation with ends and standards of its own, but an incidental attribute of his station in society" (Huntington, 1957, pp. 26–27). Nor could the nobles put on their helmets to challenge the monarch. To do so would have undermined the political, economic, and social position of the aristocracy, with its multiple dependency upon the monarchy. To the extent that it was at all conceivable, the usurpation of power as military men could only damage the soldiers' far more valued civilian positions and privileges.

The traditional model of civilian control, generalized from the Euro-

---

[8] Since it is the army rather than the much smaller air force or navy (which are sometimes nonexistent) that regularly plays the major, if not the exclusive, praetorian role in non-Western polities, the term *army* will occasionally be used to refer to the military or the officer corps as a whole.

pean monarchies of the seventeenth and eighteenth centuries, is clearly capable of maintaining civilian supremacy due to the overlap and lack of differentiation between civilian and military elites. But while this model is decidedly effective in maintaining civilian control, it has preciously little applicability in the contemporary period.[9] Military and civilian elites are markedly differentiated. Not only are the two elites made up of different individuals, perhaps recruited from different social groups, they also diverge in terms of their training, expertise, attitudes, and interests. Officers have acquired expertise in the management of force; military men prefer not to view themselves as politicians even when they serve as governors; officers are imbued with a characteristic set of political attitudes, which are much less in evidence among civilian elites; and soldiers attribute the greatest importance to the protection of the military's corporate interests, which may conflict with civilian interests. The applicability of the traditional model of civilian control is consequently much reduced, if not completely negated.

THE LIBERAL MODEL

The liberal model of civilian control is explicitly premised upon the differentiation of elites according to their expertise and responsibilities. Civilians holding the highest governmental offices—be they elected, appointed, or anointed—are responsible for and skilled in determining domestic and foreign goals, overseeing the administration of the laws, and resolving conflicts among social, economic, and political groups. Military officers are trained and experienced in the management and application of force, responsible for protecting the nation against external attack and the government against internal violence. Given the far more encompassing responsibilities of the civilians, and their presumably greater skills in executing them, the military is to accept a distinctly subordinate position. Not only must soldiers keep clear of all issues outside the national security sphere, even within that area the officers can only advise the government, having to accept civilian directives when the two groups hold divergent views.

In short, the liberal model entails the maximum possible depoliticization of the military. It is this model that has been used most often to assert civilian supremacy within the non-Western states. For example, in a 1961 speech to the cadets at the Ghana Military Academy, President Nkrumah enunciated the liberal model in no uncertain terms: "You must have confidence that the government is doing what is best for the country and support it without question or criticism. It is not the duty of a soldier to

---

[9] It began to break down in Western Europe after 1800 when education and skill replaced inherited status and wealth as the basis of recruitment and advancement within the military.

criticize or endeavour to interfere in any way with the political affairs of the country; he must leave that to the politicians, whose business it is. The government expects you, under all circumstances, to serve it and the people of Ghana loyally" (Kraus, p. 162).

Within five years of this speech some of the cadets to whom it was addressed took part in the successful coup against Nkrumah, despite his injunction that "politics are not for soldiers." Obviously the liberal model cannot rest securely upon civilian assertions, claims, and warnings. Subordination to civilian authority has to be internalized as a set of strongly held beliefs and values. Soldiers who are imbued with these beliefs and values—what might be referred to as the *civilian ethic*—are attitudinally disposed to accept civilian authority and to retain a neutral, depoliticized stance even when in sharp disagreement with the government. The civilian ethic has a restraining impact upon behavior if and when some issue or conflict sparks interventionist motives.

The liberal model rests upon a second foundation: civilians must exhibit due regard for the military. In its actions and statements the government respects the military's honor, expertise, autonomy, and political neutrality. It does not slur the officer corps, interfere in professional military affairs, interject political considerations into the armed forces (e.g., by promoting officers because of their political loyalties), or use the army for domestic political advantage. The liberal model would then appear to be an effective one for ensuring civilian control. Given civilian regard for the military, officers have fewer reasons to intervene, while the civilian ethic restrains the officers from acting upon possible interventionist motives.

Yet the liberal model is not as firm a foundation for civilian control as might appear at first glance. To begin with, civilians themselves often do not adhere to one of its cardinal rules: no trespassing on the military reservation. It is not uncommon for presidents, prime ministers, and monarchs to interfere with such exclusively military matters as the promotion and assignment of officers to particular posts. Nor have civilians consistently refrained from using or politicizing the armed forces to further their own interests and governing objectives. Such actions invariably give rise to powerful praetorian motivations. Only by intervening can the military protect its autonomy, professionalism, cohesiveness, and pride in the face of civilian transgressions.

To continue with the Ghanaian example, Nkrumah was overthrown primarily because he injected politics into the military in order to exercise more extensive control over civilians and soldiers—soldiers who had not previously contemplated a coup. Nkrumah dismissed the two highest ranking officers, replacing them with others who were more susceptible to his control; he promoted some officers because of their personal and political loyalties to him, thereby flouting the accepted promotional criteria of competence and seniority; and he made one regiment responsible to him personally rather than to the military chiefs, thus warping the hierarchical command structure and detracting from military unity. Nkrumah's repeated violations of the liberal model generated exceptionally powerful interventionist motivations. In the words of General Ocran, one of the chief conspirators, the intrusion of politics "will wreck the army" (Ocran, p. 2). And Nkrumah is far from being an isolated example of civilian governors trespassing upon the military reservation in order to extend their control.[10]

The officers' belief in the civilian ethic does have a restraining effect upon interventionist behavior. But attitudes cannot be instilled overnight. It usually takes at least a generation to socialize men into a given set of attitudes, and considerably longer for these attitudes to develop into a group tradition. It then becomes somewhat unrealistic to expect the officer corps of newly formed armies to be imbued with the civilian ethic. Those who served in the former colonial armies accepted the civilian ethic; British and French officers helped instill this ethic by word, deed, and training. However, with the postindependence expansion of the armed forces, these men now form a distinct minority within the officer corps. In addition, the internalization of the civilian ethic depends upon civilian governors who can generate widespread respect within the officer corps. But due to their own inabilities, the presence of some intractable problems, and the soldiers' inordinately high expectations of politicians, the governments of most non-Western states have not been able to win consistent approval from the military. An officer corps that does not hold successive civilian governments in high regard is unlikely to imbibe the civilian ethic.

Moreover, even firmly internalized attitudes do not *dictate* behavior. Rather, they strongly dispose men to behave in certain ways. When other salient considerations run counter to the attitudinal disposition, the latter may be more or less painfully pushed aside. The belief that the civilian government is doing irreparable harm to nation and army may be sufficiently powerful to neutralize the restraining impact of the civilian ethic. To continue with the Ghanaian example, most of the conspirators had internalized the civilian ethic of their former British commanders, which was further reinforced during their later attendance at British military academies. General Afrifa certainly identified strongly with the tradition of a nonpolitical army subordinate to the government. But after considerable soul-searching he decided to discard it:

> *I have always felt it painful to associate myself with a coup to overthrow a constitutional government, however perverted that constitution may be. Oliver Cromwell was a good general, but he did not take his rightful place*

---

[10] See pages 71–75 for additional examples.

> *in the glorious gallery of British generals because he overthrew a constitu-*
> *tional authority by force of arms. It was painful, therefore, to come to the*
> *conclusion that the coup was necessary to save our country and our people*
> *[even though] we owed allegiance and loyalty to the Government of Ghana*
> *by practice of our profession. (Afrifa, p. 37)*

Apparently the force of circumstances can overcome even the most deeply
internalized attitudes.

THE PENETRATION MODEL

The third type of civilian control may best be described as the penetration
model. Civilian governors obtain loyalty and obedience by penetrating the
armed forces with political ideas (if not fully developed ideologies) and
political personnel. Throughout their careers officers (and enlisted men) are
intensively imbued with the civilian governors' political ideas. In the military academies, training centers, and mass-indoctrination meetings, and in
the frequent discussions that take place within the smallest military units—
at these times and places intensive efforts are made to shape the political
beliefs of the military. The resulting congruity between the political ideas
of civilians and officers consequently removes a potential source of conflict
between them. Moreover, the officers' acceptance of currently orthodox
political ideas is employed as a significant promotional criterion, along with
military abilities and experience. Political conformity is rewarded. Having
had their political beliefs and loyalties tested again and again as they move
up the hierarchy, senior officers may be expected to be most accepting of
civilian control.

Along with the downward dissemination of political ideas, civilian
supremacy is maintained by the extensive use of controls, surveillance, and
punishment. "Political officers" are assigned to each military unit, at every
level in the military hierarchy. They are responsible to higher-ranking political officers and ultimately to the civilian leadership, rather than to superior "military officers." Indeed, officers with political control responsibilities
commonly take precedence over military officers with equivalent ranks. Surveillance and control may be buttressed by the employment of the secret
police and their informers within the armed forces, whose chain of command extends upward to the civilian elite. Where the dissemination of political ideas and persuasion is insufficient for exacting political conformity,
these control measures are designed to deter and prevent praetorian proclivities.

It is among the Communist regimes that the penetration model has
been applied in its most fully developed form. Civilian control is forcefully

proclaimed in the less well known second part of Mao Tse-tung's assertion: "Power grows out of the barrel of the gun. Our principle is that the party commands the gun and the gun shall never be allowed to command the party." The ideological integration of the military and civilian spheres is evidenced in the Chinese leadership's calls for an army that is both "Red and Expert." The army is differentiated from the civilian sphere in terms of professional expertise, but congruent with it in terms of a shared ideology. The extent to which the Chinese military is penetrated by political ideas is evidenced in the fact that fully 40 percent of the soldiers' training is devoted to ideological work. The scope and intensity of ideological exhortation may be quickly appreciated by taking note of a conclusion reached at an Air Force Plane Maintenance Conference: Political thought is "the soul of plane maintenance work. . . . Marxism-Leninism could drive out mechanical malfunctions" (Joffe, p. 128).

The structural manner in which the Chinese military is penetrated was set out definitively in a 1956 speech by the Minister of National Defense, Marshall P'eng Te-huai. Civilian control is founded upon a dual structure of authority within the People's Liberation Army: "Both military commanders and political commissars in our army are leaders of the armed units, and both are responsible for the leadership of the army. However, there is a division of labor between them: military commanders should be responsible for the implementation of orders and directives so far as they concern military affairs, while political commissars should be responsible for the implementation of those concerning political work" (Joffe, p. 59). From this statement it would seem that the responsibility of the political commissars is a limited one, since military matters predominate over political ones in the armed forces. But this is not true of the penetration model.

In an earlier part of his speech Marshall P'eng implicitly (but clearly) defined "political work" to encompass practically the entire spectrum of what is normally meant by military concerns, including military organization, the assignment, transfer, and promotion of personnel, logistics, and battle plans, as well as the implementation of all directives and orders issued by superior officers. This inclusive conception of "political work" thereby extends the responsibility of political commissars—along with their superiority over military commanders—into all decision-making realms (except for actual combat) so that even routine matters cannot be decided without their approval. All decisions must be in accord with party policies. The exercise of control by political officers is further reinforced by their responsibility for regularly evaluating and investigating the loyalty and efficiency of all members of their military units. Surveillance is so extensive that suspicions might be quickly aroused if some officers got together for a social occasion without inviting their (presumably not too popular) political commissar (Griffith, p. 204; Kau, p. xxiii).

Among the non-Western states the penetration model has been most fully implemented in Communist China, North Korea, North Vietnam, and Cuba. It has also been applied in milder form in Guinea and Tanzania. After an abortive mutiny by enlisted men in 1964, the Tanzanian army was disbanded; the new army of politically loyal officers and enlisted men was integrated into the single-party regime. Service in the army is limited to party members, and prior to their recruitment they must have served in the party's national youth league. The army features a political commissar in each unit, and the company commander acts as chairman of the party committee, which is elected by the enlisted men. Political penetration thereby turns the army into an officially recognized organ of the ruling single party (Lee, pp. 149–50; Bienen, 1970, pp. 374–80). Out of civilian penetration, civilian control. In President Nyerere's words, "The task is to ensure that the officers and men are integrated into the Government and Party so that they become no more of a risk than, say, the Civil Service" (Bell, p. 6).

Clearly the penetration model is a powerful one for buttressing civilian control. Looking at the evidence—there has only been one coup attempt and no successful coup in any of the countries that have implemented this model—it might even be said that penetration comes close to guaranteeing civilian control.[11] In its fully developed form it approximates the traditional model with its congruence of civilian and military beliefs. And where conflicts of political ideas and interests do arise, the civilians enjoy extensive resources for surveillance and control. The applicability of the model is, however, limited in two important respects.

Once the penetration model has been applied it is enormously effective in ensuring civilian control, but except under very special circumstances its implementation is an inordinately risky proposition. A powerful and professionally differentiated military, like any other institution or corporate group, is strongly opposed to infringements upon its autonomy. As already noted with respect to the liberal model, civilian attempts at penetration engender powerful interventionist motives; even mild infringements upon the military's autonomy have motivated interventionist actions. The model's implementation thus becomes highly problematic; it is far more likely to produce intervention than civilian control.

However, this generalization loses much of its significance under the unusual circumstances of a weak, newly created army. For example, in China the Communist party leadership simultaneously developed and penetrated the revolutionary army. In 1929—twenty years prior to the Communists' victory—there was already an elaborate political infrastructure within the Red Army, consisting of a political commissar, a political depart-

---

[11] For an important caveat to this generalization, see the remarks about civil-military relations in China and Cuba, p. 28.

ment, a party committee, a party secretariat, and party cells (Kau, p. xxii).[12] In Tanzania President Nyerere disbanded the army after the 1964 mutiny was put down by British troops whom he invited in to do just that. The army was then recreated along the lines of the penetration model at the time of its greatest weakness. And in Cuba the army was disbanded after Castro's revolutionary victory in 1959, and then recreated from above according to the penetration model.

The adoption of the penetration model is also limited to a certain kind of regime, one in which there is a single locus of power, as in personal dictatorships and highly centralized single-party regimes. It cannot be applied where there are competing centers of power (as in open regimes featuring party competition) or where power is dispersed (as in regimes with a division of powers between the executive and the legislature). The model cannot be applied in such regimes because its inherent logic requires that the military be penetrated by a single set of political ideas and controls.

For more than one set of leaders to attempt to do so would divide the military against itself, as well as promoting conflict between soldiers and civilians. All civilian elites prefer civilian control, but they want to exercise it on their own behalf. Where there are two or more power centers, at least one of them will not accept a penetration model that sharply buttresses the power of its rival. Presumably only a few attempts have been made to apply this model in regimes with two or more power centers because of the civilians' realization that it cannot be implemented and, if attempted, would draw the military into the political fray, which is just what the model is intended to avoid. The penetration model has, in fact, only been implemented successfully in regimes with a single, predominant center of power.

Considering the limitations of the three models, civilian control in the non-Western states is seen to be an uncertain undertaking. The traditional model is highly effective, but it is virtually inapplicable in the contemporary context given the fairly sharp differentiation between the military and civilian spheres. The liberal model is potentially effective. But it must be recognized that the civilian ethic requires time and propitious circumstances for its internalization, and that even then it may be painfully discarded under the pressure of events, in particular, when civilian leaders violate one of its cardinal rules by politicizing and interfering with the military establishment. The penetration model is exceptionally effective once im-

---

[12] Yet even in China, where the model has been fully implemented, the officers' concern with professional autonomy has led to serious conflicts with the civilian leadership since the mid-1950s. Two major purges were required to rid the officer corps of the tendency toward a "purely military viewpoint," and it was the issue of professional autonomy that helped spark Lin Piao's coup attempt (Kau, pp. xl–xliv).

plemented. But the attempt to do so is inordinately risky, except under the unusual circumstances of a weak army, and even then the model can only be applied within a certain type of regime.

These statements add up to the conclusion that there is no model of civilian control that is both widely applicable and exceptionally effective. This conclusion may then be read as a general explanation for the *overall* frequency of military intervention: civilian control is a more or less problematic undertaking. In Chapter 3 we shall explain why some soldiers remain under civilian control whereas others intervene.

THE PUBLIC RATIONALE OF PRAETORIANISM

Having underscored the limitations of civilian control, it becomes appropriate to turn to the public rationale for the rejection of civilian control. Immediately after the overthrow of a civilian government the officers issue a public statement to explain and justify their actions. These communiqués include some common themes because they speak to the problems facing almost all praetorians in the coup's immediate aftermath—the consolidation of their control and the legitimization of their actions.

The praetorians portray themselves as responsible and patriotic officers, these public-spirited qualities leaving them little choice but to protect the constitution and the nation from the unhappy consequences of continued civilian rule. Foremost responsibility is not due to the men who happen to be occupying the seat of government. Their overriding responsibility is to constitution and nation. The military take it upon themselves to decide if the constitution has been violated or the national interest subverted, and thus whether or not intervention is warranted.[13]

Speaking as the commander of the Argentine army, General Onganía clearly articulated these themes in a 1960 speech to the officers and cadets at West Point:

> *Obedience is due a government when its power is derived from the people, and pursues the constitutional precepts set forth by the people, for the people. This obedience, in the last instance, is due to the constitution and to the law, and it should never be the result of the mere existence of men*

---

[13] It should be noted that two-thirds of Latin American constitutions explicitly accord the military some responsibility to serve as constitutional guardians. For example, the 1946 Brazilian constitution assigned the military the responsibility for maintaining a balanced distribution of powers among the executive, legislature, and judiciary. But in no instance does a Latin American constitution promulgated under civilian auspices extend the military's responsibility to the occupation of governmental offices themselves.

or political parties who may be holding office because of fate or circumstances. It should therefore be clear that the duty of rendering such obedience will have ceased being an absolute requirement if there are abuses in the exercise of legal authority that violate the basic principles of a republican system of government, when this is done as a result of exotic ideologies, or when there is a violent breakdown in the balance of independence of the branches of government, or when constitutional prerogatives are used in such a way that they completely cancel out the rights and freedoms of the citizens.

General Onganía went on to say that under such circumstances the people have the right to resist oppression, but as unarmed citizens they usually cannot make use of this right. It is therefore the military's responsibility to act on their behalf. Power is transferred to those who are authorized to bear arms, whose mission includes protection of the constitution and the rights of the people (McAlister et al., p. 117).[14] The military have a special responsibility, a crucial mission that transcends their obligations to existing authorities. This is praetorianism's basic public rationale.

Particular coups are justified by charging the former civilian incumbents with a shorter or longer list of performance failures. The soldiers almost invariably claim that constitutional principles have been flouted by the corrupt, arbitrary, or illegal actions of the civilian incumbents. They are also commonly accused of having acted contrary to the national interest by allowing subversive groups to threaten the country's internal security, by fomenting class and communal conflicts and thereby encouraging political disorder and violence, by adopting policies that resulted in low economic growth rates, widespread unemployment, and inflationary spirals, or by failing to undertake programs of socioeconomic modernization and reform.

At the same time the praetorians confidently assert that they will restore the country to political and economical good health. They are willing and able to do so because the officer corps is highly patriotic, detached from the interests of particular class and communal groups, devoid of the politicians' weaknesses, and highly skilled in technical and managerial matters. Given these attributes, along with the determination to succeed, the military governors announce that they will eliminate corruption, root out subversive elements, curb political disorder, generate economic growth, and bring a halt to inflationary spirals. Some praetorians go on to announce their intentions to modernize the economy and implement progressive socio-

---

[14] Since General Onganía's reputation within the Argentine military was built upon his dedication to legality and the depoliticization of the armed forces, it is especially significant that he assumed the presidency two years after his West Point address.

economic policies. But the predominant theme is that of praetorians as saviors, promising to remedy and rectify past civilian failures, rather than committing themselves to the fashioning of a better or different society.

Lastly, almost all praetorians announce their intention to hand over the reins of government to democratically elected civilians in the near or distant future. They accept the principle of civilian control, yet they were compelled to intervene because of their public responsibilites to constitution and nation. Civilian rule will thus be restored as soon as possible—as soon as they have revived the economy; resuscitated the polity, and arranged for free and orderly elections. However, as we shall see in the following section, some praetorians subscribe to highly ambitious, long-range political and economic goals. In these instances civilian rule is only to be restored some time in the indefinite future when these goals have been achieved.

Whether the public rationale of praetorianism more or less accurately reflects the soldiers' real motivations, it is a relatively persuasive political idiom with which to win civilian acceptance of the coup. All the more so when the military can point to actual civilian performance failures, when the officers have not yet had their governing qualities tested in office, when they confidently assert that the nation's problems will soon be resolved, and when they promise a fairly speedy return to the barracks and the installa-tion of a popularly elected government.

A TYPOLOGY OF PRAETORIANISM: OFFICERS AS MODERATORS, GUARDIANS, AND RULERS

Praetorians share several important attitudinal attributes, such as their bias against mass political activity and politicians, they exhibit common behavior patterns, such as the defense of the military's corporate interests, and their regimes take on similar forms, such as the creation of authoritarian structures. These and other similarities make it possible to generalize about praetorian soldiers. Yet there are also important variations. A fuller understanding of any widespread political phenomenon requires the identification of differences as well as similarities.

Praetorians differ from each other most fundamentally with regard to the level of intervention, that is, the extent of governmental power that they exercise and the ambitiousness of their objectives.[15] These two dimensions of praetorianism generally vary together. The

---

[15] However, despite their differing objectives as governors, the most important motivations behind the coups are similar—the protection and enhancement of the military's corporate interests. See pp. 00–00.

greater the number and ambitiousness of the praetorians' political and economic goals, the greater the extent of governmental power that they exercise, and vice versa. Given the obvious importance of these two aspects of military intervention, and the point that they constitute the praetorians' most salient differences, it makes good sense to use them in constructing a typology of praetorianism. Praetorian officers may be classified as moderators, guardians, and rulers (see Table 1).

Table 1   The Levels of Military Intervention

	Moderators	Guardians	Rulers
Extent of power	Veto power	Governmental control	Regime dominance
Political and economic objectives	Preserve status quo	Preserve status quo and/or correct malpractices and deficiencies	Effect political change and sometimes socioeconomic change

Praetorian moderators exercise a veto power over a varied range of governmental decisions and political disputes, without however taking control of the government themselves. Civilians govern, but their power is checked by a military that does not accept anything near total civilian control. Moderator-type praetorians act as highly politicized and powerful pressure groups in relation to the civilian incumbents, sometimes backing up their demands with explicit threats of a coup. Where necessary, they may carry out a displacement coup—one in which a government is overthrown or prevented from taking office and is replaced by another group of civilians that is more malleable or acceptable to the military. Once the soldiers have made their demands known, it is up to the civilian incumbents to comply or correctly calculate the minimal extent to which the demands must be satisfied in order to retain their positions.

Just as moderator-type officers shy away from exercising governmental control themselves, their objectives are correspondingly minimal, at least relative to those of other types of praetorians. They try to preserve the status quo, maintaining the balance (or imbalance) of power among contending groups, enforcing the political and constitutional ground rules, staving off practically any kind of important change in the distribution of economic rewards, and ensuring political order and governmental stability. Moderator types consequently evidence a keen concern for the outcome of political conflicts. In Latin America, displacement coups are most commonly executed when newly activated strata (i.e., workers and peasants) are able to effect significant changes in the distribution of political power. Where a political party that is unacceptable to the soldiers is likely to come to power through an upcoming election, the army may take power briefly to prevent the election from being held. Displacement coups are also executed if the newly politicized strata have elected "too many" legislative or executive officials. The coup is used to annul the results and to seat another government, which conforms more closely to military preferences.

In short, moderator armies act as conservatives, which helps explain why they do not exercise governmental power themselves. Direct control is often unnecessary given their negative goals. It is easier to prevent change than to bring it about, and this may be accomplished from the governmental sidelines with their veto power.

Over time, praetorian moderators regularly transform themselves into guardians or rulers. Once the officers have become politicized as moderators, it is a relatively small step to exercise governmental power themselves. An officer corps that is sufficiently politicized to act as a pressure group, effectively threaten a government, prevent the accession of another government, or replace one civilian government with another, can generally carry out a coup and then retain power itself. And when moderator-type actions are unsuccessful in bringing about the desired outcomes—when their veto-type actions have to be repeated again and again—the officers conclude that the only remedy is to control the government themselves.

Argentina provides a good example of this "escalation" pattern. During President Frondizi's incumbency, between 1959 and 1962, the military acted as moderators in making numerous demands upon him. They insisted that he fire several cabinet ministers and replace them with men who were more acceptable to the officers, that he alter his policies regarding exploitation of the oil fields and educational reform, that he break diplomatic relations with Cuba, and that he severely restrict the activities of working-class and Communist parties or outlaw them altogether. The officers' views were respected in about half these instances (Finer, pp. 167–69). Although a majority of officers were opposed to a military takeover, Frondizi's decision to allow the working-class *peronistas* to participate in the legislative elections, and their surprising show of strength, eventuated in the 1962 coup.

---

[16] Moderator-type praetorianism parallels Stepan's "moderator model of civil-military relations," although his conceptualization includes additional elements, such as civilian *acceptance* of military intervention. See Stepan, 1971, pp. 62–66.

And this despite many officers' strong belief in a moderator role for the military.

Prior to the coup a group of "legalistic" officers issued a statement in which they set out their preferred conception of the Argentine military's moderator role: "We believe that the armed forces ought not to govern. On the contrary, they should be subordinate to the civil power. This does not mean that they should not gravitate in the country's institutional life. Their role is at once silent and fundamental. They guarantee the constitutional pact which our ancestors bequeathed us, and they have the sacred duty of forestallng and containing any totalitarian enterprise which may arise in the country whether from the government or the opposition" (McAlister et al., p. 118). Given the conditional acceptance of civilian supremacy, it is not surprising that the officers took control in 1962 for a two-year period. Nor it is surprising that they did so from 1966 to 1973, and again in 1976, when other civilians did not satisfy their expectations.

Just because the level of military intervention has consistently increased once the soldiers have acted as moderators, we will accord only passing attention to this type of praetorianism. For despite the considerable power exercised by moderator types, we can be somewhat neglectful of them in the confident expectation that they will soon turn up as praetorian guardians or rulers.[17] Even in the case of the Brazilian military, which is atypical in having played a moderator role throughout the twentieth century, it took control of the government in 1964. Similarly in Chile, the armed forces acted as moderator-type praetorians for more than forty years since governing the country in 1930–31, only to turn into ruler types after the overthrow of President Allende in 1973.

PRAETORIAN GUARDIANS

After the praetorian guardians overthrow a civilian government, they retain governmental power in their own hands, usually for a period of two to four years. With regard to their governing objectives, guardians are often no different from moderators in wanting to stave off political change and maintain political order, except that guardians are convinced that these goals can best be realized by controlling the government themselves. Military officers are on the whole more or less reluctant to take the reins of government into their own hands. That the guardians do so is partly attributable to the belief that they have no alternative in the absence of an elite group capable of preserving the political and economic status quo, or

---

[17] Moreover, less than adequate attention is paid to moderator types in the literature because it is exceptionally difficult to obtain information about their secretive, behind-the-scenes maneuvers.

that without a takeover, power would gravitate toward political elites whose goals are at odds with those of the military.

All guardian types are committed to the preservation of the basic status quo, which is partly defined in terms of a very recent past before the onset of civilian performance failures. These praetorians consequently aim to improve the effectiveness or alter the policy directions of previous governments, some of them also attempting to effect mild political and economic changes. Their goals may include the removal of squabbling, corrupt, and excessively partisan politicians, the revamping of the governmental and bureaucratic machinery to make for greater efficiency, and the redistribution of some power and economic rewards among civilian groups.[18] Guardians are concerned with economic growth and with the elimination of inflationary spirals, excessive public spending, and balance-of-payments deficits that developed under civilian rule. They aim to stimulate the economy—without however attempting to effect any significant changes in its contours. Basically, they intend to correct what are seen to be the malpractices and deficiencies of the previous government. They are "iron surgeons" ready to make some incisions into the body politic, but doing little to replace what has been cut out or even to ensure that the surgical operation has lasting consequences after the praetorians discharge the patient.

All military regimes are authoritarian in that they eliminate or extensively limit political rights, liberties, and competition, at least until the officers are getting ready to return to the barracks. Although political activity and organizations are sometimes entirely outlawed by the moderators, on the whole their regimes are less authoritarian (i.e., closed and restrictive) than those of ruler-type praetorians.[19] Some political parties, communal movements, newspapers, and trade unions are commonly allowed to operate, although severely limited in their activities. With regard to trade unions, for example, guardians have purged the existing leadership, curbed the statement of wage demands, or outlawed strikes, without however totally destroying the unions. Those newspapers that are allowed to publish are not permitted to criticize the government or the army.

No attempt is made to mobilize the population in order to control and channel its political and economic activities from above. This accords with the guardians' relatively limited objectives. The basic contours of polity, economy, and society are to be preserved or mildly altered, necessitating sharp restrictions upon the activities and power only of those civilians

---

18 Where the redistribution involves major losses to the majority (i.e., the lower classes), the guardians' objectives can be better described as reactionary rather than conservative.

19 See pp. 110–17 for a general typology of regime structures and its application to guardian and ruler-type praetorians.

whose goals differ from the soldiers'. But since no attempt is made to effect basic changes, it is unnecessary for the guardians to create a mobilization regime capable of penetrating the population.

Ruler-type praetorians are far less in evidence than either moderator or guardian types, constituting roughly 10 percent of all cases of military intervention. Yet the enormous power that ruler types exercise and the ambitiousness of their political and economic goals make them an especially important part of the study of praetorianism. Compared with their guardian counterparts, they not only control the government but dominate the regime, sometimes attempting to control large slices of political, economic, and social life through the creation of mobilization structures. The political and economic objectives of praetorian rulers are exceptionally ambitious, occasionally warranting their self-description as radical modernizers or revolutionaries.

It is the far-reaching nature of the intended changes, along with the realization that these changes will take considerable time to become securely rooted, that necessitates regime dominance and an indefinite period of military rule. Whereas guardians commonly promise to return power to the civilians within a few years, ruler armies make no such commitments, at most stating that a civilian regime will be reinstituted. For example, in its 1974 Declaration of Principles, General Pinochet's government clearly stated that the Chilean military will remain in power for an indefinite period "because the task of reconstructing the country morally, institutionally, and materially requires a profound and prolonged action." Only after bringing about these fundamental changes will the armed forces return governmental control to civilians through "universal, free, secret, and informed suffrage," and assume "the role of specifically institutional participation that the new Constitution assigns them . . . which will be . . . National Security, in the broad sense that this concept has in the present epoch" (Sanders, 1975c, p. 3). The reference to the "broad" national security responsibilities that the military is to exercise under a future civilian government means that even after a long period of military rule, the soldiers do not intend to accept civilian control, but to act as moderator-type praetorians.

Ruler types intend to bring about basic changes in the distribution of power by eliminating nearly all existing power centers. They invariably attempt the root-and-branch destruction of monarchies, traditional oligarchies, and political parties. To remove a traditional oligarchy from the government is insufficient without concomitantly neutralizing its power bases—large landholdings and the peasantry's near total material dependence. Nor is it sufficient to remove the leaders of mass parties from governmental positions and close the regime to popular participation, without at the same time destroying the organizational network of political parties, labor unions, peasant leagues, and communal associations.

Praetorian rulers exhibit the same economic concerns as most guardian types, namely, the revitalization of stagnant economies. But ruler types commonly believe that this cannot be achieved by alternative economic and financial policies alone; high-powered investment and modernization programs are required to bring about steady economic growth. Some praetorian rulers also intend to bring about progressive economic changes that will result in a marked improvement in the living conditions and opportunities of the poorer strata. Such changes may be achieved by the more egalitarian redistribution of incomes and occupational opportunities, by the provision of additional public benefits to the lower classes, or both. Progressive measures include land reform and liberal loans for peasants to enable them to buy land, as well as the raising of minimum wages, the expansion of social security, medical, and educational programs, the nationalization of privately owned enterprises, and the enactment of more egalitarian tax laws.

Ruler types build decidedly more authoritarian regimes than guardian types, who limit themselves to control of the government. Praetorian rulers use their power to dominate the regime. Almost all independent political and semipolitical organizations and activities are outlawed. Newspapers are either heavily censored or published and edited by governmental appointees. Repression is generally more extensive; praetorian rulers tolerate considerably less criticism and opposition than their guardian counterparts. Some ruler-type praetorians attempt to mobilize the population by creating mass parties (or movements) over which they have exclusive control. Polity, economy, and society are to be penetrated from above. Going beyond governmental control to regime dominance, and sometimes to societal penetration and mobilization from above, is thought to be required by the rulers' highly ambitious goals.[20]

In Chapters 4 and 5, we shall return to the political and economic objectives of guardian and ruler types, describing and explaining the manner in which they attempt to achieve these goals and the extent to which they are realized.

---

[20] In Chapter 4 it will be seen that ruler types rarely succeed in their attempts to create mobilization regimes, although their regimes are markedly more authoritarian than those of the guardians.

**A
CAUTIONARY
NOTE**

In this chapter a fairly sharp distinction has been drawn between civilian and military regimes. Yet this constitutes an oversimplified picture. Although our definitional criteria [21] allow us to place all but a few regimes in the civilian or military category, soldiers frequently enjoy considerable power in regimes where civilians occupy the seat of government and civilians sometimes enjoy a good measure of influence where officers are serving as governors. To distinguish between the two kinds of regimes is therefore not to suggest that one type is exclusively controlled by soldiers and the other solely by civilians.

We have already seen that moderator-type praetorians exercise considerable power in civilian regimes under the liberal model of civilian control. The officers exercise a veto power from the governmental sidelines, limiting what the civilian incumbents can and cannot do in various decisional areas. In some instances civilian presidents and prime ministers have tried to shore up their governments by asking soldiers to become cabinet ministers, as in the case of President Allende of Chile. And where civilians maintain control by means of the penetration model, senior officers may be sitting within the highest decision-making circles. In Communist China military men occupy one-third and in Cuba one-half of the seats on the Central Committee (Domínguez, p. 232). It is not possible to generalize about the degree to which soldiers have pushed their way into this position in contrast to the civilian leaders inviting them in. Although the penetration model places the civilians in a position of clear predominance, the senior officers commonly exercise considerable power in the making of both military and nonmilitary decisions.

Turning to military regimes, civilians almost always serve as bureaucratic or technical advisers in the formulation of governmental policies. In most instances civil servants, economists, lawyers, and politicians of the "correct" political coloring are accorded seats in the cabinet. In guardian-type regimes this may be done in preparation for the transfer of power to the civilians. In ruler-type regimes civilians are brought into the government for their skill in carrying out ambitious economic policies or to "civilianize" the regime as a way of attaining a measure of legitimacy. But even where civilians hold most of the ministerial portfolios, as in Egypt under President Sadat, the praetorians are not only predominant, the civilians have little if any independent power. They are present and influential largely at the sufferance of the military governors.

It is most unusual to come across a military regime in which civilian elites have their own power bases and resources, in which the soldiers

[21] As set out on pp. 2–4.

"need" the civilians almost as much as they "need" the soldiers. Syria and Thailand are two of the few military regimes whose governments can be described as military-civilian *coalitions,* despite the officers' predominance.[22] The Syrian military that came to power in 1963 has maintained a close working relationship with the socialist-nationalist Ba'ath Party. The party has supplied the praetorians with an ideology, organizational skills, and linkages to students, workers, and peasants. The Ba'ath leadership has been able to remain independent of the praetorians, it enjoys a significant measure of decision-making influence, and has even been allowed to employ its ideological and organizational skills within the army (Ben-Dor, pp. 322–23).[23]

The case of Thailand, which has been governed by the military during almost the entire post-1945 period, is quite different with respect to the nature of the military-civilian coalition. Political parties, mass organizations, and ideologies are of little significance. Politics is limited to the elite arena. Thailand's leading praetorians attained and exercised power through the formation of cliques (or patron-client relationships) with wealthy businessmen, high-ranking civil servants, and other military officers. They purchase elite support by granting legal and illegal favors relating to government contracts and appointments to lucrative positions on the boards of public and private enterprises. These are awarded to civilians and officers alike on the basis of their personal loyalty to one or another of the leading praetorians. The distribution of power is a product of the competition between two or three military-civilian cliques, with financial favors serving as the medium of exchange and cohesion within the cliques (Welch and Smith, pp. 97, 102–3).

Having pointed out the occasionally fuzzy dividing line and overlap between military and civilian regimes, we need to recall that in the great majority of cases it is possible to distinguish between the two types of regimes. Military regimes are those in which soldiers have seized power through the coup d'etat, officers or former officers hold the highest governmental positions, and they rely primarily upon the officer corps in retaining them, even though civilians play a greater or (most commonly) a lesser role.

---

[22] Although it has been said that most Latin American countries are governed by military-civilian coalitions most of the time (Ronfeldt), the term *coalition* is used in an overly encompassing manner.

[23] The military and the Ba'ath in Iraq have developed a strikingly similar relationship.

A
POLITICAL
SOCIOLOGY
OF
THE OFFICER
CORPS

2

For political patterns to be fully understood and explained it is necessary to examine the ways in which they are influenced by both political and societal factors. Political sociologists begin with the premise that many of the important explanations underlying political phenomena are to be found in several societal realms. These include the class structure, the distribution of social status, cultural patterns, socialization experiences in the family, school, and workplace, organizational patterns, and the rate and level of economic modernization, among others.

The present chapter examines those sociological characteristics of the officer corps that are thought to have a significant impact upon praetorianism. The sociological variables include the organizational features of the military establishment, the officers' class backgrounds, their present class and status positions, their inherited memberships in religious, racial, linguistic, and ethnic segments, the education and training that turns them into professional soldiers, and the socialization patterns that engender certain attitudes toward politics and government. We shall describe the nature of these sociological characteristics and suggesting how and why they influence various aspects of praetorian behavior.[1]

---

[1] Admittedly, far more empirical research needs to be done on the internal characteristics of the officer corps and their impact upon political attitudes and behavior before the generalizations that follow can be accorded a high degree of confidence. However, it is thought that the descriptive and explanatory hypotheses do enjoy considerable plausibility on the basis of theoretical reasoning, existing empirical work, and the near absence of findings that call them into question. Moreover, the generalizations take the form of stronger or weaker tendency statements, which allow for a certain number of exceptions. For a summary statement regarding the different interpretations of the military's political behavior held by those writers who focus upon its internal features and those who concentrate upon the interaction with its "environment," see Cox, pp. 6–11.

This chapter does not, however, mean to imply that praetorianism can be understood and explained by dealing with sociological factors alone. What we discuss here will be integrated with the relevant political factors in the following chapters to provide a comprehensive analysis of praetorianism. For example, in this chapter it is suggested that the bureaucratic features of the military help account for the emergence of negative attitudes toward politicians and political activity. But it is only in the later chapters that these attitudes are placed alongside certain political (or "environmental") variables, which together help account for the decision to intervene, the praetorians' characteristic governing style, the legitimacy of military governments, and their ways of dealing with severe communal conflicts.

Nor should this focus on the officer corps' internal characteristics be interpreted as an acceptance of various interpretations of the military as an insulated, self-encapsulated, fully cohesive, hierarchically controlled institution. It does indeed approximate these features, which go a long way in shaping the officers' politically relevant attributes. However, the officer corps is also permeable to outside influences, ranging from the officers' social backgrounds to contemporary political currents, and its formal organizational structure is sometimes barely capable of containing a factionalism stemming from personal rivalries and ambitions, differences in age, training, and rank, and conflicting attachments to political leaders, parties, and policies. In other words, this chapter is informed by the "ideal type" features of the military as an insulated and unitary organization, but these are not accepted unquestioningly. They are "tested against reality" and often found to be wanting.

THE OFFICER CORPS AS A MIDDLE-CLASS PRESERVE

All students of military intervention agree on one proposition if no other: The officer corps is recruited predominantly from men who come from middle-class backgrounds. And given the small size of the non-Western middle class, these officers are disproportionately represented within the officer corps. It is quite common to find an officer corps in which three-quarters of its members were born into the middle class, while this class constitutes only one-sixth of the total population. Although the concept is vague, we can say that the middle class is situated somewhere in the "middle," between the tiny upper class of wealthy entrepreneurs, large landowners, and highly successful professionals on the one hand, and the huge lower class of employed and unemployed workers, small-holding peasants, tenant farmers, and landless agricultural laborers on the other. The middle class is thus rather diverse, including as it does, teachers, civil servants, lawyers, technicians, shop owners, traders, medium and small entrepreneurs and land-owners along with military officers.

The fathers of today's officers typically held such middle-class positions in countries as socially and economically diverse as Brazil, Peru, Argentina, Chile, Egypt, Iraq, Turkey, India and Nigeria.[2] Among those cadets who entered the Brazilian Military Academy between 1941 and 1943, 20 percent came from traditional upper-class families, 76 percent from middle-class families, and 4 percent from lower-class families. By the early 1960s upper-class recruits had dropped to 6 percent of the entering classes, lower-class recruits had risen slightly to 9 percent, while the middle class continued to predominate with 78 percent of the new officer recruits (Stepan, 1971, pp. 32–33). However, at least one significant variation is apparent. Compared with the African and Middle Eastern officer corps, which draw heavily from the lower middle class, those of Latin American and Asia feature a larger proportion of men with solidly middle-class and upper-middle-class backgrounds.

In accounting for middle-class predominance within the officer corps it is useful to ask first why the upper and lower classes do not provide more recruits. The sons of wealthy entrepreneurs, large landowners, and prestigious professionals are not especially attracted to the military as a career. Given their social, financial, and educational advantages, they can confidently expect to attain far more lucrative positions in the civilian sector. Although they may well assume positions of power within the army after many years of service, such positions of influence can be more quickly and confidently attained elsewhere. And while officers enjoy considerable social status, their prestige is lower than that of other occupations open to men from upper-class backgrounds.

The very small number of officers with lower-class backgrounds stems from just the reverse reasons. Many would not hesitate to apply for an officer's commission, entailing a great measure of upward social mobility, except for want of the opportunity to do so. Entrance into a military academy or an officer training school requires the completion of primary schooling and at least some secondary education. But the sons of lower-class fathers have had either an overly brief education or none at all. They rarely continue past the elementary level, if indeed they get that far. Even where secondary education is free, their labor is commonly needed to supplement the family's meagre income. In the newly independent states a significant

---

[2] For data and descriptive summaries on the social backgrounds of these officer corps, see Stepan, 1971, pp. 30–36; Astiz, 1969A, pp. 143–44; Astiz, 1969B, p. 868; de Imaz, pp. 56–58; Sanders, 1975B, p. 2; Be'eri, pp. 321, 331; Janowitz, 1971, p. 313; Yalman, pp. 129–30; Cohen, pp. 184–86; and Luckham, p. 111. In contrast, a majority of Indonesian and Burmese officers have been recruited from the upper class (Willner, p. 271).

number of men entered the officer corps after having served as enlisted men and noncommisisoned officers in the colonial army. These were the only trained men capable of filling the newly created positions. But once these positions were filled from the ranks, primary and secondary schooling has been required of successive applicants.

For men with middle-class origins, a military career is a real possibility because of their educational attainments. It is also a desirable one, since the income, security, and status of an officer are as high as, or higher than, those of most middle-class occupations. Men from solidly middle-class families who become officers maintain, and often enhance, their social and economic standing. For those from lower-middle-class families, an officer's commission constitutes an upward step on the mobility ladder. For secondary school graduates who aspire to a university degree, but who cannot afford it or who are unable to win one of the scarce places, education in the national military academy is both free and easier to attain. And it often constitutes a near educational and status equivalent to a university degree.

THE MODEL OF THE PROGRESSIVE-MODERNIZING SOLDIER

How then do the officers' social backgrounds affect their political attitudes and behavior? To what extent can the latter be explained in terms of their middle-class origins? According to one influential interpretation, the officers' social backgrounds have engendered decidedly progressive political and economic attitudes. Military officers approximate what may be called the model of the progressive-modernizing soldier.

Shils has suggested that the lower-middle-class origins of many officers—their fathers being traders, craftsmen, and small farmers—make them painfully aware of the distance that separates them from the wealthy and powerful. These officers are not sympathetic to big businessmen and conservative politicians. Their values are egalitarian (Shils, p. 17). Referring to the officer corps of Southeast Asia, Pauker states that they "are not the product of social classes with feudal traditions. . . . Their natural tendencies are progressive" (Pauker, pp. 339–40). With respect to Latin America, Johnson claims that the increasing recruitment of officers with lower-middle-class backgrounds makes for a military that is "more inclined than formerly to gravitate toward positions identified with popular aspirations and to work with the representatives of the popular elements" (Johnson, p. 152).

According to Janowitz, the absence of men from aristocratic and wealthy families among the Middle Eastern officer corps engenders an outlook that is "congenial to social change" (Janowitz, 1971, p. 317). Then there is Halpern's strong contention that in the Middle East and North Africa, the officers have shown "an acute awareness of the chronic ills of their countries," having joined the military in order to escape from the economic frustrations of civilian life (Halpern, p. 295). In addition, Halpern maintains that these officers are bent upon wide-ranging reforms because of their close connections with "the new middle class." The defining feature of this new middle class is its salaried position, in contrast with the propertied and landowning middle class. It is made up of teachers, administrators, technicians, lawyers, engineers, white-collar workers, and military officers. This class is said to be committed to the refashioning of society; it is only through social and economic reforms that careers will be opened and secured for people like themselves who constitute a meritocracy rather than an established class. Acting with, for, and as members of this new middle class, the military becomes the vanguard of socioeconomic reform (Halpern, pp. 52–54, 253, 258).

THE MODEL REVISED

A major strand of this broad interpretation is acceptable. The officers' middle-class, and especially lower-middle-class, origins help turn them into opponents of aristocratic, landowning, and wealthy upper-class strata. Where these strata are politically and economically dominant, in control of a highly inegalitarian if not semifeudal regime, the officers' resentments may help inspire their intervention. And once in the governmental saddle, they often strip these groups of their power and wealth. However, neither this generalization nor any of the others noted above warrant the conclusion that most non-Western officers are imbued with progressive values, that their political behavior is inspired by an abiding concern for the great majority of the people, namely, the lower classes. When the military does act against the upper class, in its own behalf or in that of the middle class, this is rarely of any direct benefit to workers and peasants. And the officers' middle-class origins may very well predispose them to act contrary to the interests of workers and peasants.

Moreover, the model of the progressive-modernizing soldier attributes an exaggerated importance to the officers' class origins—the relative disadvantages, marginality, insecurity, and degradation that many of them experienced before entering the military. These experiences provide a forceful impetus for individual mobility. But they need not, and usually do not, instill a broader concern for the plight of less fortunate strata. In fact, the realization of individual aspirations is commonly followed by a reduced concern for collective mobility.

Undoubtedly the iniquities experienced by some officers were sufficiently poignant, and their memories vivid enough, for them to retain some concern for the lower classes after their achievement of middle-class positions. But rather than assume that childhood and adolescent socializing experiences are generally more salient than adult class and status positions, where there is a discrepancy between the past and the present in this regard, it is the latter that usually has a greater impact upon political attitudes and behavior. Whatever sense of absolute and relative deprivation soldiers from lower-middle-class backgrounds may have experienced, as current members of the solid and upper middle class they tend to identify with its interests—an identification that is further supported by status concerns, marriage and family connections, social contacts, property ownership, and business interests.[3] And for those soldiers born into the solid middle class who did not experience any material or social inequities, their preadult socialization experiences engender an added attachment to the established middle class.

Rather than accept the model of the progressive-modernizing soldier, it would seem that a somewhat different formulation is warranted. Military officers are inclined to act in accordance with middle-class interests.[4] The extent to which they pursue modernizing and progressive economic goals or defend the status quo is then partly dependent upon the *nature* of these middle-class interests, which vary markedly depending upon the prevailing distribution of political power and the shape of the class structure. The middle class is interested in the preservation of its privileged material position where it is already firmly entrenched economically, and the enhancement of its position through economic expansion and modernization where it is not yet securely established. Although there may be significant divisions within it, the middle class is interested in the defense of its political power base where one already exists, and the enhancement of its power where it is weak.[5]

Officers consequently tend to act as a force for change under certain conditions and as ardent defenders of the status quo under others. Where a traditional landowning oligarchy is politically and economically dominant and the miniscule middle class's economic position is not secured, the praetorians begin to approximate the model of the progressive-modernizing soldier. They may destroy the traditional oligarchy and its supporting power bases and then carry out reforms that are intended to increase the size and mobility opportunities of the middle class. In societies featuring a relatively

---

[3] One telling indication of the officers' middle-class identities comes from Peru, where military ranks are discussed in class terms. Junior officers, lieutenants, and captains are identified with the lower middle class; majors and lieutenant colonels, with the solid middle class; and colonels and generals, with the upper middle class (Einaudi and Stepan, p. 41).

[4] Perhaps it is partly because the middle class is objectively and subjectively situated in the "middle," between the tiny upper class and the vast lower class, that the officers tend to equate its interests with the national or public interest.

[5] But the praetorians are far more devoted to the enhancement of the military's corporate interests, and to those of the communal segment into which they were born, than to middle-class interests.

large, politically powerful, and economically established middle class, praetorian actions are quite different. Here middle-class interests are regularly challenged by politicized workers and perhaps peasants as well, prompting military coups and policies designed to preserve the political and economic status quo—one in which the middle class has an enormous stake.

Thus in one type of society praetorianism commonly involves middle-class gains at the expense of the traditional upper class, whereas in the other type—of which there are about twice the number—the soldiers defend existing middle-class privileges against the threat from below, intervening and governing to the general detriment of lower-class interests (Huntington, 1968, pp. 221–22; Nordlinger, 1970, pp. 1132–33, 1142–43). In Chapters 3 and 5 this hypothesis will be developed further and applied to the incidence of coups and the socioeconomic policies of military governments.

COMMUNALISM AND THE MILITARY

All societies are divided along class lines. Most non-Western societies are also divided along communal lines—inherited attributes of race, religion, region, language, and ethnicity sharply distinguish one part of the population from another. In many of these societies communal divisions give rise to intense conflicts. The conflicts revolve around issues that are thought to be of the greatest importance—the communal segments' social identities, cherished cultural values, most-sought-after material rewards, and political rights. Besides the conflict issues themselves, the segments commonly exhibit invidious beliefs, unflattering stereotypes, long-standing jealousies, and deeply imbued prejudices toward each other, out of which emerge strongly felt and emotionally charged antagonisms. All forms of violence, including national disintegration through civil war, are thus real possibilities.

The relationships between communalism and praetorianism largely center on the answer to this question: Is it generally the case that common military training and socialization experiences break down the officers' communal attachments, concomitantly instilling secular, national attitudes? The answer has an important bearing upon the likelihood of military intervention in the midst of intense communal conflicts, and the performance of military governments in averting widespread violence in such deeply divided societies.

THE MODEL OF THE SECULAR-NATIONALIZING SOLDIER

Most political scientists who have discussed the officer corps of communally divided societies claim that military training, socialization, and organization markedly weaken communal identities and antagonisms, simultaneously instilling a national, secular outlook among officers recruited from different communal segments.

According to Janowitz, officers evidence a powerful sense of national identification which turns the military into "a strong source of anti-communal sentiment. . . . The capacities of the military for developing national identifications derive from the unity of its organizational environment. Its members are aware that they belong to a group which has a unified and indivisible military function. . . . In the military, as compared with other institutions of a new nation, the probability of equal treatment is greater. The result is a sense of cohesion and social solidarity, because men of various regional and ethnic backgrounds are given a common experience and come to think of themselves as Indians, Egyptians, or Nigerians" (Janowitz, 1964, pp. 63, 81).[6] Pye gives somewhat more emphasis to purposeful socialization efforts within the military as these help develop national concerns and a modern outlook, also pointing to the recruits' isolation from civilian life and their induction into the impersonal military world as these break down attachments to communal groups (Pye, 1962A, pp. 82–84). Lefever claims that "the more disruptive aspects of tribalism within African military establishments [are being] mitigated by statistical balance, integration of certain units, transtribal deployment, and selection and promotion based on competence rather than kinship" (Lefever, p. 178). Referring to Ghana and Nigeria, Gutteridge similarly maintains that military training helps turn the officer corps into "cohesive entities with a strong national consciousness"; the military units serve as "melting pots in which soldiers tend to lose some of their regional and tribal characteristics" (Gutteridge, 1966, p. 40).

These generalizations and a few others have been summarized in a threefold comparison of the officer corps and the civilian political elite: the officer corps is more broadly recruited from different communal groups than is the political elite; the officers' training and socialization experiences are more uniform and national in orientation than are those of the political elite, making for a relatively unified officer corps; and due to the rigorous discipline and the value placed upon cohesiveness, the military is less divided than are political elites (Jahan, p. 279). These statements add up to a model of the secular-nationalizing soldier. The officers are thus relatively immune to the political currents of communalism and effective in integrating their divided societies. Their attachments to the army as a national, communally indivisible institution, and their primary identification with

[6] The military itself has made such claims. According to the 1965 *Indian Armed Forces Year Book*, "The portals of the [military] academy are open to all young men. There is no distinction or discrimination on the grounds of class, creed or religion. The academy, in fact, is a meeting ground of young men from distant parts of the country, living and learning in utmost harmony despite the differences in class, creed or religion. Living together, cadets start on the same footing and grow up in an atmosphere of a healthy secular outlook."

the nation rather than with its subgroups, reduces the likelihood of communally inspired intervention while promoting the effective regulation of communal conflicts on the part of those soldiers who do take power.

THE MODEL REVISED

Yet there is reason to doubt the validity of these generalizations. For one thing, they are based upon a premise that is unfounded in many, if not most, communally divided societies: that the officer corps is roughly representative of the society, that it contains a significant number of officers from each of the major communal segments, with the military thereby bridging communal differences and antagonisms. Yet it is quite common for some communal groups to have little or no representation within the officer corps, while others are heavily overrepresented. Of the thirty black African armies, only ten are ethnically balanced (Shabtai, pp. 107–12). And the imbalance can be extreme. In the Sudan, for example, with its northern and southern regions divided along racial, religious, and linguistic lines, virtually the entire officer corps was made up of northerners, which had a decisive impact upon that country's prolonged civil war. And prior to the secession of East Pakistan and the civil war that eventuated in its establishment as an independent Bangladesh, 95 percent of Pakistani army officers were recruited from West Pakistan.[7]

Clearly the model of the secular-nationalizing soldier has limited applicability where the great majority of officers are recruited from a single communal group. Communal identifications and loyalties are not markedly weakened within the military. The officer corps may well be cohesive, but its unity does not grow out of secular and national values. It stems from communal homogeneity and exclusiveness. When such soldiers do come to power, they are consequently more than likely to exacerbate communal conflicts by wielding it in the interests of their own communal segments, even attempting to "neutralize" or "eliminate" the opposing segment, as in the Sudan and Pakistan.

Nor is military cohesiveness especially strong where two or more communal segments are represented in the officer corps. The model of the secular-nationalizing soldier exaggerates the impact of the military in eradi-

---

[7] The overrepresentation of certain communal groups is due to various historical, cultural, educational, and political circumstances. Some communal groups predominate because the former colonial government purposefully recruited from politically "safe" or "martial" segments, because the groups' cultural patterns define a military career as attractive, because some groups contain a disproportionate number of secondary school graduates who are eligible for the military academy, and because some governments have thought it advantageous to maintain communal imbalances within the army.

cating communal loyalties. True, the officer corps is relatively cohesive, more so than the civilian political elite as a whole. Common training and socialization, national symbols, distinctive functions, equal treatment, segregation from civilians—all these factors make for a relatively high level of cohesiveness. On the other hand, the officers' values have been strongly shaped within their communal environments during childhood and adolescence. Their adult identities are partly defined in terms of inherited communal characteristics, and they are by no means so isolated from civilian life and events that these have no effect in maintaining communal loyalties. This is not to deny the impact of the military experience in forming a national consciousness and a secular set of values. Yet these neither eradicate nor replace communal loyalties. They constitute an additional set of values, the two existing together despite their inherent contradictions.

When civilians are involved in an intense communal conflict, the officer corps may then divide along identical lines as their communal attachments override the value placed upon military cohesiveness and national unity. For example, despite a communal imbalance within the Nigerian officer corps, this had few political consequences during the first years of independence. Only after "shafts of illumination from the immediate political environment—the sequence of political events from 1964 to 1966—brought into focus the ethnic and regional identities in the army, [were they] invested with a political significance and potentiality for fratricidal conflict between the soldiers" that helped spark the 1966 coup (Luckham, p. 9). In Lebanon, a country where Moslems outnumber Christians, the officer corps has been predominantly, but not exclusively Christian. At the outset of the civil war that began in 1975 the army managed to avoid involvement in the fighting. But then Moslem officers deserted to join their own communal militiamen, followed shortly by the total disintegration of the Lebanese army. An army that remained "above" an intense communal conflict for some thirty years, largely because the predominantly Christian officer corps found itself under Christian dominated governments, was quickly pulled apart when the communal conflict turned into civil war.

Where more than one communal segment is represented within the officer corps, it is not only the existence of severe civilian conflicts that can divide the army against itself. In these "mixed" officer corps communal resentments, jealousies, suspicions, and factionalism may also develop due to issues that are internal to the military, especially the criteria to be used in the recruitment and promotion of officers.[8] Should recruitment and pro-

---

[8] Communal tensions may even be more strongly felt within the army than in civilian society because the requirements of cooperation, obedience, and command are far greater within the military (Stepan, 1971, p. 11; Luckham, pp. 107–8).

motions be based upon merit criteria alone, or upon some formula of quotas to ensure proportionate representation according to population size?

Communal groups with a relative abundance of secondary school graduates believe that the merit principle should govern the allocation of public service positions, including military ones. Communal groups that are educationally disadvantaged, especially when they are underrepresented in the public services, maintain that a certain number of positions at each rank should be reserved for them until they have attained a percentage that is equivalent to their relative population size. The employment of one or another of these two divergent criteria clearly effects the interests of individual officers and their communal segments. It is then no wonder that officers prefer the merit or proportionality principle according to their communal identities. And given existing jealousies, resentments, and mistrust, the promotion of individual officers on the basis of merit criteria may be scrutinized in communal terms. It is suspected that one officer rather than another was promoted because of his communal identity—a suspicion that may turn into a firm belief despite the absence of communal biases.

This kind of communal divisiveness within the officer corps was clearly evident in Nigeria, the issue of tribal-regional representation generating mutual resentments and fears. The small number of Hausa-Fulani officers resented the Ibo officers whose educational achievements had given them a predominant position within the higher ranks; and they suspected that the Ibo officers would use their predominance for their own interests and those of their segment. The Ibo officers were afraid that the use of proportional quotas would mean the favored promotion of Hausa-Fulanis to rectify the communal imbalance at the middle and highest levels. Although communal biases did not affect promotions significantly, in a suspicion-charged atmosphere many officers who fell behind in promotions concluded that they had been unfairly penalized in the past and would be affected adversely in the near future.

The Ibo majors who carried out the first Nigerian coup in 1966 did so partly in the belief that they had suffered or would suffer promotional discriminations, along with the fear that they would eventually be forced out of the army to make room for Hausa-Fulanis who had recently been recruited according to the proportionality principle. The countercoup, which occurred six months later, was partly inspired by the sharp reaction of Hausa-Fulani officers to the many Ibo promotions that occurred after the first coup, although these were made in accordance with preexisting seniority rules (Luckham, p. 192).[9] A conflict over recruitment and promotion criteria, in combination with considerable mutual suspiciousness, thus played

[9] The promotions occurred because many of the middle- and high-ranking Hausa-Fulani officers had been killed during the first coup.

a significant part in motivating the first coup which brought the Nigerian army to power, as well as in motivating the second "revenge" coup which eventuated in a deadly civil war.

Evidence of the marked salience of communal attachments within the officer corps comes from a survey of the grievances behind coup attempts against both civilian and military governments between 1946 and 1970. Among the countries of Africa, almost all of which are more or less sharply divided along communal lines, 27 percent of the coups were related to the praetorians' perceptions of a threat to their own segments.[10] In the Middle East 19 percent and in Asia 12 percent of the coups were significantly related to communal grievances (Thompson, pp. 29–31). Moreover, in Congo/Brazzaville, Dahomey, Togo, and Uganda, it was found that "military juntas have been as prone to favor certain ethnic groups as the civilian regimes they replace." In each of these countries military governors have promoted officers, policemen, and civil servants belonging to their own regional-tribal segment, sometimes purging those of other communal groups (Decalo, p. 30).

To assess what has been said about the model of the secular-nationalizing soldier, it is accurate to depict the officer corps as relatively cohesive. Even in communally divided societies it is no more factionalized than is the civilian political elite. Recruitment patterns, promotional criteria, the content of military education, and shared socialization experiences do help instill a secular-nationalizing outlook. On the other hand, the officer corps is frequently in the nearly exclusive hands of a single segment, whose political behavior is then very much geared to the interests of its "own people." Where the officer corps is roughly representative of the major communal segments, national loyalties and military cohesiveness may be highly valued, without however overcoming the soldiers' communal attachments. Moreover, the keen interest in the recruitment and promotion issues, further stirred up by mutual resentments, jealousies, and suspicions, sometimes inflame divisions within the military. Communal conflicts may consequently pull or push the soldiers into the political arena, the coup itself and the praetorians' actions as governors then exacerbating the conflict.

In Chapter 5 we shall return to the relationship between praetorianism and communal conflict. After introducing additional considerations, the officers' political attitudes and governing style in particular, we will analyze the impact that military governments have upon the political integration of communally divided societies.

---

[10] According to another study of thirty-two coup attempts in Africa, communal considerations played an important part in eleven and a less significant role in six (Shabtai, pp. 240, 250–51).

<table>
<tr><td>

**THE
MILITARY
AS A
BUREAUCRATIC
ORGANIZATION**

</td><td>

The internal structure of political groups—the patterned relationships among their members, roles, and units—may influence the members' political attitudes, their definition of what constitutes the group's vital interests, and the group's ability to dominate or compete against other groups. As a potential or actual political group, the military's most salient structural features are bureaucratic in

</td></tr>
</table>

nature. They have significant consequences for the officers' attitudes and behavior, from the decision to intervene to the praetorians' governing style.

THE BUREAUCRATIC CHARACTERISTICS

The distinguishing characteristics of the ideal typical bureaucracy include the use of achievement criteria in the determination of promotions, a strong commitment to the rationality principle in the decision-making process, and a strictly hierarchical ordering of offices and their individual occupants. The vast majority of military establishments *approximate* this bureaucratic model.

Promotions are consistently based on achievement criteria, which include relative standing in one's graduating class from the military academy, attendance at advanced training centers, seniority, and proven ability. Careers are very much open to talents within the officer corps. Every competent lieutenant figuratively carries a colonel's eagle or a general's stars in his pocket. Particularistic criteria, such as personal friendships and family connections, and inherited criteria, such as class backgrounds and communal identities, are seldom significant. However, personal and political loyalties may be salient in officer corps that have been politicized by civilian chief executives or through their own intervention.

Decision making tends toward the highly rational, centering around the calculation of the most efficient, most effective, and quickest means for the realization of specific goals. Soldiers are not primarily concerned with value choices or the determination of goals. They deal with strategies, tactics, and logistics; the goals of national security and military victory are taken as givens, as is the principle of civilian supremacy in some armies, which relieves the officers of the responsibility for deciding among decisional options. Considerations other than those relating to task-oriented behavior, such as traditional values, moral concerns, individual preferences, and the goals of other organizations, are generally ignored. They are irrelevant to the officers' decision-making calculus and thus "nonrational." Rational decision making, as actuality or as an ideal to be approximated, helps engender the related belief that there is a single correct solution to every problem—a solution that can be identified when extraneous (i.e., "nonrational") considerations are ignored.

Like other bureaucracies, the military is structured hierarchically: authority flows downward and responsibility upward. But the military differs from all but a few civilian bureaucracies, such as Communist parties and the Catholic church, in the forcefulness, extensiveness, and explicitness of its hierarchical structure.

In most bureaucracies hierarchy is partly premised upon future rewards; obedience influences salary increases, promotions, and desirable assignments. In the armed forces hierarchy is also punitive, based upon the threat of the harshest disciplinary measures, and a normative belief in unquestioning obedience inculcated from the very outset of military training.[11] Although some officers adopt a "managerial approach," which recognizes the morale building advantages of informing, consulting, and persuading their subordinates, its adoption is totally the superior's prerogative, and thus does not constitute a weakening of the hierarchical structure. In fact, insofar as effective control is partly premised upon consent, loyalty, and morale, the "managerial approach" may strengthen command-control relations.

The scope within which the hierarchical imperative is applicable is inordinately extensive. It applies to the military as a "total institution," from the correct decorum on social occasions to the execution of near-suicidal missions. There are often rifts between senior, middle-level, and junior officers, staff officers and troop commanders, academy and nonacademy graduates, and various personal cliques. However, they are not necessarily related to political divisions regarding possible coups or the policies of military governments. And as such, they have little impact upon the hierarchical structure. Only when the officer corps becomes politicized is the hierarchical structure's forcefulness and extensiveness threatened.[12]

In addition, the military's hierarchical structure is more highly articu-

---

11 The forcefulness of the hierarchical imperative is ultimately justified by the *raison d'être* of the military—victory in armed combat. Victory requires a centralized command capable of directing the separate units, along with field-grade officers who can instantaneously order their men into battle even in the face of vastly superior forces.

12 Internal divisions, including violent ones on rare occasions, are more likely when a politicized military establishment includes a navy and an air force, not just an army. For each of the services is a self-contained hierarchy, coming together only at the very highest level under the authority of the chief of staff. The division of the military into three sizable services is most commonly found in Latin America. And it is there that the services have occasionally engaged in violent but short clashes with each other in attempting to impose their political views. In 1955 and 1963 the Argentine navy was pitted against the army and

lated and clearly exhibited than that of any civilian organization. Positions of superiority are constantly symbolized, formalized, and recognized by salutes, uniforms, insignia, spatial positioning, and differential personal perquisites. As one sociologist put it, throughout history "few things have been as explicitly structured [i.e., articulated and exhibited] as religious ritual, magical practices, and armed forces organizations" (Levy, p. 45).

THE CONSEQUENCES OF BUREAUCRACY

How then do these bureaucratic features affect political attitudes and behavior? Although by no means one of the most important explanations for the incidence of coups, the prevalence of achievement criteria and the rationality principle help form a mild interventionist disposition under certain conditions. The non-Western military commonly views itself as the most "modern" group in society; it sees itself as a highly capable and efficient organization. Officers tend to withdraw their respect for governments that are ineffective, those characterized by factional squabbling, continued vacillation, and decision making based upon personal and partisan advantage. The disposition to intervene is heightened in the self-confident belief that they, as capable and efficient officers, can do a better job at governing than the civilians.

The soldiers' self-image as highly competent and rational decision makers helps shape their characteristic governing style, that of decision making without politics.[13] In arriving at their decisions the praetorians frequently employ managerial and technical criteria in deciding among policy options. Other considerations, such as the attainment of widespread popular support, are to be shunted aside. They also tend to believe that virtually all problems are soluble if only the correct course of action is identified in a rational, task-oriented manner, and then forcefully pursued. Military men are somewhat unrealistic in assuming that political, social, cultural, economic, and institutional patterns can be readily altered in the desired directions. Only after the first year or two in power do they realize that many grave problems are more or less intractable, that some civilian failures were due to recalcitrant circumstances confronting any government, military or civilian.

Powerful interventionist motives are invariably engendered whenever a civilian government attempts to tamper with the highly valued hierarchi-

---

air force, and the air force and army fought each other in Ecuador (1961) and Guatemala (1962). But in these and other instances the sense of institutional cohesiveness helped minimize the number of casualties and the duration of the conflict.

[13] See pp. 117–24 for a fuller discussion of their governing style and its other formative influences.

cal structure and the immense power derived from it. To challenge the hierarchical principle is viewed as an unwarranted attack upon the military's corporate interests.[14] Civilian governments have done so in attempting to win the direct political loyalties of officers, sergeants, and enlisted men, when they have allowed mutinies to go unpunished, and when, as we have already seen in the Ghanaian case, they have made certain units directly responsible to themselves rather than to the military chiefs.

Whether or not the military chooses to use it for praetorian purposes, tight organization serves as a critical power factor. Due to its hierarchical structure the military may be described as an organizational weapon with guns. Even those politicized armies that are sorely divided, that are not tightly controlled by the senior commanders, are relatively well organized. Where factionalism is found within the military, it is at least equally evident among the civilian elites. The officer corps is almost the single most powerful group in society because the hierarchichal imperative gives the officers control over a much larger number of men who wield guns.

The power conferring aspect of the hierarchical principle may be taken one step further by asking: To whom is primary obedience owed? The question does not receive an easy answer. For while the hierarchical principle accords ultimate authority to the senior commanders, the principle also includes the dictate that primary obedience is owed to immediate, face-to-face superiors. *Direct* orders are always to be obeyed. And it is the middle-level officers—the colonels, majors, and captains—who are the highest-ranking immediate superiors of the men who wield the guns. When a major orders the officers and enlisted men in his command to execute a coup, his orders are almost invariably obeyed, even when the senior officers support the government.[15]

This aspect of the hierarchical imperative is sharply illustrated by one aspect of the first Nigerian coup. Hausa-Fulani sergeants and enlisted men obeyed the (sometimes unarmed) Ibo majors when ordered to assassinate Hausa-Fulani political leaders and high-ranking Hausa-Fulani officers (Luckham, p. 31). What more telling example of obedience to immediate superiors than an unquestioning compliance with orders to murder govern-

---

[14] The concept of corporate interests is developed in Chapter 3.

[15] Be'eri has described the rank and file of the Arab armies as "potters' clay" in the hands of their coup-minded commanders—a description that is equally applicable to other non-Western armies. "[The enlisted men] have not shared in the planning, have not been asked for their opinions nor deemed to have any opinions of their own. It has always been axiomatic that the Arab soldier obeys his commander blindly, whoever the enemy, even though the commander himself may be manifesting extreme disobedience towards those to whom he has sworn allegiance . . . Only rarely has a commander thought it necessary to persuade doubting soldiers to obey his orders" (Be'eri, p. 260). The 1964 Brazilian coup is one of the rare instances in which an officer justified his orders to move against the government to the enlisted men under his command.

ment ministers and senior officers, belonging to the same communal group, upon orders from lower-ranking officers from another much despised communal segment, who were themselves acting against the army high command and the prevailing principle of civilian supremacy?

Thus due to the specific nature of the hierarchical imperative—primary obedience is owed to face-to-face superiors—middle-level officers are sometimes able to act independently of the senior commanders before, during, and after the coup. Field-grade officers can carry out coups on their own initiative, overthrowing the generals along with the civilian governors.[16] Generals who are planning a coup cannot simply order middle-level officers to take part; the introduction of political issues weakens a chain of command premised upon purely military considerations. The colonels and majors must somehow be persuaded to help execute the coup, or at least not to oppose the conspirators. And after a military government has been installed, its leaders (who may themselves have formerly been field-grade officers) are often forced to alter their policies or are overthrown by the current troop commanders.

OFFICERS AS PROFESSIONALS

Military officers are professional managers of force and violence. They direct the application of force and violence to enhance national security in the face of potential and actual threats ranging from subversion to all-out conventional warfare. Like other professionals—doctors, lawyers, teachers, engineers, and scientists—military officers are professionals in the sense that they place a high value upon autonomy, exclusiveness, and expertise.[17]

THE DIMENSIONS OF PROFESSIONALISM

Officers attach an overwhelming measure of importance to their autonomy. Civilians are not to trespass on the military reservation. As a professional body officers assert their right to decide questions of military strategy, the requirements for recruitment into the military academy and the officer corps,

---

[16] However, there have hardly been any Latin American coups since 1945 that were led by colonels and majors against the generals.

[17] This formulation overlaps Huntington's focus on expertise, but departs from his conceptualization by expanding his "corporateness" dimension of professionalism to include exclusiveness and autonomy, and by omitting professionalism as service and responsibility to a client (Huntington, 1957, pp. 7–16). Service and responsibility to a client, which in the case of military officers is the government as the agent of the state (Huntington) or the nation (Abrahamsson), is not employed here as a dimension of professionalism because near tautological generalizations could easily result when it is used to explain the incidence of coups.

the content of the training curriculum, the criteria governing promotions, promotions themselves, and the assignment of officers to particular responsibilities and units. Autonomy entails the exclusion of civilian interference within the military establishment; civilians are not to influence the officers in the execution of their military responsibilities.

Officers place an inordinately high value upon their exclusiveness. They alone have the right to bear arms in the nation's defense. "The legal right to practice the profession is limited to members of a carefully defined body. His commission to the officer is what his license is to a doctor" (Huntington, 1957, p. 10). In other words, the military is not to have any serious functional rivals, namely, national militias that are less than "professional." If these are sufficiently enlarged and well armed, they are viewed as highly unwelcome threats to the military's exclusive responsibility for national security.

Officers are also professionals due to their expertise. They are more or less well trained and skilled in directing, administering, and operating an organization whose primary activity is preparing for the application of force and violence. (The degree to which professionalism as expertise is correlated with effectiveness in combat is left as an open question.) Officers have attained special abilities in the management of force and in directing the enlisted men who actually apply the violence. This expertise is attained in a training program that includes courses in strategy and tactics, troop command, weapons technology, transport of men and supplies, and usually basic engineering and administration.

Some military academies and advanced training centers also offer courses in political science, history, psychology, sociology, and economics. In fact, Huntington suggests that military expertise "requires a broad background of general culture for its mastery," bringing the insights of the social sciences to bear upon military problems and decisions. The officer "cannot really develop his analytical skill, insight, imagination, and judgement if he is trained simply in vocational duties. The abilities and habits of mind which he requires within his professional field can in large part be acquired only through the broader avenues of learning outside his profession" (Huntington, 1957, p. 14).[18]

The post-1945 period has witnessed a two-fold growth of military expertise. First, in some military academies and advanced training centers the curriculum has been broadened to include courses in the social sciences and public policy issues that relate to national security broadly defined, such

---

[18] There are some similarities between the bureaucratic and professional features of the military. Concern with professional autonomy includes the maintenance of the hierarchical structure; professionalism as expertise overlaps the rationality principle in decision making and achievement criteria in determining promotions.

as inflation and agrarian reform. Second, the emergence of military managers and technologists, both in number and rank, constitutes a heightened professional expertise within the officer corps as a whole. Professionalism has been increased as organizational, logistical, engineering, and intelligence-gathering skills have been added to the battlefield ideals of combativeness and heroism. Both kinds of change indirectly relate to the officer corps' management of force and violence on behalf of the nation's security.

THE RELATIONSHIP BETWEEN PROFESSIONALISM AND INTERVENTION

How then do these dimensions of professionalism affect the incidence of coups? Civilian governments that threaten the military's autonomy or exclusiveness regularly generate powerful interventionist motives. It is the actions or inactions of the civilian incumbents, rather than the level of professionalism, that determine whether such motives do or do not appear. What varies is not the value assigned to professional autonomy and exclusiveness, which remains very high, but the frequency and extent to which they are threatened by civilian leaders.[19]

Civilian impingements upon the military's autonomy and exclusiveness generate powerful interventionist motives because they do far more than detract from the professional pride and self-image of the officer corps. When civilians interfere with military matters they usually have an adverse effect upon the career interests of many officers, lower the competence of the officer corps, detract from military effectiveness, warp the hierarchical command structure, hurt morale, and threaten the unity of the officer corps. When civilians create or expand existing militia forces they call into question the military's ability to execute its exclusive national security responsibility, reduce the political standing of the armed forces, allow for a reduction in the size of the officer corps, and perhaps threaten its very existence, since the military might be dissolved and replaced by the militia.[20]

With regard to the third dimension of professionalism—expertise that is directly or indirectly related to the management of force and violence—there are plausible reasons for thinking that greater expertise both contributes to and detracts from the likelihood of intervention. According to Huntington, the greater the expertise of the officer corps, the less likely

---

[19] However, these statements do not apply to those few cases in which unusual circumstances allowed for the extensive implementation of the penetration model of civilian control.

[20] Autonomy and exclusiveness constitute two of the four dimensions of the military's corporate interests whose defense consistently engenders interventionist motives. (See pp. 71–78).

is their intervention.[21] The individual officer's positive self-image, and the outlet for his ambitions and energies, are then bound up with the pursuit of military excellence, that is, expertise. In contrast, where military competence is not highly valued, the officers are left with little to do in the way of perfecting their national security capabilities, while personal ambitions do not find an outlet in the acquisition of expertise as a means of winning promotions. Such officers are consequently more inclined to engage in politics as an extracurricular activity. Moreover, officers who pride themselves on being experts are reluctant to support praetorian forays in the belief that these would detract from the competence of the officer corps as managers of force and violence. An officer corps' involvement in politics reduces the time and energy available for the maintenance and development of military skills. (Huntington, 1957, p. 71).

Both points are plausible: officers who are primarily devoted to the attainment of military expertise are concomitantly less interested in political issues, and they are concerned that intervention will lower the standards of military excellence.

On the other hand, there are persuasive reasons and some evidence for thinking that there is a positive rather than an inverse relationship between the level of expertise and the likelihood of intervention. Officers who have graduated from the military academy, who have taken advanced training courses and have attended war colleges, who have specialized intelligence-gathering, managerial, and logistical skills—it is these well-trained officers who are most likely to harbor disrespect and disdain for civilians who cannot govern competently. These officers are also the most likely to believe that their military skills can be transferred to the civilian sphere where they will decidedly improve governmental performance, thereby engendering a mild interventionist disposition toward ineffective civilian governments.

Another set of reasons for thinking that expertise sometimes encourages intervention takes us back to Huntington's statement that officers with educational backgrounds in the social sciences are not only more competent professionals, military excellence requires such broad training over and above strictly vocational courses in strategy, tactics, logistics, and military history. The broadly educated soldier is the better-trained soldier. Is it then not possible that advanced training in nonmilitary subjects promotes a concern with civilian affairs? Would not a study of political and economic subjects make officers more critical of civilian governors? And

---

21 However, Huntington's generalization is not stated in "isolation," for he includes two other dimensions of professionalism (corporateness and responsibility to a client) in arguing that heightened professionalism reduces the probability of intervention.

might they not also learn that internal security is not solely related to military power—that it also depends upon political and economic policies—thereby widening their perceived responsibilities to encompass what are normally considered civilian concerns? At a minimum, these "leading" questions suggest that heightened professional expertise may engender interventionist dispositions when civilian governments are performing inadequately.

Evidence that this is more than a possibility comes from Brazil and Peru. It is not just that the praetorian officer corps of these two countries are probably the most professionally competent ones in Latin America.[22] Their intervention is partly related to a broadened training program that was developed prior to the 1964 and 1968 coups. What is true of Brazil in this regard finds some decided parallels in the Peruvian case, which is discussed in Chapter 5.

The Brazilian officer corps exhibited a high level of professional expertise throughout the post-1945 period, as seen in the requirement that each major promotion necessitated attendance at an advanced training school. Before officers can assume a troop command, they must have spent four years at the military academy. Lieutenants cannot be promoted to captain unless they spent a year at the junior officers' school. To be eligible for promotion to general, middle-level officers must pass the difficult examination qualifying them for the General Staff School—which only one out of four applicants succeeded in doing—and then attending its three-year course. Success in the Brazilian army is thus closely related to academic achievement.

Starting in the 1950s the Higher War College offered a course of study that extended far beyond the usual military curriculum. Three of the seven academic divisions were devoted to political subjects, psychological-social studies, and economic affairs. The middle- and high-ranking officers who attended the college studied inflation, agrarian problems, banking reform, electoral laws, transportation, and education. They dealt with the political, economic, and social conditions facilitating the growth of radicalism and violence among workers and peasants. According to the major doctrine developed at the Higher War College—which was disseminated to key troop commanders through military publications—internal security is very much dependent upon governmental policies that promote economic growth and modernization.

Out of this broadened military expertise came a further politicization of the officer corps. Instead of the gap between the military and political spheres widening, the new professionalism led to a belief that there was a fundamental interrelationship between the two spheres, with the military

---

[22] The Argentine officer corps, which is also interventionist, is the only one in Latin America with an equally high level of professional expertise.

playing a key role in interpreting and dealing with domestic political problems owing to its greater technical and professional skills in handling internal security issues." It was this greater expertise, although only indirectly related to the officers' management of force and violence, that helps account for the 1964 increase in the level of intervention. The officers had intervened as moderator-type praetorians in 1945, 1954, and 1955; in 1964 they took control as guardians and soon thereafter transformed themselves into ruler types. On the previous occasions they thought themselves too deficient in political and economic training to serve as governors. By 1964 their further professionalization led them to conclude that the military could and should assume control of the government. They had developed a doctrine relating internal security to socioeconomic development, the trained cadres to implement the doctrine, and sufficient confidence to think of themselves as more able than the civilian governors (Stepan, 1971, pp. 50–51, 176–80, 183–84; Stepan, 1973, pp. 50–51, 56–58).

These reasons for thinking that professionalism as expertise encourages interventionist proclivities, rather than the acceptance of civilian control, are supported by several comparisons of officers with greater and lesser training within the same praetorian armies. The fourteen-man Executive Committee of the Free Officers' Association that overthrew the Egyptian monarchy in 1952 included five men (Nasser among them) who had the distinction of having graduated from the Staff College. Whereas one-third of this group had received advanced training, at the time of the coup less than 3 percent of the Egyptian officer corps had attended the Staff College (Be'eri, pp. 84–85). In a comparison of the 142 officers who took part in the 1961 South Korean coup with a sample of nonparticipants, it was found that 52 percent of the conspirators had graduated from the military academy, whereas only 19 percent of the nonparticipants had received such extensive training (C. I. Eugene Kim, 1968, p. 315). A markedly disproportionate number of the leaders of the first (but not the second) Nigerian coup had previously been chosen for the highly selective, intensive, intellectually demanding two-year training course at Sandhurst, England. That their professional competence was far above the average is also suggested by the fact that most of the eleven conspirators alternated between training and staff assignments (Luckham, pp. 6, 36–37). In Brazil, the generals who had attended the Higher War College were notably overrepresented among the active plotters in the 1964 coup. Among the generals who had studied at the college, 60 percent were active in planning the coup, whereas only 15 percent of those generals who had not attended were among the conspirators (Stepan, 1971, pp. 183–84). And within the Peruvian military, officers with advanced military educations have been disproportionately involved in political activities (including the 1968 coup) compared with their less well trained counterparts (Einaudi and Stepan, p. 59).

When these considerations are taken together, it would seem that professionalism as expertise is somewhat more likely to promote intervention than the acceptance of civilian control. Plausible reasons have been offered for the reverse relationship, yet on balance these are probably outweighed by those that we have just discussed and the supporting examples. However, it should be noted that the hypothesis takes the form of a weakly stated generalization: a high level of professionalism as expertise encourages intervention, but this is not one of the most important explanatory variables. With regard to the other two dimensions of professionalism, autonomy and exclusiveness are highly valued within almost all military establishments. Civilian interference with internal military affairs and the creation of rival militias consequently trigger powerful interventionist motives. But whether or not such motivations arise depends upon the *civilian* governors, who may or may not threaten the military's autonomy and exclusiveness.

THE OFFICERS' POLITICAL ATTITUDES

Attitudes are made up of beliefs, values, and norms —beliefs about the nature of reality, values regarding the kind of reality that is desired, and norms about what reality ought to be like. Although attitudes do not invariably shape behavior—if a conflict exists between attitudes and certain immediately pressing concerns, the former may be ignored or contradicted [23] —the political attitudes of military officers have an especially pronounced impact upon their actions.

The most salient of the officers' political attitudes refer to political order, political activity, and the governing of states. They are both characteristic and distinctive of the officer corps. They are characteristic of the officer corps insofar as most officers adhere to them. They are distinctive of the officer corps in that each of them is far more frequently found within the military than among most civilian groups, and the combination of the three is almost exclusively found within the officer corps.[24]

---

[23] For example, it was seen that the set of beliefs, values, and norms that strongly disposed the Ghanaian officers to accept civilian control was overcome by Nkrumah's interference with military autonomy, albeit with considerable difficulty.

[24] The only group whose political attitudes closely approximated those of the officer corps is the higher civil service, which helps account for the latter's notable influence with military governments. See pages 121–22 for a development of this point.

Officers place an inordinately high value upon the maintenance of political order. Political order is desired, desirable, and necessary. Institutions that permit disorder are condemned. The men who purposefully encourage disorder, as well as those whose inactions inadvertently allow for disorder, are dangerous. Officers are so sensitive to the possibility of disorder that even in the absence of deep societal divisions, a raucous or highly competitive politics is viewed as undesirable and threatening. It is one thing to place an extremely high value upon order in the context of a dangerously fissiparous politics; it is quite another when it becomes an overriding concern in the context of a merely cacophonous politics.

What then are the roots of the characteristic military attitude toward political order? The high value placed upon the preservation of political calm is primarily shaped by the military's exceptionally forceful, extensive, and clearly exhibited hierarchical relations. The officers' deep respect for, and belief in, the necessity of hierarchy, are then generalized to the civilian sphere. Out of military discipline, a belief in political order. It is psychologically difficult for men to compartmentalize attitudes, holding one set to be appropriate in one context and another set elsewhere. There is a tendency to generalize attitudes, transferring them from the most salient context—in this instance the military sphere within which they are essential—to other spheres. As a rigorously ordered institution, any threat to the military's hierarchical order takes on enormous significance. Without distinguishing very much between the appropriateness of this concern for the military and civilian spheres, it is also applied to the latter.

In carrying out their chief responsibility of guaranteeing the nation's security, officers tend to overestimate the degree to which it is threatened. Their very reason for being, their ultimate purpose, is national security. And as such, they are extremely sensitive to the possibility that it may be endangered. What others accept as the ineluctable (and perhaps "healthy") currents of political conflict, officers tend to interpret as challenges to the regime itself, or as the tip of the iceberg of an impending threat. Their responsibility for national security almost dictates that they overestimate the power of actual opponents, react to potential challenges as if they were actual threats, and assume that what might happen is likely to happen unless preventive actions are taken, out of which comes the inordinate concern for political order.

That concern also stems from their strong aversion to being forced to act as policemen. Officers see themselves as professional [25] and heroic man-

---

[25] Unless otherwise indicated, from this point on *professionalism* will be used solely to refer to one of its three dimensions—that of military expertise.

agers of violence. They are ready and willing to use force against similarly trained and armed soldiers, hopefully from another country. To do so against their "own people," against men who are unorganized, untrained, and sparsely armed, is an unpalatable task, at least in the absence of intense animosities toward a particular class or communal group. It impugns their professional standing, martial qualities, and heroic image. But when the police are unable to maintain order, it is the army that has to put down riots, break up unauthorized demonstrations, guard politically sensitive buildings, and patrol the cities. Officers are consequently much (or overly) concerned that a disorderly politics may get out of hand, requiring that they demean themselves as policemen.

Turning to its consequences, the exceptionally strong attachment to political order affects the incidence of coups, the structure of military regimes, and the economic policies of military governments. In a few instances, governments that were unable to preserve order have been overthrown by officers who were required to undertake the unsavory role of policemen. More importantly, when other interventionist motives are present, political turbulence strengthens the resolve to act upon these motives. Intervention can be more readily justified and rationalized when the government is unable to meet its primary responsibility of maintaining public order. Soldiers do not regularly recognize that disorder is often beyond the control of politicians and governments—that it is the product of long-standing communal animosities and the unsettling consequences of social and economic change. The unquestioning belief in the necessity of order prevents the officers from distinguishing between those politicians who ineptly or purposefully foment demonstrations, riots, and violence and those politicians who are doing an effective job of keeping disorder within relatively safe bounds. Soldiers are disposed toward intervention in both situations.

We have already noted that all military regimes are either partially or completely closed. Authoritarian structures are preferred because mass participation and political competition are thought to be closely related to political turbulence and the possibility of violence. The maintenance of political calm requires a greater or lesser degree of regime closure, depending upon the particular political context.

One of the most important decision-making touchstones of military governments is the preservation of political order. Unless there is an internal "enemy" that is to be defeated, no policy will be adopted that threatens the much-desired state of political calm. This point is particularly applicable to the minority of military governments that do have a serious interest in promoting major economic changes of a modernizing or progressive variety. For unless such changes are carried out within the context of a mobilization regime, a kind of regime that praetorians are unwilling or unable to create, they contain the potential for an unwieldly, difficult to control, and highly turbulent politics. When political disorder is expected to follow from the implementation of modernizing or progressive policies, the praetorians' commitment to these changes becomes notably diluted.

ATTITUDES TOWARD POLITICAL ACTIVITY

The soldiers' attitudes toward political activity as the more or less strenuous pursuit of group interests are decidedly negative. Political activity tends to be seen as excessively self-serving, as well as harmful in its exacerbation of societal differences. Latin American officers (and others as well) commonly believe that "politics is 'dissension'; political parties are 'factions'; politicians are 'scheming' or 'corrupt'; and the expression of public opinion is 'insubordination'" (McAlister, p. 152). More than any other elite group, military officers view political parties as undesirable agents of disunity. While president of Pakistan, General Ayub Khan stated that parties "divide and confuse the people" and allow for their "exploitation by unscrupulous demagogues." Nasser declared that parties would "divide us and create differences between us" (Huntington, 1968, pp. 243–44).

Officers are especially ill disposed toward mass participation insofar as it constitutes a more extensive and intensive type of political activity. The expression of popular interests is seen as narrow minded and selfish; adamantly stated demands on the part of the masses are disparaged as the absence of respect for authority; their crude formulation and emotional overtones detract from the respectability of mass politics; and the organized pursuit of group interests is considered unnecessarily divisive. This is not to suggest that soldiers are negatively disposed toward democratic regimes in principle. Rather, they are biased against what are viewed as the excesses of democratic (or mass) participation. An "ideal" democratic regime is even highly valued. But the military's ideal is decidedly unrealistic insofar as it leaves little room for the extreme partisanship, strenuous competition, and intense conflict that are often part and parcel of democratic participation.

Negative attitudes toward political activity are firmly rooted in two closely related features of the military establishment: hierarchy and cohesiveness. We have already noted that military officers, like most men, tend to generalize what is learned within the major sphere of their activity to other spheres. Since hierarchy and cohesiveness characterize or ought to characterize the military, they are thought to be desirable and realizable within the polity. Just as the hierarchical imperative does not permit the expression of personal interests within the military, so too should politics minimize the articulation of individual and group interests within society.

Just as enlisted men and subordinate officers respect and obey their superiors, citizens should maintain themselves in a state of political acquiescence toward their governors. Just as the military constitutes a highly cohesive organization, the officer corps a "brotherhood," so too should the society approximate a consensual model. Just as differences within the military—between officers and enlisted men, between senior-, middle- and junior-level officers, and between the various units—usually do not and certainly should not give rise to divisions, so too should class, regional, and communal differences not form the bases of political conflicts within society.

In some armies the assessment of political activity as less than honorable stems from the officers' desire to attain or maintain positions of high social status within society, as well as the desire to preserve or enhance their professional self-image. The military career becomes more respected and respectable with the denigration of the role of another elite—that of the politicians. The Nigerian officers' tendency to disparage political activity derives from their "rather low status compared with other elites, motivating them to provide honour for themselves on their own terms through emphasis on the distinctive values of martial life, which were contrasted with the more complex and dubious morality of the politicians" (Luckham, pp. 107, 203). The military career is both different from and "superior" to that of the politicians.

The negative disposition toward political activity often has a significant effect upon the decision to intervene. Given the existence of one or more interventionist motives, the resolve to act upon them is measurably strengthened by the greater or lesser contempt for politicians and the inability to appreciate their possible contributions. Considering their numerous responsibilities, the many pressures that are placed upon them, and the need to balance conflicting interests and considerations, it is easy to be critical of politicians. Soldiers are exceptionally so. When in actuality the civilians are blatantly opportunistic, self-serving, corrupt, factious, and incompetent, the critical bias turns into sharp resentments and animosities. When motivated to do so for other reasons, it is then obviously easier to act against men who are little respected, whose contributions are unappreciated, and who are generally thought to be parasitic, unproductive, or positively harmful.

Once in power, the negative attitude toward political activity has a pronounced effect upon regime structure. Since political organizations are unnecessarily divisive and mass participation borders on insubordination, the regime is to be closed to popular participation and competition, at least until the polity can be sufficiently regenerated to allow for the election of a new civilian government. The impact of attitudes upon actions is poignantly exemplified by the title of the 1961 law that outlawed political parties in South Korea. The praetorians called it the Political Activities Purification Law. And a few newly established military governments in Africa even arrested and deported some politicians who had opposed the previous civilian government and favored a military takeover (Zolberg, 1968, pp. 89–90).

In addition, the soldiers' bias against political activity leave them unable to appreciate the uses of mass political parties that they themselves control. Such organizations could help buttress and legitimize their power, and they are sorely needed to ensure the implementation of ambitious economic reform programs. Yet few military governments have attempted to build mass parties, and where they have been created they turned out to be ineffectual structures because genuine participation was not permitted. The praetorians' antipolitical biases make it difficult for them to recognize the nature of political reality at the grass-roots level. They are disinterested in attracting and organizing the masses, and without the political skills to do so.

ATTITUDES TOWARD THE GOVERNMENTAL PROCESS

Officers have an apolitical vision of the governmental process, a nonpolitical conception of how society can and should be governed. "Even more so than other groups in society . . . their goal is community without politics, consensus by command" (Huntington, 1968, p. 244). To put it most starkly, societies should be governed in a political vacuum. The governors are to act in accordance with the national (or public) interest, with the soldiers concomitantly believing in its palpable and identifiable existence. According to this unrealistic vision of governors acting as political eunuchs, they are charged with the seemingly straightforward responsibility of identifying and implementing policies that are in the national interest. This is also to say that partisanship, bargaining, and compromise not only are unsavory in and of themselves—this is not how governors should act—but have harmful consequences in subverting the public interest.

Considering their powerful normative attachment to the nation,[26] it is no accident that the military tend to believe in the existence of a singular public interest. Those differences and conflicts that do arise should be submerged in favor of an identifiable public interest, which is somehow equiva-

---

[26] The officers' powerful nationalistic sentiments are explicable in terms of the connections between military and nation. The nation can hardly be viewed in critical or neutral terms since the military is responsible for defending it, simultaneously expressing its power, symbolizing its sovereignty, and incorporating its special qualities. Closely bound up with the nation, it serves as a source of pride and identification for the officer corps.

lent to the shared interests of the nation's constituent parts. The military tend to believe that there is such a thing as the national interest because their very existence is premised upon the defense of the nation as a whole; their reason for being is national service. To view the nation as made up of conflicting interests or incompatible parts is to downgrade the importance and purpose of the military. Men who act according to a different conception of the nation, especially workers who believe that their interests conflict with those of the middle class, are to be condemned.

The devaluation of bargaining and compromise is also rooted in the heroic and martial traditions of the military (Janowitz, 1964, p. 66). Military honor and victory are gained by relentless, undeviating action against the enemy, rather than by averting his forces, minimizing bloodshed or negotiating truces. Just as soldiers should not waver on the battlefield, decision makers should not temporize or depart from their principles. Bargaining and compromise are consequently not only devalued but taken as indications of weakness or unprincipled behavior. These normative judgments are further buttressed by the officers' enhancement of their self-image in asserting the moral superiority of the martial virtues, as well as the hierarchical structure of the military, which leaves little room for any give-and-take between superiors and subordinates.

As might be expected, the soldiers' apolitical attitude toward the governmental process has its most direct impact upon their own governing style—the characteristic way in which authoritative decisions are considered and reached. Among praetorian governments it tends toward decision making without politics.[27] One of its dimensions relegates the demands, preferences, and views of politicians and citizens to a position of secondary importance at best. So far as possible they are not to find their way into the decision-making process. To take into account the interests and concerns of the masses and their leaders is to subvert the public interest—one that can best be identified by the praetorians themselves, possibly with the advice of selected individuals such as civil servants and technocrats. To make decisions in a different, political, manner would produce illogically constructed compromises, temporary palliatives, ineffectual actions, or clearly detrimental policies. It would also involve the praetorians in the demeaning and distasteful business of compromise and bargaining.

The apolitical attitudes of military governors have particularly unhappy consequences in societies that are experiencing severe communal conflicts. When confronted with intense ethnic, religious, linguistic, and regional conflicts, military governors tend to negate the possibilities of compromise agreements designed to avert the outbreak of major violence. They do not see the need for them, besides being ill disposed and unskilled

[27] The praetorians' characteristic governing style is discussed on pp. 117–24.

in working out an artful political balance. Instead, the military governors of deeply divided societies tend to assume that the conflicts can be resolved, and the divisions that gave rise to them can be eradicated by "national solutions" imposed from above. These "solutions" are to be identified and applied without temporizing or compromising the goal of national unity. Yet deep-seated divisions and emotion-charged conflicts cannot be eliminated in the short run; the attempt to do so can only exacerbate them. To aim for national unity as an expression of the public interest rather than work out partial agreements that could mitigate the conflict's intensity is likely to result in violence, repression, and political disintegration. And this is especially so when the favored "solutions" are imposed in an uncompromising, heavy-handed, forceful manner.[28]

Praetorians sometimes return governmental power to the civilians earlier than intended when they find themselves acting like "unsavory" politicians. Instead of being able to govern according to their apolitical predilections, they find themselves dealing with incompatible goals, responding to group pressures, and confronting recalcitrant problems which force them to depart from their original principles. Their apolitical self-image becomes soiled. As they see themselves becoming more and more like the politicians whom they overthrew, withdrawal from government appears increasingly attractive. The desire to return to the relative political purity of the barracks helps explain the short duration of most military regimes.[29]

THE PRONOUNCED IMPACT OF ATTITUDES UPON BEHAVIOR

Political attitudes have a decided impact upon the officers' behavior before and after the coup. For the degree to which attitudes affect behavior is especially pronounced when one or more of three general conditions are satisfied: the particular attitudes form a mutually reinforcing pattern; they are the product of an extensive and intensive socializing experience; and they are reinforced by powerful conformist pressures. Each of these conditions is found within the officer corps.

Rather than the officers' political attitudes being unrelated and thus unsupportive of each other, their attitudes toward political order, political activity, and the governing of states form a mutually reinforcing pattern. Each of the three attitudes implies, and thereby strengthens, the other two. For example, the strong preference for an apolitical government helps

---

[28] For the impact of the apolitical governing style upon the civil wars in the Sudan, Pakistan, and Nigeria, see pp. 156–65.

[29] This is one of the reasons for the inherent instability of military regimes. See pp. 138–47.

induce a negative attitude toward political activity, since the latter invariably allows partisanship, competition, and conflict to affect governmental decisions. Similarly, the pronounced sensitivity to political disorder heightens the antipathy toward political activity which frequently results in a disorderly politics. A moment's thought will indicate that these statements are also valid when stated in reverse—that is, the negative attitude toward political activity deepens the soldiers' attachment to the ideal of an apolitical government and the strong predilection for political order. Indeed, it can be seen that each of the attitudes reinforces the others.

The officers' political attitudes are firmly internalized because of the intensive and lengthy socialization experiences they undergo. Beginning at age fifteen or sixteen when they enter the military academy, and throughout their advanced training and career experiences, politically relevant attitudes are purposefully learned, implicitly instilled, and latently internalized.[30] Be'eri is not exaggerating the socializing impact of the military when he writes that "apart from monastic orders there is no comparable social body that so sets its stamp, for so much of a man's life, on every individual belonging to it" (Be'eri, p. 294).

The officers' characteristic political attitudes are then maintained and further strengthened by conformist pressures—pressures that are more forcefully felt than in almost any other political group. For the military comes close to being a "total institution": officers work and live within its confines, military life is sharply differentiated from civilian life, officers are often segregated and occasionally isolated from civilians, and they remain within the same institution throughout their careers.[31] Moreover, the function of the military requires unity, cohesiveness, and an *esprit de corps*. There is often a deliberate fusion of personal and military life in the officers' mess and the barracks in order to foster cohesion and "brotherhood." For potentially deviant officers to challenge the prevailing political beliefs, values, and norms in the face of powerful conformist pressures is highly problematic.[32]

---

[30] In Brazil almost all the cadets at the military academy previously attended military high schools. About 90 percent of the officers thus began their military education when they were about twelve years old (Stepan, 1973, p. 64). For an extensive and insightful study of the socialization of officers, see Luckham's analysis of the Nigerian military "as a social system," pp. 83–197.

[31] However, to say that "the barracks becomes the world" due to "separate housing in purely military quarters" and the "systematized nomadism [of] moving from one garrison town to another" (Finer, p. 9), exaggerates the self-encapsulation of the officer corps.

[32] These last few points are significantly less applicable to some very small, poorly trained, ethnically heterogeneous, and factionalized African officer corps, such as those of Congo/Brazzaville, Dahomey, and Sierra Leone.

THE
COUP
D'ETAT

3

Our approach to the problem of explaining the incidence of military coups is premised upon an apparently simple but crucial statement: the coup d'etat is a consciously conceived and purposefully executed act. It is purposefully undertaken in order to achieve consciously formulated goals, with an awareness of the possible costs and risks involved. The coup d'etat is thus analyzed and explained from the perspective of the soldiers themselves.[1]

In this chapter we will develop some general answers to the dual question, Why and when do soldiers intervene? The question of why they do so gets us into the realm of motivations.[2] What do the officers intend to prevent or accomplish in overthrowing civilian governments? It will be suggested that by far the most common and salient interventionist motive

---

[1] An alternative approach begins not with the decision to intervene but with the various factors that are thought to explain it. This approach may turn out to be overly mechanistic insofar as it identifies various explanatory factors without spelling out exactly how and why they influence the decision to intervene. Our own approach and the hypotheses derived from it are indirectly buttressed by the findings of Hibbs's exceptionally sophisticated quantitative analysis of the successful coups that occurred between 1948 and 1967. For there were no significant associations between coups and four explanatory factors that have been offered by writers on military intervention, but which are not dealt with in the present study. These alternative explanatory factors include the level of economic development, social mobilization, political participation, and political institutionalization (Hibbs, pp. 90–109). Since Hibbs's data include all independent states, the analysis was repeated for the non-Western states alone, without any significant differences appearing in the statistical associations.

[2] Since both motives and attitudes shape praetorian actions, it may be helpful to distinguish between them. Motivated behavior is undertaken *in order to* accomplish certain goals. Attitudinally determined behavior is undertaken *because of* particular dispositions to act in certain ways.

involves the defense or enhancement of the military's corporate interests. After examining the ways in which corporate interests engender powerful interventionist motives, the following section departs from the book's organizational format in concentrating upon a single area of the non-Western world. For it is only in Latin America that the level of politicization among the lower classes is regularly high enough to be seen as a challenge to the military's corporate interests, as well as the interests of the middle class on whose behalf Latin American officers are sometimes motivated to intervene.

The most important answers to the second part of the question—When do soldiers intervene?—are to be found in the civilian governments' performance failures and their resulting loss of legitimacy. Performance failures (e.g., the inability to preserve public order) strengthen the officers' resolve to act upon their interventionist motives insofar as they come to hold the incumbents in greater or lesser contempt. The officers can more easily rationalize and justify their coups when acting against incumbents whom they see as incompetent or worse. More important, performance failures lead to the deflation of governmental legitimacy within the politicized stratum of the civilian population. It is this factor that encourages and allows the officers to act upon their interventionist motives. Despite the enormous power enjoyed by the military, there are several reasons why it is almost never used against civilian governments unless (or until) they have lost their legitimizing mantle. Legitimacy deflations are crucial in facilitating the transformation of interventionist motivations into coup attempts.

After having analyzed the factors that explain the decision to intervene, the final section of this chapter deals with the coup itself. The success of some coups—those in which the officer corps is united in its opposition to the incumbents—is virtually guaranteed from the outset. But in most cases it is a more or less risky undertaking. There are nearly as many failures as successes. Some general answers are then offered to the question of how successful coups are planned and executed. These take the form of three "rules" of interventionist prudence, whose implementation markedly heightens the probability of success.[3]

---

[3] It should be noted that none of the explanations for the decision to intervene or the coup's success refer to foreign interference. Although the United States in particular has occasionally tried to bring about or forestall military coups, these efforts have rarely had a significant impact. For example, the Chilean armed forces would have overthrown Allende even without the CIA's "destabilizing" effort. The 1954 Guatemalan and 1962 South Vietnamese coups are two of the few cases in which American involvement had a significant effect on the outcome.

THE MILITARY'S CORPORATE INTERESTS

Every public institution—whether it be the civil service, the legislature, the executive branch, the judiciary, the police, or the armed forces—is much concerned with the protection and enhancement of its own interests. And these institutions perceive their interests in broadly similar ways. They all share an interest in adequate budgetary support, autonomy in managing their internal affairs, the preservation of their responsibilities in the face of encroachments from rival institutions, and the continuity of the institution itself. These will be referred to as the institutions' corporate interests. The defense or enhancement of the military's corporate interests is easily the most important interventionist motive.

Public institutions that are highly cohesive, imbued with an *esprit de corps*, and endowed with considerable power resources pursue their corporate interests in a determined and effective fashion. They are energized and able to do so with relatively little risk of internal disunity. The military differs from most public institutions in its cohesiveness and *esprit de corps*; it differs from all others in the enormous power derived from its hierarchical structure and force of arms. The military has consequently been remarkably successful in protecting or enhancing its corporate interests through the *coup d'etat*.

Two preliminary points need to be raised. First, there is the disparity between the praetorians' public justifications for their coups and the motivations that are attributed to them here. After the coup the military assert that they acted for public-spirited reasons in protecting the constitution or nation from the unhappy consequences of civilian rule.[4] Here it will be seen that the praetorians are primarily, often solely, motivated by the defense or enhancement of military interests, and they act upon them even when these conflict with constitutional rules and norms, and what may appear to others as the best interests of the nation. Yet the two kinds of explanations are not necessarily contradictory, at least in the minds of the praetorians.

For given the self-image of the officer corps as leading nationalists, they are commonly able to rationalize away or sincerely justify even their predatory actions. Since they identify with the nation, what is to the advantage of the military is also good for the country. This kind of thinking is further enhanced by the reverse identification—the identification of the nation with the military. National honor, sovereignty, and power reside with and within the armed forces. It is almost as if coups necessarily promote the national interest because the officers identify with the nation and the nation is identified with the military. This point is even made by

---

[4] Praetorianism's public rationale is discussed on pp. 19–21.

a student of the Latin American military who is rather critical of their actions: "The generals are not capricious ogres whose only interests are destroying democracy and raiding the national treasury . . . [Officers] view themselves as sincere patriots. Their intervention, they believe, is always in the national interest—to save their country or protect their institution, which they consider the very embodiment of nationhood" (Lieuwen, 1964, p. 98). The soldiers consequently intervene on behalf of their corporate interests with preciously few qualms or inhibitions, especially since they act against civilian governments that have suffered legitimacy deflations.

Second, the personal interests of officers—their desire for promotions, political ambitions, and fear of dismissal—are important motivating factors in a significant number of coups (Thompson, pp. 26–28; Decalo, pp. 17–22). However, the presence of individual interventionist interests does not weaken the primary importance of corporate interests as interventionist motives. For personal interests are more or less significant in explaining any kind of elite behavior; there is no reason to suppose that they are especially salient in accounting for the interventionist behavior of military officers. And in developing explanatory generalizations about elite behavior what is most important is not the various personal interests themselves, but the extent to which they coincide with, and their behavioral expression is facilitated by, other, more general factors. With regard to military coups, there is usually a close parallel between individual concerns and corporate interests, as when civilian interference with institutionally prescribed promotional patterns adversely affects those officers who have been passed over because they are not in favor with the chief executive. Moreover, the officer corps' concern with corporate interests provides personally ambitious or discontented officers with the necessary support for their coups. Even a student of the African military who lays great stress on individual interests in accounting for coups, and who describes General Idi Amin's coup in Uganda in 1971 as "a classic example of a takeover triggered by personal fears and ambitions," goes on to say that "an army rife with grievances . . . facilitated the coup and assured it a measure of support" (Decalo, p. 18). In short, despite the relevance of personal interests to interventionist behavior, their explanatory importance is sharply reduced because they generally coincide with, and can often be realized through, the activation of corporate interests.

BUDGETARY SUPPORT

Turning to the first of the military's corporate interests—adequate budgetary support—civilian governments sometimes try to cut back expenditures or refuse to increase them at the military's insistence. The incumbents do not see any security threats on the horizon; they think it necessary to adopt a policy of financial austerity; the funding of modernization or welfare programs takes greater priority; or the civilians perceive the officer corps as hostile. It is then not uncommon for the senior commanders to threaten a coup, with the threat swiftly materializing if their demands are not met. For adequate budgetary support, as determined by the military, constitutes one of its chief corporate interests.

Once having installed themselves (or a new civilian government) in power, the "necessary" budgetary adjustments follow. In this regard the history of military intervention in Peru is atypical only in a matter of degree. Two patterns emerge from the many coups that took place between 1912 and 1964. Every civilian government that reduced the proportion of the national budget assigned to the Peruvian military was overthrown, and this despite continual increases in the absolute size of military expenditures. And the new civilian or military government that was installed by the officers invariably increased military expenditures (Villaneuva, 1969, p. 194). The 1948 Peruvian coup, for example, was explained and justified by the statement that the civilian government had not "built even one military base" while adopting "the inconceivable project of reducing the military forces by one-third, for economic reasons" (Astiz, 1969A, pp. 138–39).

The regularity with which military spending is increased *after* the coup indirectly suggests that intervention has often been prompted by budgetary concerns. At least until 1960, whenever a military government came to power in Latin America, defense expenditures were increased even though a sizable (many would say an excessive) proportion of the budget was already being spent on the armed forces (Lieuwen, 1960, pp. 147–48). When the twenty Latin American countries are classified according to the extent of military intervention between 1956 and 1965, and these scores are then related to defense spending as a percentage of gross national product, a .55 correlation emerges (Putnam, p. 100). This correlation suggests that 25 percent of the variation in military expenditures is related to the level of intervention. In another study the Latin American countries were divided into three groups: those in which the military controlled the government *circa* 1960, those in which the officers were politicized (i.e., they acted as moderator types), and those in which they accepted civilian supremacy. In the latter group of countries 9 percent of central government expenditures were devoted to the military, this proportion increasing to 14 percent and 19 percent with the increases in the level of military intervention (Schmitter, pp. 438–39).

The relationship between praetorianism and defense spending is not limited to Latin America. Civilian governments in the non-Western areas have devoted an average of 14 percent of total public expenditures to armed forces; military governments have spent 21 percent (or 50 percent more) on the armed forces (Kennedy, p. 163). Among those seventy-four non-Western countries to which the United States extended some foreign aid in the 1957–62 period, the military accepted civilian control in thirty-six and intervened extensively in the other thirty-eight. It then turns out that the average proportion of gross national product allocated to defense expenditures was almost twice as high in those countries with a praetorian officer corps (Nordlinger 1970, p. 1143).

Although these findings do not provide direct evidence about interventionist motives, the markedly higher defense expenditures in countries with a praetorian officer corps suggest that one of their chief motivations in taking power is to increase the defense budget, or at least to prevent budgetary reductions. Taking our analysis one step further, the question becomes: What exactly is it about the defense budget that motivates intervention? [5]

Most obviously, budgetary allocations affect the material well-being, usually the privileged position, of the officer corps, including salary scales, the number of promotions, retirement benefits, housing facilities, and other perquisites. Budgetary changes also serve as a telling indicator of the political power and prestige of the armed forces, with reductions in expenditures signaling a loss of influence and standing. And expenditures influence the officers' perception of the military as a modern, professional organization.

The presence of each of these motivating factors is exemplified in the overthrow of President Nkrumah in 1966. That a reduction in the material privileges of the Ghanaian officer corps helped motivate the coup is brought out in the memoirs of one of the leading conspirators. "By late 1965," writes General Ocran, "the going was getting tough for most senior officers. The salaries introduced in 1957 meant little in 1965. They were worth only a

---

[5] There is an alternative or additional explanation to the ones that are about to be suggested. Expenditures are significant not for the satisfaction of corporate interests but for the preservation of the nation's security from external and internal threats. Given the soldiers' defense responsibilities we would expect them to adhere to more demanding standards of national security than do the civilians. It is better to err on the side of additional safety by spending more on men and weapons. Yet this interpretation of the praetorians as acting on behalf of their functional responsibilities rather than their corporate interests runs squarely up against several difficulties. First, only a small number of non-Western countries are threatened from abroad, and where such threats have appeared, civilian governments have been more than generous in supplying and enlarging the armed forces. Second, even in the internationally conflagrated Middle East, the praetorians have not justified their coups in terms of national security considerations. And third, with regard to the possibility of internal subversion and guerrilla warfare, unsatisfied budgetary demands rarely relate to expenditures for expanded counterinsurgency capabilities. Instead, additional expenditures are generally used to increase military pay and to purchase expensive weapons (tanks, planes, ships) that have little if any utility in meeting insurgency threats.

third of their value." And he goes on to mention the perquisites that the officers were losing under Nkrumah's rule. "One day [the officers] were to pay for their electricity; the next day they were to lose their training allowances; the following day they were to lose their travelling facilities. We all wondered what was happening to us" (Ocran, p. 43). The officers consequently increased the military budget during each of the three years that they controlled the government.

And it might be added that the same kinds of motivations prompted the second Ghanaian coup in 1972, which overthrew the civilian government that was installed in 1969. Given the precarious economic situation resulting from plummeting cocoa prices and the huge indebtedness inherited from the Nkrumah regime, President Busia's popularly elected government undertook severe austerity measures. The military suffered a 10 percent budgetary reduction. The leader of the coup, Colonel Acheampong, stated that Busia "started taking from us the few amenities and facilities we in the armed forces . . . enjoyed even under the Nkrumah regime." His description of the specific material deprivations that the officer corps was suffering under the Busia government resembles statements of their plight under Nkrumah. High on the official list of reasons for the coup were Busia's defense reductions, the loss of many army fringe benefits, and the erosion of the purchasing power of military salaries (Decalo, p. 31; Welch, 1972, pp. 212–13).

Changes in the size of the defense budget are a telling indicator of the politcial power and prestige of the armed forces. Governments that impose reductions or refuse to accede to demands for enlarged budgets are signaling officers and civilians alike that the influence and standing of the military is on the wane. There may very well be a decline of morale and pride within the officer corps, along with the belief that it is (or soon will be) in a weaker position to defend its other corporate interests. Both General Ocran and General Afrifa interpreted the privileges of the President's Own Guard Regiment—the unit that was made directly responsible to Nkrumah and favored with better pay and equipment at the expense of the regular army—as a decline in the officer corps' political influence and as a slap in the face to its pride (Ocran, pp. 28–39; Afrifa, pp. 97–98).

Defense expenditures also affect the self-perceptions of the officers as members of a professional, modern organization. Increased firepower, sophisticated weapons, large installations, and even the quality of uniforms are taken as indicators of modernity and professional expertise. Officers who are denied funds for the purchase of such equipment may then develop interventionist motives out of wounded pride and resentment toward their civilian "detractors." The effect of military expenditures upon professional pride may have been especially pronounced in Ghana. Unlike some other coups which were motivated by the desire for very expensive equipment,[6] the Ghanaian officers felt deprived of the bare essentials of a "proper" army. General Afrifa's wounded professional pride is evident in his description of the third-rate condition of the military under Nkrumah:

> *The army was rendered incapable, ill-equipped, [having] virtually been reduced to a rabble. By Christmas 1965 a number of our troops were without equipment and clothing, things essential for the pride, morale, and efficiency of the soldier . . . It was shameful to see a Ghanaian soldier in a tattered and ragged uniform, sometimes without boots during his training period. [Afrifa, pp. 103–4]*

General Ocran voices similar sentiments in setting out the conspirator's motives:

> *The commanders were really hard put to it. They had known and had been accustomed to a high standard of turnout and cleanliness. What then, could they do to soldiers who turned out on parade in torn uniforms . . . with no polish or shine on their boots or with their toes showing through their canvas shoes? . . . Even the officers went about in very unpresentable uniforms. [Ocran, pp. 45–47]*

Many coups are thus the product of a conjunction between the officers' interest in adequate budgetary support and the unwillingness or inability of civilian governors to satisfy them. Civilian governments are often aware of the likely impact of their actions—an awareness that helps account for what might be viewed as excessive defense spending. They have more or less grudgingly accepted the soldiers' budgetary expectations in the hope of staving off a coup, sometimes increasing expenditures in order to "buy off" the military.

For example, President Betancourt of Venezuela (1958–63) managed to serve out his entire constitutional term of office—the first time this had occurred in that country's military-dominated history—by providing the officers with better salaries, rapid promotions, and a generous allotment of fringe benefits. And he was able to do so despite the adoption of expensive agrarian reforms and developmental programs. He assured the officer corps that these costs would not detract from their economically privileged position since enormous oil revenues were then beginning to replenish the national treasury (Lieuwen, 1964, pp. 86–91; Taylor, pp. 48–53, 67–71).

---

[6] For example, it was the air force of the Dominican Republic, whose $6 million request for new planes had just been rejected by President Bosch, that sparked the 1963 coup (Lieuwen, 1964, pp. 60–61).

Yet in other instances the military have intervened despite budgetary increases designed to stave off a coup, as in the 1973 coup against President Allende of Chile. Allende was overthrown despite military salary increases which were greater than those for equivalent civilian grades, better fringe benefits, and the purchase of additional equipment, including new ships for the navy despite a severe balance-of-payments deficit (Michaels, p. 12).[7]

MILITARY AUTONOMY

Civilian refusals to satisfy budgetary interests do not always engender strong interventionist motives. Interference in the internal affairs of the military almost invariably does so.[8] Even minor trespasses upon the military reservation may be seen as attacks upon its corporate interests. Military autonomy excludes civilian involvement in shaping the educational and training curriculum, the assignment of officers to particular posts, the promotion of all but the most senior officers, and the formulation of defense strategies. And autonomy certainly excludes any attempt to penetrate the officer corps or the enlisted ranks through the introduction of political ideas or personnel.

Civilian interference has a multiple and decided impact upon the officers. Such actions generally lower the professional competence and self-image of the officer corps by substituting political for achievement criteria, call into doubt the soldiers' identities as independent and respected officers, factionalize an otherwise cohesive officer corps, warp the hierarchical structure, and weaken the officers' power to defend their other corporate interests. Considering the several important ways in which civilian interference adversely affects the military, we can begin to appreciate why it almost always inspires interventionist motives.

The overthrow of the Egyptian monarchy in 1952 was largely motivated by the king's interference in military affairs. The first infringement occurred in 1948 when King Farouk ordered the inadequately prepared

---

[7] For other cases of civilians attempting to "buy off" the military, see Schmitter, p. 484, and Cox, pp. 207–8.

[8] This statement is not meant to apply to those armed forces that have already been penetrated by the government. Recall the generalizaton offered in Chapter 1: the penetration model is exceptionally effective in ensuring civilian control once it has been implemented, but except under very unusual circumstances the attempt to do so invariably engenders powerful interventionist motives. In Congo/Brazzaville, for example, the attempt to transform the military into a "People's Army" under the direct control of the radical single party, with a Political Directorate to supervise its ideological indoctrination, generated sharp civilian-military frictions that eventuated in the 1968 takeover (Decalo, pp. 150–55).

army to attack Israel contrary to the advice of the general staff, which correctly predicted an Egyptian defeat. The cabinet originally accepted the military argument based on detailed reports showing the state of military unpreparedness. It also accepted the right of the military to decide the strategic issue of the attack's timing. The cabinet then suddenly reversed itself at the insistence of Farouk and his chief of staff lackey. After the humiliating defeat it became known that the king had irresponsibly committed the army to war, which generated the first wave of military resentment against the monarch. Disaffection was further deepened in 1950 when certain irregularities in the behavior of the king and his circle became known. Especially galling was the purchase of defective weapons for the 1948 war, which constituted direct, irresponsible, and corrupt interference in military affairs (Vatiokitis, pp. 32–36, 42, 59–60). As Nasser was to write later, Egypt "has been deceived and forced into a battle for which she was not ready, her fate the toy of greed, conspiracy, and lust, which left her without weapons under fire" (Nasser, p. 23).

Up to this point the Free Officers group only verbalized their grievances and resentment. They took no action until the king and his advisers again intruded into the military sphere by promoting and shifting officers according to their loyalties to Farouk. After the king usurped cabinet responsibility by forcing the selection of his own unqualified candidate as supreme commander, almost the entire high command came to hold its positions at Farouk's sufferance. The resolve to intervene was irrevocably hardened when the king appointed his highly unqualified brother-in-law as minister of war (Vatiokitis, pp. 39, 59, 66).

Brazil's President Goulart also managed to bring about his own overthrow in 1964 by trespassing on the military domain. Previous Brazilian presidents had influenced promotions and assignments as a means of ensuring the military's political loyalty. Goulart did so with notably greater frequency. In the years before he reached the presidency thirty-four out of seventy-three (or 47 percent) of the line officers promoted to the rank of general had graduated first in one of their military classes. During Goulart's four years in office only five out of twenty-nine (or 17 percent) of those officers promoted to general had exhibited such exceptional abilities, indicating that promotional criteria had been significantly politicized by Goulart. Many senior officers resented this interference because it adversely affected the military's high professional standards and hierarchical relations at the top. The men passed over for promotions felt unfairly treated and resented those who had been advanced. That President Goulart's handling of senior officers was significant in bringing about his own overthrow is evidenced in the disproportionate number of coup activists found among the generals who had not been promoted during the Goulart presidency. And the new military governors purged a disproportionate number of those generals who had been promoted under Goulart (Stepan, 1971, pp. 165–67).

The Brazilian officer corps also became alarmed over the politicization of the enlisted ranks, especially the noncommissioned officers, with its direct threat to military discipline and hierarchy. Afraid that he would be overthrown because of his left-wing policies and connections with militant trade unions, Goulart attempted to prevent a coup by openly seeking political support among the sergeants. In return he promised to back their demands for greater political rights and increased material benefits, such as the provision of special housing. Trade unions also exerted themselves in attempting to politicize the sergeants, as did a few of Goulart's leading supporters. By 1963 politicization had progressed to the point where the chief speaker at a national meeting of sergeants and warrant officers insisted that congress pass agrarian reform measures, also warning that in the event of an attempted coup, the sergeants would take action themselves. A few months later the sergeants burst into action in protest against a supreme court ruling which upheld the disqualification of enlisted men from competing for public office. They occupied strategic centers in Brasilia and held a supreme court judge, the president of the congress, and a few military officers as hostages. Goulart adopted an ambiguous position toward the short-lived revolt, calling it an emotional outburst without real political content. Some of his supporters went so far as to defend the justice of the revolt (Stepan, 1971, pp. 160–62).

The coup was finally triggered by Goulart's further interference with military discipline. His reaction to a sailors' mutiny was instrumental in bringing the moderates within the officer corps to support the activists who had been waiting for some further action that would finally discredit the president's formidable asset of constitutional legality. The navy minister ordered the arrest of a sailor who was attempting to organize a leftist union within the navy. When the navy minister moved against the leader and the Sailors' Association, over one thousand sailors revolted by barricading themselves in a building. Rather than support the minister, Goulart replaced him with a compliant retired admiral proposed by the leaders of the national trade union movement. The new navy minister granted a full amnesty to the besieged sailors—a move that hit the officer corps like a bombshell. Manifestos were issued denouncing this action as an attack upon military discipline and the hierarchical principle. And if this was not enough, a week later Goulart spoke to a televised gathering of sergeants where he refused to disassociate himself from the sailors' revolt (Skidmore, pp. 284–302; Schneider, pp. 95–97, 358).

He was overthrown the next day. His interference in military affairs had become sufficiently blatant to dissuade any officers from supporting him, including those who agreed with the president's socioeconomic policies and who had been promoted under his auspices.

In Ghana, Nkrumah's interference constituted a concerted attempt to achieve complete control and political conformity by influencing promotions and assignments.[9] In 1965 he ordered the early retirement of the two highest ranking officers because they objected to the removal of the President's Own Guard Regiment from the army chain of command. The impact upon the officers' self-esteem can be gauged from Afrifa's comments: "This was not the way to treat Generals. . . . As a result of this action the Ghanaian officers and men felt that the profession of men-at-arms had been disgraced and that their Generals as well as they themselves had been humiliated." The dismissals were said to be a "major reason" for the coup (Afrifa, pp. 99, 102). The new army commander was well respected, but his close ties to Nkrumah caused some discomfort and anxiety, particularly after it became evident that other officers were also being promoted and their commands shifted because of their attachments to Nkrumah and his ideology. "Nkrumah was beginning to manipulate certain officers for the purpose of undermining the authority of the Military Command. The policy of divide and rule was actively pursued among all ranks of the armed forces. It had become difficult to trust one's colleagues" (Afrifa, p. 100). Factionalization and a weakened hierarchical structure often follow the military's politicization.

Nkrumah also challenged the autonomy principle by building up a "private army" within the military. In 1965 the President's Own Guard Regiment was detached from the army chain of command and was made directly responsible to the president. While the regular army was beset with all kinds of shortages, Nkrumah lavishly outfitted the POGR and increased its size to twelve hundred men, one-eighth the size of the regular army. The issue of the POGR thus affected the hierarchical command structure, military cohesiveness, and the officers' self-esteem. It was this particular

---

[9] He also attempted to use the Convention People's Party to gain political control over the army and to induce the officer corps to conform to his own political ideas. "For a long time the Convention People's Party had made a steady assault on the Army with a determined programme to indoctrinate it with the ideology of Nkrumahnism. I remember that a branch of the Convention People's Party was even opened at the Teshie Military Academy for this purpose. There was an occasion when officers were made to join the Party by force. Forms were sent out from the Minister of Defense, to be completed. I refused to complete this form on the principle that the Army must be above party politics" (Afrifa, p. 99). Afrifa exaggerates the pressures placed upon the officer corps—he himself and the majority of officers did not join the party—but it is clear that Nkrumah was trying to destroy the army's autonomy.

challenge to the autonomy principle that, more than any other single griev-
ance, apparently motivated the coup (First, p. 197; Kraus, p. 185).

THE ABSENCE OF FUNCTIONAL RIVALS AND THE SURVIVAL OF THE MILITARY

The third and fourth dimension of the military's corporate interests—the
absence of functional rivals and the very survival of the army—are closely
related. They are almost always affected by the same threat: the creation
or expansion of a militia under civilian control.[10]

The creation of functional rivals is almost as galling and threatening
as civilian manipulation and penetration. The establishment of a sizable
popular militia calls into doubt the military's adequacy and reliability as
guarantors of national security. The dilution of this responsibility and its
assignment to professional inferiors with insufficient training, expertise, and
experience can only be interpreted as a stinging insult within the officers
corps. The political power and prestige of the military are also affected
by the loss of its monopolistic control over the means of coercion. A relatively large militia force serves as a powerful counterweight to the regular
army, thereby reducing its ability to ensure adequate budgetary support
and noninterference in military affairs. It also represents a clear signal to
the military: the armed forces are replaceable. The creation of a powerful
militia may be followed by a sharp reduction in the size of the military,
widespread dismissals, and enforced early retirements, if not the dismemberment of the regular armed forces. Even if these possibilities do not material-
ize, there is a very real concern that they might.

After winning its independence from France, Algerian politics revolved
around the personal and ideological rivalry between President Ben Bella
and Colonel Boumédienne, the army chief of staff. Ben Bella's major supporters were found among the locally based political chieftains, each of
whom controlled a remnant of the guerrilla forces dating from the war of
national liberation against France. To maintain his political power Ben
Bella insisted that the irregular guerrilla forces not be disbanded, while
opposing the professionalization and expansion of the army. Colonel
Boumédienne carried out his 1965 coup when it became evident that the

---

[10] In Ghana, however, it was the expansion of the POGR that posed this threat.
"In all this plan to build a second Army one thing stood out prominently: and
that was a plan gradually to strangle the Regular Army to death" (Ocran, p.
37). Among other justifications for the coup, Nkrumah was charged with using
his private army "as a counter-poise to the Ghana Armed Forces," and afterward plans were found for the elimination of the regular army (Bebler, pp.
34, 39).

president was planning to further solidify his political base by transforming the former guerrillas into a people's militia as a counterpoise to the army (Zartman, pp. 223–42).

President Keita of Mali was overthrown for similar reasons. At the time of the 1968 coup the paramilitary People's Militia outnumbered the army by roughly three to one and undertook night patrol work and border surveillance. In addition, the militia enjoyed a privileged position as an integral part of President Keita's single-party regime, thereby challenging the army's special status even before it became known that it was intended to replace the army. The officers' pride was deflated further when illiterate youths with machine guns questioned their authority. Since the senior army commanders were politically and personally loyal to the president, it was left to a group of lieutenants to execute the coup, after which the militia was immediately disbanded (Bebler, pp. 85–88, 110). The apparent lesson was not learned in neighboring Niger, where President Diori steadily undermined the army's position during the early 1970s. The hostility and wounded professional pride engendered by Diori's goal of gradually replacing the Nigérien army with a militia organized within his single-party regime eventuated in the 1974 coup (Higgott and Fuglestad, pp. 393–95).

The 2,500 man Civil Guard had been created several years prior to the 1963 coup in Honduras. The issue was then not the expansion of the militia but its political role and relative power. The man who had created the militia, President Villeda Morales, was supporting another Liberal Party leader in the upcoming presidential elections. Largely because Villeda had employed the Civil Guard as a counterpoise to the army, the officers voiced their preference for a Nationalist Party victory. The conflict grew more heated when President Villeda appointed the Civil Guard to supervise the election. The armed forces, which had served as the guarantors of institutional and constitutional integrity, were being deprived of one of their customary responsibilities. The coup occurred immediately after the Liberal Party's presidential candidate publicly proclaimed his preference for the Civil Guard and boasted that he was prepared to put the army in its place (Lieuwen, 1964, p. 66).

A critical factor in the Chilean armed forces' overthrow of President Allende in 1973 was the arming of his most radical supporters. Believing that a military coup constituted the greatest danger to the Socialist government, the Movement of the Revolutionary Left and other extreme leftist groups armed themselves and factory workers in the urban areas. Organizing and arming to resist a coup, the government and its radical supporters helped bring it about. For over and above sharp policy disagreements with the government, within the officer corps as a whole an exceptionally pressing concern was the expansion of parallel armed organizations that were undermining its monopoly of force. It was feared that the armed radicals would try to take power, the military being unable to control them short of civil war. The defense of corporate interests was at least as important as opposition to Allende's reformist and progressive policies in motivating the coup (Sanders, 1975B, pp. 3–8; Michaels, pp. 17–18).[11] Immediately after the coup the praetorians eliminated the threat in an unusually repressive and bloody manner, with the death toll reaching two thousand in the first week alone.

Latin American armies are fearful of Communist movements. But their opposition does not stem solely from Communist economic objectives, their atheism, or fermentation of disorder. Opposition to communism, even when it is no more than a specter on the domestic horizon, is perhaps chiefly motivated by its perceived threat to the military's corporate interests. If Communists attain a notable measure of political power, they will try to create a functional rival to the military; if they attain governmental control, they will replace the regular army with a militia (Lieuwen, 1964, pp. 101–2; Needler, 1969, pp. 240–41; Stepan, 1971, p. 155).

For example, in a newspaper interview after the 1964 coup the Bolivian commander in chief stated that Paz Estenssoro, the deposed president, was not a Communist. "But some of the leaders of his party are, as they showed during their time in office [since] they armed militias, wanted to put an end to the army, and sponsored communist movements" (Needler, 1969, p. 241). From this remark, it would seem that the army may go considerably further than opposing the Communists themselves as a threat to the military's corporate interests. Politicans who favor the militia over the army are denounced as Communists, and then opposed as such.

In ousting Ecuadorian President Arosemena, the army justified its action by accusing him of being "soft" on communism. When Needler began his study of the 1963 coup, he first assumed that the army's decidedly antagonistic reactions to the Communist party were related to its espousal of radical economic objectives, publicly proclaimed atheism, and leadership of disorderly mass demonstrations. However, it turned out that these were not important. Institutional self-preservation motivated the coup; if the Communists came to power, they would purge the officer corps and replace the army with a militia (Needler, 1964, p. 41).

Lieuwen's interpretation of the same Ecuadorian coup differs significantly in pinpointing the source of the threat, but not its nature. He too

---

[11] Military autonomy was also being challenged. The extreme left was trying to organize among the rank and file for better living conditions and greater political rights. The hierarchical structure was most directly threatened by the encouragement given to enlisted men to disobey particular officers who were known to favor a coup (Michaels, pp. 26–27; Sanders, 1975B, pp. 6–7).

points out that the prime motivation was institutional self-preservation, but the Communist threat and the government's Communist sympathies were purposefully exaggerated to justify the coup. The army was actually fearful of former President Ibarra's likely victory in the upcoming election. Having been ousted by the army only two years before, his return to power would probably mean a wholesale purge of the officer corps. He did not return (Lieuwen, 1964, pp. 46–48).

In short, interventionist motives are consistently and sharply activated when the civilian governors fail to provide adequate budgetary support, interfere with military autonomy, create or expand militia forces, and thereby threaten the dissolution of the regular army. The great majority of coups are partly, primarily, or entirely motivated by the defense or enhancement of the military's corporate interests.[12]

Evidence for this generalization comes from a survey of 229 successful and unsuccessful coup attempts in fifty-nine countries between 1946 and 1970. Thompson utilized political histories, case studies, regional news digests, and newspapers to identify the "grievances" that motivated the coup makers. Although our four types of corporate interests do not correspond exactly to his coding categories, there is enough overlap between them to allow us to make some use of his data. It turns out that 23 percent of the coups were motivated by "corporate positional grievances," which overlap with what we have referred to as the preservation of autonomy, the absence of functional rivals, and the maintenance of the military's political power to protect its corporate interests. Thompson also found that 33 percent of the coups were related to "resource grievances," which are similar to the concern with military expenditures and autonomy. And 31 percent of the coups were "preemptive," being designed to prevent political parties and individuals from taking power who were perceived as direct threats to military interests (Thompson, pp. 12–26, 32–39).[13]

---

[12] This does not mean that the soldiers consistently act upon their interventionist motives. Whether or not motives are translated into behavior depends upon certain facilitating conditions, namely, the performance failures of the government and its resulting loss of legitimacy in civilian eyes.

[13] Unfortunately, these categories are not mutually exclusive. The fact that they are partially overlapping prevents us from simply adding up the percentages to get the exact proportion of coups that have been triggered by corporate interests. In fact, these figures are significantly higher for coups against civilian governments—which is our concern there. The 229 coup attempts included in the survey refer to actions by praetorian soldiers against both military and civilian governments; Thompson does not distinguish between them. Since civilian governments jeopardize corporate interests far more often than do military governments, we can safely assume that such threats have engendered a much higher proportion of coups against civilians.

**LOWER-CLASS
POLITICIZATION
IN LATIN AMERICA:
THE THREAT
TO CORPORATE AND
MIDDLE-CLASS
INTERESTS**

Having suggested that the protection of corporate interests is decidedly the most important interventionist motive, our explanation of military coups may be taken one step further by asking, *Which* civilian governments are commonly seen as potential or actual threats to these interests? It would seem that there is only one *general* answer to this question. Governments whose primary support comes from the lower classes, and those that might come to power with the support of politicized workers and peasants, are most often seen to jeopardize military interests. Among the non-Western countries, it is in Latin America that the lower classes are most politically aware, active, and organized. Only in Latin America, with its relatively high levels of urbanization, literacy, and mass-media exposure, have the lower classes often attained sufficiently high levels of politicization to constitute a serious threat to the military.

Lower-class politicization also affects middle-class interests, which we have already seen to be protected or promoted by some praetorians. These interests are endangered by governments whose primary support comes from workers and peasants, and threatened in the near future if heightened popular participation is allowed to affect the election of governments and the selection of policies.

It is only in Latin America that the threat to middle-class interests often comes from below. Only in this area of the non-Western world has socioeconomic modernization reached sufficiently high levels to foster the emergence of a sizable urban working class and a politicized lower class. A strong lower-class challenge to middle-class (and military) interests has yet to appear in the great majority of African, Middle Eastern, and Asian countries due to their relatively low levels of socioeconomic modernization. Moreover, Latin American politics is free of those severe religious, linguistic, racial, and ethnic conflicts that either cut across or submerge class conflicts. Unlike the many countries of Asia, Africa, and the Middle East featuring sharp communal conflicts which bring together the members of different classes, Latin American societies are almost exclusively and most sharply divided along class lines. In this one section of the book our discussion is therefore limited to a single geographic area.

Before analyzing how lower-class politicization in Latin America helps motivate intervention in defense of corporate and middle-class interests, it should be recalled that the resolve to act upon these motivations is strengthened by the negative attitude toward political activity and extreme sensitivity to political disorder. Unlike the middle and upper classes, which are able to express their interests and flex their political muscles without recourse to high-pitched political activity, the lower classes must rely upon highly overt means. Their major power resource is the more or less disorderly activation of numbers—the activation of voters, strikers, marchers, and demonstrators, as well as land seizures, illegal strikes, and violence. The resolve to act against Latin American governments that permit or encourage mass political activity is consequently strengthened because it runs counter to the officers' characteristic political attitudes.

LOWER-CLASS POLITICIZATION AS A THREAT TO MILITARY INTERESTS

Latin American officers have good reason to view a politically active, organized lower class as a more or less direct threat to their corporate interests. Most generally, the emergence of an additional contender for political power entails a concomitant reduction in the power of the others to shape governmental decisions. Lower-class politicization, detracts from the relative political strength of the military to further its interests.

Considering the recent histories of most Latin American countries, in which the military frequently opposed leaders with widespread mass support, there is reason for these leaders or their successors to be hostile toward the officer corps. Popular leaders who have been denuded of their political rights, whose electoral victories have been neutralized and organizational work destroyed, may not be ready to forgive and forget when their turn comes. Even where such popular leaders have tried to conciliate the military in order to attain or maintain governmental power, the officer corps has usually played it safe by interpreting such gestures as shams. Since revenge is a distinct possibility, the seemingly safest course is to prevent leaders with lower-class support from exercising governmental power. Otherwise the officer corps might be purged or replaced by a militia.

There is also the issue of resource allocation. Are scarce public funds to be devoted to expensive welfare, land reform, and modernization programs or to military pay increases and the purchase of additional equipment and weapons? Progressively inclined governments have rarely slashed defense expenditures, but not because they agree with military estimates of adequate budgetary support. They have desisted in the hope of averting intervention. The officers can thus never be fully confident of continued or increased financial support. Nor can they be certain that a relatively expensive military establishment will not be replaced with a less costly militia where the lower classes are politically active and organized.

These considerations have taken on greater significance since Castro came to power in 1959. The military have become more fearful of the lower classes, and their threat has taken on more immediacy, after seeing a tiny guerrilla army overturn a civilian regime with military support. The Cuban Revolution also led Latin American officers to identify lower-class movements with communism even more strongly than previously. For Castro started out as a middle-class reformer who had no recourse other than guerrilla warfare within Batista's authoritarian regime, yet he ended up pursuing radical Socialist goals with Communists as allies. And his dismemberment of the regular army further underscored the conflict between military and lower-class interests. Even weak moderates may shortly turn into powerful radicals who then destroy the armed forces.

Evidence for the impact of increasing lower-class politicization upon interventionist motives and actions comes from data on the frequency with which coups occurred just before or after national elections. It is then that the heightened politicization of the lower classes becomes most evident; it is in the electoral arena that their power can be effectively employed. We would therefore expect the military to prevent elections from taking place or to annul the results more often as lower-class politicization increases. Needler's data for the period between 1935 and 1964 bear out this generalization. In 1935–44 only 12 percent of Latin America's successful coups occurred just prior to, or right after national elections were held. This figure increased to 32 percent in 1945–54, and still further to 56 percent in 1955–64 (Needler, 1968, p. 65). Since this thirty-year period saw the fairly rapid expansion of the urban working class and the heightened politicization of the lower classes as a whole, these data suggest that the proportion of coups directly or indirectly motivated by the threat from below has increased due to its heightened immediacy.

The military's determined opposition to a politicized lower class is exemplified by the 1963 Dominican coup, sparked by an air force whose demands for new jet aircraft had just been rejected. President Bosch refused to purchase these expensive weapons because the funds were needed for economic programs designed to benefit his lower-class supporters. The coup was also motivated by Bosch's organization of urban and rural labor, resulting in the creation of new power centers which could be employed as counterweights to the military (Lieuwen, 1964, p. 61). After 1963 the military repeatedly prevented Bosch from regaining the presidency, which his popular support would have ensured in a free election. Those who took part in the original coup and the moderator-type veto actions that prevented his return had good reason to believe that they would be dismissed, or worse, if Bosch or his outlawed party should return to power. As one Dominican colonel said, "If Bosch ever comes back, he will throw me into a jail so deep I will never find my way out" (Needler, 1968, p. 73). Once the praetorians have acted against a popular leader and his party, the hostility may become self-perpetuating.

The multiple threat of a politicized lower class also led to continued intervention in Guatemala. The army that overthrew President Arévalo in 1954 prevented his return to power in 1963. Three weeks before the election the army announced that it would not permit Arévalo to regain the presidency if he won the election, which he was fully expected to do. Throughout the campaign, Arévalo toned down his radical statements, contesting the election as an anti-Communist, moderate, democratic reformer. Yet the officers were not convinced. They did not allow themselves to forget his former connections with workers, peasants, Communists, and radical politicians who had all threatened the armed forces. "Having eliminated these threats in [their 1954] coup, the officers took every precaution to guard against their resurrection only a decade later. For not only do they now oppose social reform in principle, but they feel they now must protect themselves against the revenge that would surely be forthcoming if Arévalo and the labor-left should return to power. Thus, institutional self-preservation was a prime motive for the 1963 coup" (Lieuwen, 1964, pp. 42–43; Weaver, p. 68).

LOWER-CLASS POLITICIZATION AS A THREAT TO MIDDLE-CLASS INTERESTS

As suggested in Chapter 2, the military tends to act in accordance with middle-class interests, although not nearly as consistently or forcefully as it does on behalf of its own corporate interests. The political "direction" of its intervention is shaped by the particular political and socioeconomic context. In the presence of a miniscule middle class, a powerful agriculturally based upper class, and an insignificantly politicized lower class—three conditions that are commonly found together—the growing middle class will at some point oppose the traditional oligarchy. Military intervention within this context is more than likely to benefit middle-class attempts to enhance its political power and economic opportunities. Where the lower class is politicized, the middle class is economically and politically established, and the upper class is relatively powerless or aligned with the middle class—in this type of society the threat to middle-class interests comes from below, despite the heterogeneity of that class and thus the diversity of its interests. The middle and lower classes come into conflict over the distribution of political power, access to education and desirable jobs, the allocation of public funds, and the redistribution of the middle class's liquid and landed wealth. The military then tends to defend the status quo against the politicized workers and peasants.

That Latin America's praetorians have acted in accordance with middle-class interests, and that they have consequently come to oppose the politicized workers and peasants, is seen in the related changes in middle-class interests and coup objectives during the last forty years. In the 1930s a small professional, commercial, and entrepreneurial middle class had developed in many Latin American countries, followed shortly by a significant growth of the urban working class. These two classes had a common interest in challenging the political predominance of the large landowners, the men who constituted the political and economic elite. The middle class and urban working class coalitions worked for industrialization, expansion of the domestic market, increased consumption levels, unionization, and heightened distributive and regulative capabilities on the part of the government. After 1945 the alliance between them was replaced by open conflict as the middle class became politically and economically established, often aligning itself with a weakened upper class. The labor-leftist leaders were opposed for being too radical; their insistence upon the immediate implementation of agrarian reform schemes and social welfare programs would lead to economic ruin.

The military often acted in accordance with these middle-class interests. When the middle class wanted political and economic change in the 1930s, the praetorians often helped bring it about; when the middle class wanted protection for its newly won political and economic predominance after 1945, the military regularly did just that (Nun).

This generalization is supported by Needler's data on the successful coups that took place between 1935 and 1964, which he classified as "reformist" or "nonreformist." Beween 1935 and 1944, when the middle classes were trying to alter the political and economic contours of their societies in the face of upper-class predominance, 50 percent of the coups had reformist (i.e., change-oriented) objectives. Between 1945 and 1954, after the middle class had become established and was now being threatened by the increasingly powerful lower classes, the proportion of reformist coups dropped by half to 23 percent, falling further to 17 percent between 1955 and 1964 (Needler, 1968, p. 65). Additional evidence comes from a survey of thirty successful coups—about half of the total number—that took place between 1943 and 1967. Of the seven cases in which the military intervened to make reformist changes, six occurred between 1943 and 1948, and only one between 1948 and 1967 (Solaún and Quinn, pp. 45–50). That the praetorians became stalwart defenders of the status quo during the last two decades is also suggested by the previously cited data which indicate that the proportion of coups occurring around election time has grown steadily since 1935. Since the increasingly politicized lower classes could effectively flex their political muscles in the electoral arena, the soldiers have increasingly stepped in to prevent or abrogate election outcomes that threatened the middle class, the military, or both.

Latin America's largest middle class, as well as its largest and most extensively politicized working class, is found in Argentina. The relationships between class conflict and military intervention are thus most appropriately illustrated by that country's recent political history. Colonel Perón came to power in 1946 and held on to it until 1955. The middle class supported him because of his industrialization efforts; the workers did so because he enhanced their political and economic status. In the early 1950s Perón's interclass balancing act began to break down. The middle class withdrew its support with the onset of an economic downturn, the favoritism shown toward the trade unions, and the further politicization of the working class. It was this threat to the privileged position of the middle class, along with Perón's impingement upon the corporate interests of the military, that motivated his overthrow in 1955.[14]

Despite the exile of their revered leader, the working-class *peronistas* continued to be seen as a threat to the Argentine middle class, the military consequently intervening several times since 1955 in order to meet the challenge from below. In 1962 the officers even overthrew the leader of the largest middle-class party. President Frondizi allowed the *peronistas* to compete in the 1962 elections on the incorrect assumption that the movement had spent itself. He convinced the senior commanders that the *peronistas* had begun to forget their exiled leader and were ready to vote for the moderate middle-class parties, also claiming that political calm could not be restored as long as legal restrictions and force were used to suppress the working-class vote. To Frondizi's surprise and the officers' consternation, the Peronist Front won a third of the votes, more than that received by any other single party. The officers' own middle-class conservatism, their commitment to the Argentine middle class, and the maintenance of their predominant political position in the face of the challenge from below—these factors account for the opposition to the *peronistas* in 1962 (Beltrán, pp. 330–33; Di Tella, pp. 114–15).

They also help explain the military's continuing opposition to the *peronistas* up to the present. It was only in 1973 that the praetorians allowed them to take full part in national elections and the exiled Perón to take up the presidency. But even then—with the *peronistas* out of power for twenty-three years, their leader tamed by old age, and the movement's radicalism having been largely jettisoned—the decision did not grow out of a markedly lessened hostility to the workers. Rather, severe economic problems and continuous demonstrations, along with strikes and assassinations triggered by the restrictions placed upon Perón's followers, made the country "ungovernable." The praetorians perceived only two choices: to crack down even harder on the *peronistas*, which would generate even more

---

[14] Perón is one of the few praetorian governors to have acted against military interests. In order to control the military he interfered with promotions and assignments, these coming to be based on the officers' political loyalties. In order to balance the military off against the working class, he allowed the formation of workers' militias.

disorder, or to allow them into the political arena. In 1973 they opted for the latter. By 1976 the mounting violence led them to opt for the former in unseating Perón's successor, his widow Isabela, and taking power themselves.

In short, the extensive politicization of Latin America's lower classes since 1945 has led the military to overthrow civilian governments on its own behalf or that of a middle-class minority incapable of meeting the challenge from below.[15] Given a common opponent, the two groups' interests are often sufficiently congruent to turn them into allies in defending the political and economic *status quo*.[16] However, in estimating the relative importance of military and middle-class interests, it is the former that always takes precedence, even when there are no contradictions between them. This ordering of priorities is exemplified by the 1948 overthrow of Venezuela's reformist government. The officers could not accept the government's public "promises to socialize the land for the Venezuelan peasants or to lead the workers towards Venezuelan socialism. Even more dangerous to them—as members of a profession rather than a social class—was the new proposal . . . that the army and its officers be reduced in size and influence and replaced by workers' and peasants' militias. The idea of trade union battalions and campesino rifles was anti-military. . . . It was stopped" (Bernstein, p. 61).

THE PERFORMANCE FAILURES OF CIVILIAN GOVERNMENTS

Praetorians invariably charge the civilian governments whom they have overthrown with serious performance failures. Unconstitutional and illegal behavior (especially widespread political corruption), responsibility for economic downturns or inflationary spirals, and an inability to handle political opposition and discontent without their erupting into disorderly and violent actions—these are the three most frequent performance failures used to justify the overthrow of civilian governments. These charges commonly correspond to the reality of the situation, thereby making it all the easier for the praetorians to rationalize and justify their actions on behalf of constitution and nation.

But while performance failures regularly precede coups, only a few

---

[15] In a speculative vein, the future may witness soldiers turning to the lower classes more frequently as their increasing politicization requires their cooperation for the maintenance of political order. However, this possibility is premised on the ability of party leaders to control their followers, dissuading them from disorderly and violent actions. In Argentina, neither Juan Perón nor his successor, Isabela, was able to do so.

[16] The Peruvian case deviates somewhat from this generalization. See pp. 177–82.

coups have been significantly motivated by these performance failures, or in reverse fashion, few have been undertaken in order to improve governmental performance. Evidence for this assertion comes from the previously mentioned survey of 229 coup attempts between 1946 and 1970, of which only 19 were motivated by "strikingly reformist" motivations. A mere 8 percent of coup attempts were undertaken in order to correct injustices and abuses of an economic, social, *or* political nature (Thompson, pp. 44–45). There is more than enough overlap between the goal of improving governmental performance and the implementation of various kinds of reforms for us to conclude that the former is rarely an important motivation for intervention. In fact, prior to the seizure of power the soldiers have few developed ideas of any kind regarding their governing goals.

How then does the poor performance of civilian governments increase the incidence of coups? In part, civilian failures strengthen the resolve to intervene when other motives—the protection of the military's corporate interests in particular—are present. They heighten the soldiers' disrespect and disdain for the civilian governors; officers are more likely to act upon their interventionist motives against incumbents whom they hold in contempt. One type of performance failure—the inability to maintain order—affects the decision to intervene insofar as it may require the officers to act as policemen while highlighting the government's total dependence upon the military. Moreover, performance failures regularly produce or indicate a loss of governmental legitimacy in the eyes of the politically aware *civilian* population. This point is developed in the following section which deals with the crucial importance of legitimacy deflations in facilitating the translation of interventionist motives into coup attempts. Performance failures do have a decided impact upon intervention, but not in the way that the praetorians have publicly claimed.

ILLEGAL ACTIONS

With regard to the first type of performance failure, the praetorians charge the civilian incumbents with various unconstitutional and illegal acts. These include the arbitrary application of the laws, the extension of their powers into areas that are prohibited by the constitution, the retention of their offices beyond the constitutionally prescribed limits,[17] and by far the

---

[17] Charges of the unconstitutional extension and retention of power are largely limited to Latin American interventions against popularly elected governments, as in the 1964 Brazilian coup, which is discussed in the following section. Allende's government was charged with the illegal extension of its power; the intended changes were too far reaching to be constitutionally implemented by a government elected by only one-third of Chile's voters. The charges included

most frequent accusation, the flouting of legality in permitting or engaging in widespread corruption. Higher and lower governmental officials are charged with the outright pilfering of public funds, the granting of benefits and exemptions to political supporters, the sale of favors, and the acceptance of kickbacks from contractors. The illegally acquired funds are used not only to enrich those who already have official positions but also to help ensure their continuation in office by financing party activities, patronage networks, and electoral campaigns. Since accusations of corruption are made far more often than other charges of unconstitutional and illegal behavior, we shall concentrate on the connections between these and military intervention.

According to the praetorians themselves, their coups are inspired by the goal of political regeneration, eliminating venal practices and guaranteeing adherence to high standards of public honesty. Several writers on the non-Western military have referred to its "puritanical" outlook and ascetic standards. "The military demands these qualities not only for itself, but for society as a whole, and it sets itself up as a standard-bearer of hard work and unflinching dedication" (Janowitz, 1964, p. 64; Shils, p. 24; Pauker, p. 339). Luckham agrees with this generalization and suggests that the puritan ethic was of some importance in motivating the majors to carry out the first Nigerian coup (Luckham, pp. 230, 282–83). Under civilian rule Nigeria certainly exhibited an inordinate amount of political corruption, whether gauged in terms of the diversity of corrupt practices, the number of politicians who engaged them, or the high offices that they occupied. The politicians regarded the illegal translation of authority into profit, power, and party advantage as acceptable perquisites of public office.

There is, however, reason for skepticism. "The charge of corruption and misappropriation is frequently made to justify military coups in Africa as elsewhere. The question is not whether it exists—it is clearly rampant in many states—but whether it is of any great importance in promoting such events . . . Reading the various commissions of inquiry into these matters in Ghana [after the first coup], one is left with an impression that, though the revelations are scandalous, this is almost a ritual exercise of justifying in another and conventionally accepted way [a coup for] which most Ghanaians did not need any elaborate apologia" (Gutteridge, 1969, pp. 150–51). A similar conclusion emerges from an analysis of seven Latin American coups that occurred in the early 1950s. In each instance the officers justified intervention because the civilian governments had become "inept, ineffective and corrupt." But these were largely irrelevant justifications, for even if the governments were performing poorly, in at least four of these cases they were near

---

the unconstitutional disregard of decisions made by the legislature, judiciary, and comptroller.

the end of their terms in office. Thus the coups were not directed so much at the incumbments as at their probable successors (Lieuwen, 1964, pp. 106–7).

And while it might be that most non-Western officers adhere to ascetic standards while residing in the barracks, these are apparently not sufficiently salient to shape their behavior once in power. Judging from their actions as governors—in Ghana, Nigeria, Uganda, the Sudan, Pakistan, Thailand, Indonesia, South Vietnam, Colombia, and Venezuela—the soldiers do not regularly conform to their publicly proclaimed standards of honesty and self-abnegation.[18] They are not above the temptation of using public offices to acquire luxuriant trappings for themselves, and as such, it is not especially plausible to argue that interventionist motives include the desire to eliminate political corruption.[19]

Although political corruption itself rarely motivates coups, it is more than a pretext. When other interventionist motives are present, widespread corruption strengthens the resolve to act upon them. It does so by transforming the soldiers' antipolitical attitudes into intensely felt resentments toward the politicians. They are seen as venal, egregiously self-serving individuals, living a luxuriant life-style at public expense while the officers reside in the relatively austere barracks. Moreover, civilian transgressions make it easier for officers to contemplate unconstitutional acts, especially for those who adhere to the civilian ethic. Once the civilians have shown their disrespect for the constitution, the military is encouraged to accept the possibility of an illegal coup. Lastly, there is the legitimacy deflation experienced by some governments that are manifestly corrupt. Corrupt incumbents are rarely respected and are sometimes intensely resented outside their partisan "territory," which can only detract from governmental legitimacy.

ECONOMIC DOWNTURNS

A government's economic record is a critical performance criterion since economic growth is highly valued the world over and all governments are held at least partly responsible for the country's economic health. Even when the actual cause of a downturn is beyond governmental control—a sharp drop in commodity prices on the international market, for example—the incumbents are often blamed. And since virtually all governments publicly assert their commitment to economic growth, the economic record takes on further significance as a criterion of governmental performance.

18 See pp. 126–28 for some details on the corruption found among military governments.

19 To the extent that civilian corruption actually motivates coups, it may do so by highlighting the possible ways in which the soldiers can enrich themselves once in office.

Intervention against governments during periods of economic decline, stagnation, or inflation is more common than at times of economic good health. The number of Latin American coups between 1951 and 1963 was 60 percent greater in "deterioration" years (in which GNP had fallen relative to the preceding year) than in "improvement" years (in which GNP had increased relative to the preceding year) (Fossum, pp. 236–37). Military coups in Asia occurred about twice as frequently in the year following a drop in the total value of exports (Hoadley, pp. 194–95). What then are the connections between intervention and deteriorating economic conditions? [20]

Economic stagnation and inflation generally have negative consequences for middle-class salaries and incomes, the value of its savings, and the profitability of its commercial and industrial enterprises. On occasion the military have intervened during times of economic adversity to protect these middle-class interests. This is most likely to occur when stagnation and inflation are attributable to economic decisions that are intended to benefit the government's lower-class supporters. Such decisions include the nationalization of industry, which may decrease output and discourage private investment; the redistribution of landed wealth, which is often followed by reductions in agricultural productivity; and increased expenditures for welfare and reformist programs, which sometimes help fuel inflationary spirals.

These kinds of considerations played a significant, but by no means the most important, part in motivating the Brazilian and Chilean coups. During the 1950s, Brazil's economic growth rate was one of the highest in the world. Under the Goulart presidency it was one of the lowest. And at the same time the spiraling inflation cut into the actual incomes, salaries, and savings of the middle class. The workers were blamed for pushing up prices by their bitter strikes and wage struggles; the leftist government was criticized for giving in to labor demands (Stepan, 1971, pp. 139–40). As in Brazil, the Chilean officers overthrew Allende to the applause of a middle class whose economic position was declining. The government's nationalization and income redistribution policies were thought to be the cause of consumer shortages, an inflation rate that steadily moved up until it reached 323 percent just prior to

[20] There is the possibility that economic difficulties will lead to a curtailment or refusal to increase the defense budget, as in the previously mentioned second Ghanaian coup against a government whose retrenchment policies included a 10 percent cut in military expenditures. However, economic malaise does not usually affect military budgets; economic growth rates commonly decline without any reductions in military spending. Defense budgets are well protected against economic adversity due to military pressure, civilian fears that reductions will spark a coup, or civilian estimates of national security needs which coincide with those of the officer corps.

the coup, and a decline in GNP during Allende's last month in office (Sanders, 1973A, pp. 5–8).

Although soldiers are occasionally motivated to overthrow civilian governments because their poor economic performance has adverse consequences for the middle class, there are two other connections between this kind of performance failure and intervention that have a more frequent and greater impact upon the decision to intervene. Economic performance failures can only solidify and intensify the military's disrespect for the incumbents, heightened further by the belief that as highly competent professional officers, they could turn in a far better performance as economic decision makers. And the notable impact of economic performance failures upon the loss of governmental legitimacy goes a long way in facilitating the translation of motives into coup attempts.

DISORDER AND VIOLENCE

All governments are faced with greater or lesser political opposition and discontent; they differ significantly in their ability to deal with it. Governments are performing poorly when their unresponsiveness, ineptness, or excessively arbitrary actions foment widespread disorder and violence among the discontented. They are unable to fulfill their most basic responsibility: the preservation of public order, the protection of life and property.

Evidence for the existence of a significant connection between this kind of performance failure and military intervention comes from a survey of 105 successful Latin American coups that occurred between 1907 and 1966. Almost two-thirds of them took place during periods of public disorder (Fossum, pp. 234–36). And in a survey of 229 coup attempts between 1946 and 1970, it was found that 29 percent were associated with some kind of political disorder (Thompson, p. 45). [21]

One connection between this kind of performance failure and coup attempts relates to the use of the military to preserve public order when the police are unable to do so. Soldiers are brought in to quell disturbances, prevent riots, patrol cities, break up labor strikes, guard politically sensitive buildings, and impose martial law. Trained, organized, and equipped to fight similarly prepared enemies, the officers' professional standing, martial qualities, and heroic image can only suffer when they act as policemen. Their self-image is demeaned; their public prestige may suffer a corresponding de-

---

[21] Although many of the coups in these two surveys involved the overthrow of military governments by officers outside the governing circle, there is no reason to suppose that the percentage of coups that occurred during periods of disorder varies significantly according to the civilian or military makeup of the government.

cline. Coups consequently become more likely as the officers develop deep resentments toward governments whose incompetence has forced them to undertake the unsavory role of policemen. Presumably other governors can restore order more effectively, thereby relieving the officers of a demoralizing task.

One impetus behind the first Nigerian coup is found in the conspirators' hearty disdain for political leaders whose corruption and inability to keep conflict among themselves and between the regions within bounds had necessitated the use of the army as a police force. It was used to pacify Tiv tribesmen in 1960 and 1964, and again in 1965–66 to quell massive disturbances in the Yoruba heartland that were sparked by the incumbents' electoral manipulations (Luckham, pp. 201–2, 231; Bell, p. 270). In 1966 the army took power in Upper Volta after economic difficulties forced the government to issue an austerity budget. The announcement touched off a wave of strikes and demonstrations, with violence threatening unless the government rescinded the wage reductions. As in Dahomey one year earlier, military commanders were faced with the choice of firing on rioting crowds to maintain the government in power or overthrowing it themselves. In both instances they chose the latter course (Gutteridge, 1969, p. 127; Bell, p. 270).

In the month prior to the 1960 Turkish coup the army's ire had been aroused when ordered to serve as a police force. It was especially galling for infantry officers to suppress meetings of the major opposition party (which the great majority of officers much preferred to the governing party), to quell student demonstrations, and to impose martial law in the two major cities (Ozbudun, p. 14; Hurewitz, p. 214). The Colombian coup of 1953 further underscores the point because political alignments were the reverse of those found in Turkey. The rural violence between Liberals and Conservatives had been raging for several years, the officers' revulsion increasing steadily with their continuing employment as policemen for the Conservative government. They overthrew it even though the majority of officers preferred it to the Liberal opposition (Dix, p. 113 and *passim*).

Moreover, when turbulence becomes endemic and violence escalates, the officers realize that the government has become critically dependent upon them. Without their support the government could easily collapse, thereby presenting them with an interventionist opportunity if motivated to take it. This conjunction of factors—a government weakened by disorders, the officers' recognition of its dependence upon them, and the motivation to intervene—is illustrated by the first Syrian coup: "On November 30, 1948 the demonstrations marking the first anniversary of the United Nations resolution on Palestine turned into antigovernment riots; on December 2 a state of emergency was declared, and the army called out to restore order. The officer corps sensed that the life of the government depended upon them. In

March 1949 the High Command demanded an increased military budget, but the government either would not or could not comply. It was even rumored that the army allocation would be reduced. On March 20 the Chief of the General Staff, Colonel Za'im, called a secret meeting of army leaders and it was decided that the military would take matters into its own hands" (Be'eri, p. 55). It did just that.

And given the keen sensitivity to political disorder, the resolve to act upon interventionist motives can only be strengthened when demonstrations, strikes, land seizures, riots, and violence become widespread. Politicians who were formerly held in fairly low regard are now held in contempt for being unable to fulfill their chief responsibility: the preservation of public order.

Lastly, a highly turbulent and violent politics helps deflate the government's legitimacy, and often indicates that a legitimacy deflation has already set in. When numerous people engage in the politics of the street, this indicates an exceptionally intense opposition to the government, a rejection of the "rules of the game," or both. The government does not enjoy the moral right to govern in civilian eyes, which, as we shall now see, is crucial for facilitating the translation of the officers' interventionist motives into coup attempts.

THE LEGITIMACY DEFLATIONS OF CIVILIAN GOVERNMENTS

Governments are found along the entire length of the legitimacy-illegitimacy continuum. Varying proportions of the population believe that the government has a moral right to govern, consequently believing that its laws and directives ought to be obeyed. Here we will consider a government to be less than legitimate when many politically aware citizens do not accept its authority; a sizable proportion of the politicized population, ranging from those who are merely interested in national politics to the leaders of political parties, believe that the government is not deserving of its allegiance. Where the overwhelming majority of the politicized stratum believes that the government does not have a moral right to govern, it is thoroughly illegitimate. There is sometimes much difficulty in distinguishing between extensive opposition and the loss of legitimacy, but the two do differ qualitatively. Governments may be extensively and vociferously opposed for all sorts of reasons—they are decisionally ineffective, heavily biased against certain groups, and so on—without at the same time having their right to govern called into question. Widespread opposition is qualitatively transformed into a withdrawal of legitimacy by its intensification and moral condemnation.

There are various ways in which governments come to lose their legitimacy. As it turns out, the most common ones have already been identified in discussing the three kinds of performance failures that most often precede intervention. The government's legitimacy is generally eroded when nonelites resent and lose respect for incumbents who are enriching themselves at public expense, when regime rules are flouted for the exclusive advantage of the incumbents, and when illegal acts close off the hope that other groups and leaders will be able to share in the perquisites and spoils of office. Constitutionally and legally derived legitimacy loses its hold. Economic failures engender legitimacy deflations because economic growth is held to be one of the government's chief responsibilities, and economic well-being constitutes one of society's highest values. Continuous political turbulence and major incidents of violence markedly reduce a government's legitimacy, since it is unable to fulfill its most basic responsibility. Indeed, widespread disorder and violence usually indicate the onset of a legitimacy deflation.

LEGITIMACY DEFLATIONS AS A FACILITATING CONDITION

Most students of military intervention agree that variations in governmental legitimacy are an exceptionally important explanation for the incidence of coup attempts. In fact, it has been claimed that "the legitimacy enjoyed by a government affects the political role of its armed forces far more than any other environmental or internal factor" (Welch and Smith, pp. 29, 249). Despite the general agreement on the importance of the legitimacy factor, the hypothesis' underlying reasoning has not been extensively developed. What are the *connections* between legitimacy and intervention? This question becomes all the more important and intriguing, since an officer corps that is motivated to intervene almost invariably has the power to do so against illegitimate, nonlegitimate *and* legitimate governments. There are seldom any civilian groups that are large enough, sufficiently cohesive, and well armed, to prevent a military coup.

Here we will be developing the proposition that the presence of a legitimizing mantle sharply inhibits the translation of interventionist motives into coup attempts; the absence or loss of governmental legitimacy is easily the most important factor that facilitates this transformation. Soldiers may not be motivated to overthrow nonlegitimate or illegitimate governments, but when the motivation is present they consistently try to do just that.

Only one connection between legitimacy and intervention has been proposed and commonly accepted: "In countries where attachment to civilian institutions is strong and pervasive, the attempts of the military to coerce the lawful government, let alone supplant it, would be universally regarded as usurpation. This, the moral barrier, is what has prevented the military, for all its organization, prestige and power, from establishing its rule throughout the globe" (Finer, p. 22). Soldiers do not intervene when a "moral barrier" stands in their way, when their actions would be condemned as "usurpations" of power.[22] Officers are, in effect, no different from other political actors insofar as they would much prefer popular approval to opprobrium.

Although the "moral barrier" to intervention set up by the population is significant, it is by no means decisive. Coup-minded soldiers are not *overly* discouraged by the popular criticism that would be forthcoming due to certain internal characteristics of the officer corps. Given the soldiers' unshakable patriotic self-image, their actions can be rationalized as public spirited, even in the face of quite different civilian interpretations. Their self-image as responsible and loyal officers allows them to ignore or denigrate popular views when these conflict with their "higher" duty to constitution and nation. Considering their strong attachment to the hierarchical imperative, they can readily interpret popular opinion as irrelevant, while its expression through political activity can be viewed as "insubordination." The disapproval of politicians can be easily written off as another indication of their self-serving behavior; they want governmental power for themselves. And lastly, popular disapproval loses some of its potency because the military is differentiated, partially segregated, and occasionally isolated from the civilian sector. Expectations of widespread public censure do affect the decision to intervene, but in and of themselves these do not decisively inhibit coup-minded officers. Several additional aspects of the legitimacy deflation are at least equally important.

One of these goes beyond popular condemnation per se, to its behavioral expression. There is a reasonable if not high probability that the overthrow of legitimate governments will spark mass protests, general strikes, riots, sporadic violence, and possibly armed resistance. The soldiers are not inhibited from overthrowing legitimate governments in the expectation that they would be stopped by civilians, even if armed resistance were to develop. Rather, the exceptionally high value that officers place upon political order makes them reluctant to undertake coups that would make for a period of raucous and demonstrative politics. They would not only be responsible for triggering or escalating the level of political turbulence, they would have to govern in this highly unpalatable context. And the military would probably have to undertake the unappealing and demoralizing task of subduing unarmed, untrained nationals. It would be thrust into the professionally de-

---

[22] The same point is commonly made in a slightly different manner. For example: "Military intervention rarely occurs in countries marked by a high degree of legitimacy . . . Establishment of a military regime would run counter to popular sentiment. In the face of articulate, mobilized public opinion, officers would find their attempt at seizing power greeted not with gratitude for salvation, but with sullen resentment" (Welch and Smith, p. 27).

meaning role of a police force. Soldiers thus rarely overthrow legitimate governments because they do not want to bring on, or deal with, the disorderly and violent behavioral expressions of popular censure.

Moreover, in most officer corps there is a larger or smaller group that adheres to the civilian ethic—the normative-legalistic belief in the principle of civilian supremacy. Whether these officers support a coup attempt, remain neutral, or oppose it, is significantly influenced by the legitimacy factor. The civilian ethic is more easily ignored or contravened when the governors have lost their legitimacy, particularly if they have done so by undertaking unconstitutional or illegal acts themselves. Incumbents who are accorded the moral right to govern by politicized civilians are usually accorded that same right by those officers who subscribe to the civilian ethic.

Most importantly, soldiers are decidedly reluctant to overthrow legitimate governments because such attempts are not only sure to fracture military cohesiveness, they are also likely to fail. Military cohesion, and thus the successful execution of the coup, are severely jeopardized when the conspirators must deal with those who oppose the overthrow of legitimate governments for the reasons that were just mentioned: the aversion to crossing the "moral barrier," the reluctance to foment and deal with disorderly opposition, and a belief in the civilian ethic. The conspirators must somehow persuade most of these officers to join them or remain neutral, which is improbable given the incumbents' legitimacy. A coup attempt would consequently threaten the much-valued cohesiveness of the military and elicit active opposition within the officer corps. It is most unlikely to succeed, at least not without the coup makers having to do the unthinkable in taking up weapons against their "brothers-in-arms." [23]

THE BRAZILIAN CASE

The 1964 Brazilian coup clearly illustrates each aspect of the legitimacy argument. Governmental performance failures produced a sharp legitimacy deflation; powerful interventionist motives were present for some time, but the soldiers acted only after the government had lost its legitimacy; and their reasons for intervening only after the legitimacy deflation had set in correspond to the connections between legitimacy and intervention that were just identified.

We have already seen that President Goulart's multiple challenges to the military's corporate interests, and to a lesser extent to those of the middle

---

[23] See the discussion of the South Korean coup in the following section for an important caveat to this generalization.

class, triggered powerful interventionist motives. The economic performance failures of the government—the zero growth rate and the spiraling inflation —touched off widespread middle-class opposition, which was qualitatively transformed into a loss of legitimacy when Goulart was seen to be acting unconstitutionally.

Three weeks prior to the coup, before a mass audience of his workingclass supporters, Goulart indicated that he might very well try to alter the constitution so that he could serve another presidential term, with the congress being suspended in the process. The statement that regime norms were likely to be pushed aside touched off the legitimacy deflation, along with a corresponding flurry of messages to the officer corps that the time had come to act. The newspapers that had previously advised the military to abstain, despite the mounting opposition to Goulart, now urged intervention in defense of the constitution. The officer corps was criticized for continuing to obey the "illegal" orders of the president, as in this typical editorial statement: "No one is obliged to accept and obey an abusive order, much less to give protection to those who challenge and break the laws and who agitate in a public square for a Communist revolution. The Congress is one of the powers of the Republic and the armed forces have a duty to respect it, and defend it against those who attempt to destroy it."

The legitimacy deflation was then compounded by Goulart's handling of the previously mentioned naval mutiny. By allowing the politicized mutineers to go unpunished, not only did Goulart challenge the military's autonomy and its hierarchical structure, his legitimacy was further impaired within the civilian sector because his inactions were seen to sanction illegality. Newspaper editorials throughout the country now told the still somewhat reluctant officers that their duty and legal obligation to maintain law and order left them no choice but to unseat Goulart (Stepan, 1971, pp. 95, 201–7).

How then did the legitimacy deflation affect the decision to intervene? Why did the interventionist-minded officers not act until after the government had lost its legitimacy? Why did Army Chief of Staff Castello Branco make his support of the coup conditional upon the president's violation of the constitution? (Schneider, p. 90).

To some extent governmental legitimacy served as a diffuse "moral barrier." Partly because of its historical origins as a popular force, there was a widespread conception of the military as "the people in uniform." Civilians and officers alike cherished this popular image. And as such, the military has regularly been hesitant to intervene without civilian approval, that is, unless the government lost its legitimacy (Stepan, 1971, pp. 43–45). However, this consideration was of secondary importance. Not only is there little evidence of its saliency prior to the coup, its secondary importance may be inferred from the arbitrary, unusually repressive, and highly unpopular actions taken by the Brazilian military governments since then. If the image of themselves as "the people in uniform" and the related desire for civilian approval were especially salient before the coup, the praetorians would not have resorted to extensive coercion and widespread torture to maintain themselves in power after the rapid loss of their own legitimacy.

More important than public censure itself were the likely consequences of crossing the "moral barrier"—the possibility of extensive violence and the threat to military unity. The Brazilian officers' twofold imperative— no bloodshed and no splits within the military—could only be realized if the soldiers acted against a nonlegitimate government. The high value placed upon these goals and their relationship to the legitimacy factor are forcefully stated in the comments of two generals who led the 1964 coup:

> Military activists for or against the government are always a minority. If a military group wants to overthrow a government, they need to convince the great majority of officers who are either strict legalists or simply nonactivists. Activists do not wish to risk bloodshed or military splits, so they wait until a consensus has developed. Thus movements to overthrow a president need public opinion to help convince the miltary itself.

Another leading conspirator offered a similar interpretation:

> Many military activists were ready to overthrow Goulart in 1963, but they waited until public opinion pushed them further and created unity so there was no risk of civil war. By late March the [civilian] journals were asking the military to solve the problem. This and events like the [middle classes'] São Paolo march in favor of legality pushed the military into activity. Military unity is extremely important. Only if the military is split will there be a civil war. The optimum course is if we have unity and are on the right course. But the most fundamental thing is to stay unified. [Stepan, 1971, p. 97] [24]

[24] One of the activist generals drew a comparison between the 1964 coup and the abortive 1961 attempt, in which the military chiefs ordered a coup to prevent Goulart from taking office. That order was ignored by all the military commanders because "the military chiefs acted against public opinion," Goulart's recent constitutional elevation to the presidency having given him the moral right to govern. The 1961 coup attempt "was a disaster for the army," the fear of again splitting the military thus acted as a major inhibition in 1963 and the early months of 1964 (Stepan, 1971, p. 189). Indeed, except for the abortive attempt in 1961, the post-1945 Brazilian military has only intervened after the legitimacy of the government has been called into question, usually in terms of its alleged plans to subvert "democratic" institutions and perpetuate itself in office (Schneider, pp. 356–57).

In short, given the high value assigned to the preservation of military unity and the avoidance of bloodshed, the coup was put off until a legitimacy deflation allowed for intervention without endangering either one.

The interventionist-minded officers also waited for Goulart's illegal designs and acts to "neutralize" the civilian ethic, thereby creating military unity on behalf of a coup whose success was then ensured. Only if a majority of the legalist officers—those who subscribed to the civilian ethic—were to remain neutral or actively support the coup would it have a significant chance of success. It was after the mass rally in which Goulart announced his intention to alter the constitutionally prescribed distribution of power that a letter written by a senior general began to have a pronounced effect upon the legalistically minded officers. They now had to ask themselves whether obedience is due a president who is himself planning to alter regime structures unconstitutionally. Would they defend a government in the name of civilian supremacy which itself intended to violate other, equally basic constitutional principles? And when the sailors' mutiny went unpunished, those officers who accepted obedience to the president "within the limits of the law" as prescribed by the constitution were confronted with a president who had seemingly acted contrary to the laws (Schneider, pp. 82, 92; Stepan, 1971, pp. 204–7). In the end, the activists were able to persuade an overwhelming number of officers to support, or at least not to oppose, the coup by pointing to the legitimacy deflation and the less than legal actions and designs that brought it about.

The effect of Goulart's illegal designs and actions upon military unity, and the importance of military unity for the decision to intervene, are even seen in the operations order issued by the first general to move against Goulart. He explained that an attempt to overthrow Goulart before he had flouted the law would have itself smacked of illegality: "It would have attracted to his side a forceful sector of the armed forces who lack confidence in politics and are committed to legal formalism." But once Goulart stepped beyond the bounds of the law, intervention became both necessary and possible. In the general's slogan, "He who breaks the law first is lost!" (Stepan, 1971, p. 205).[25] Not a single officer died on Goulart's behalf.[26]

The Brazilian case thus fully bears out the importance of the legitimacy factor as well as its several underlying generalizations. However, without

[25] The issuance of operations orders to subordinates which state anything other than the times, places, and targets of troop movements—which offer any rationale or justification for the coup—are exceedingly rare. See pp. 46–47.

[26] In Chapter 2 it was also said that the further enhancement of an already high level of professionalism (as expertise) engendered sufficient self-confidence among the conspirators for them to take control of the government themselves, rather than displacing Goulart and then replacing him with another civilian president, as had occurred in past coups.

diluting the content of the general argument, it should be realized that this case differs from many others in such a way as to inflate the already critical importance of the legitimacy factor as a facilitating condition. It took on even greater importance in Brazil because of the officer corps' unusually strong commitment to the civilian ethic. Where the civilian ethic is more extensively and deeply implanted, the government's legitimacy must be more severely deflated before the legalist-minded soldiers will act or step aside. The legitimacy factor also takes on even greater importance where there is a relatively high level of politicization, as in Brazil. In that context, the overthrow of legitimate governments would make disorder and violence far likelier and more extensive.

PLANNING
AND
EXECUTING
THE COUP

Having identified the most important interventionist motives and the conditions that facilitate their translation into coup attempts, we are left with two questions pertaining to the planning and execution of the coup. First, what are the probabilities that a coup attempt will succeed? How difficult and risky is the interventionist enterprise? Second, what makes for successful or unsuccessful coup attempts? What factors need to be taken into account in planning and executing the coup in order to heighten the likelihood of success?

THE RISKY NATURE OF MOST COUP ATTEMPTS

It might appear that the coup is a relatively simple exercise. The military enjoys overwhelming coercive power, its forces can be readily mobilized against the government, little civilian opposition is possible, and none is likely since soldiers rarely attempt to overthrow legitimate governments. It would thus appear quite simple for a small group of officers to lead their men into the chief executive's residence, perhaps using tanks to cover their approach and rifles to batter down some doors. The president, prime minister, or king is ordered to resign, arrested, or shot. It all happens rather quickly and smoothly, as in this characterization of a fairly typical Latin American coup:

> *In the wee hours of the morning, a detachment of troops, sometimes abetted by tanks, suddenly arrived at the executive residence and seized the President. At the same time, other troops seized control of the communications media—the telephone exchanges, the radio and television stations, and the progovernment presses. Meanwhile, firepower was concentrated at focal control points to meet any possible civilian resistance. At dawn*

> *came the* pronunciamento, *the announcement by the armed forces to the people that they had assumed control of the government, that the President and Congress were deposed. [Lieuwen, 1964, p. 108]*

This coup may indeed have been a rather simple affair. The political conditions were apparently propitious, since there was no resistance by civilians or soldiers, and the coup was seemingly well planned and efficiently executed. But most coups are anything but simple. They may appear deceptively simple just because they have been successfully and quickly executed. The demanding and risky nature of most coups becomes more apparent when it is realized that they may fail at various points in the coup-making process. The conspirators may be discovered at the outset, when they first discuss their opposition to the government. They may be foiled during the planning stage of the coup, which usually requires several months of preparation. In executing the coup, they may fail to capture all the critical installations, civilian incumbents, and high-ranking officers who are opposed to the coup. They might also fail after taking these crucial targets, the coup attempt being put down by other military units who remain loyal to the government. Of those coups that do not succeed, the great majority are foiled during the first and second stages; only a small proportion fail after the orders are given to move against the government. Thus the bloodless nature of most coups.

Even successful praetorians are sometimes faced with major difficulties at each stage of the coup-making process, as in the 1952 Egyptian coup which brought the Free Officers to power. Judging from the following account the Egyptian coup looks considerably more difficult and risky than might be supposed from its almost immediate, bloodless, and complete success:

> *The Free Officers' difficulty was that they were staff officers and had no fighting troops (or they were stationed outside of Cairo). The circle of conspirators therefore had to be widened. Al Shafi of the armoured cavalry agreed and so did Shawki of the infantry; but Mehenna of the artillery not only refused but gave reason to believe that he was actively hostile. The date chosen was August 5, when the Court and the cabinet would be at Alexandria, the summer capital. However, on July 20 news arrived that . . . all fourteen of the conspirators were to be arrested. They thereupon decided to strike in the next forty-eight hours and met on the appointed day to lay their final plans. It now appeared that the Chief of the General Staff had wind of [their immediate] plot, so they decided to march one hour earlier than arranged. Shawki and his 13th Infantry Regiment, together with Sadiq's tanks, occupied General Headquarters and arrested the Chief of the General Staff. Muhieddin's armoured cars threw a cordon*

around the miltary areas of Abbassia and Heliopolis. Al Shafi's tanks, mean-
while, occupied the strategic points in the centre of Cairo and seized the
telephone exchange, the broadcasting station, the railway and the airports.
By 3 a.m. the conquest was complete and the Free Officers in General Headquarters proclaimed General Naguib as Commander-in-Chief of the army
. . . At 4 a.m. the Prime Minister telephoned from Alexandria to General
Naguib to find out what had happened, but was inclined to make light of
the affair. The decisive moment occurred when the conspirators learned
that the powerful El Arish garrison had come over. Only now did the conspirators make their appeal to the public. General Naguib explained to the
reporters that the officers' aims were legality, continuity and democracy;
and at 6 a.m. the pronunciamento of the movement was broadcast. . . . Two
days later the army presented its ultimatum to the King, who had no choice
but to agree and abdicate . [Finer, pp. 158–59]

Even this highly successful coup was clearly no simple matter. The conspirators were identified, almost arrested, forced to alter their plans on two occasions, and compelled to act before being able to recruit additional officers
with troop commands in the Cairo area. And despite having captured the
critical installations and personnel, the final outcome remained in doubt until a key garrison decided to support them.

That the outcome of most coups is uncertain is persuasively supported
by the large proportion of failures. In a survey of 107 coup attempts that occurred in non-Western countries between 1945 and 1967, it was found that
30 percent were unsuccessful (Luttwak, pp. 204–7). According to a survey
of 284 coup attempts (against both civilian and military governments) between 1945 and 1972, 50 percent were failures (Kennedy, pp. 337–44). Of
the 41 coups that were attempted by Middle Eastern officers between 1936
and 1969, 44 percent did not succeed (Perlmutter, 1970, p. 291). Whatever
the exact proportion of failures, from slightly less than a third to a half, it is
obviously considerable. Since officers are not given to rushing headlong into
interventionist adventures, the notable number of unsuccessful efforts underscores the considerable complexities involved; coup makers must have en-
countered and overcome some very real difficulties.

Although most coups are more or less risky enterprises, a significant
proportion involve few if any risks.[27] Success is almost certain when a clear
majority of officers agree upon the desirability of a coup or remain un-
opposed to the conspirators. Civilian governments simply cannot retain
power when the officer corps is completely or fairly well united
against them. For example, there was no doubt about the outcome of the

[27] This point may be inferred from the fact that in the Middle East between
1936 and 1967 there was no serious opposition to the conspirators in fifteen
of the thirty-seven coup attempts (Be'eri, p. 255).

1966 coup in Argentina that was planned by the commanders of the three services and a majority of senior officers. As early as ten months before the overthrow of President Illía, the news media were reporting accounts of the soldiers' intentions and plans, thereby demonstrating their supreme confidence in the expected outcome [28] (Astiz, 1969B, p. 875). About one-fifth of all coup attempts are virtually certain to succeed because the officer corps is fairly well united in its opposition to the incumbents.

What then of the roughly 80 percent of all coup attempts that are fairly risky enterprises? What factors account for the probability of success or failure? Although the outcome depends upon numerous factors, it is possible to identify what are probably the three most important ones. If these are ignored the likelihood of failure is quite high. It is therefore appropriate to refer to them as "rules" of interventionist prudence. This is not to suggest that their fulfillment guarantees success; there are other, more specific and unpredictable circumstances that could still spell failure. But if the three requirements are not met, failure is most likely except of course where the military is united in favoring a coup, which makes them almost superfluous.[29]

Rule 1   The active participation of strategically situated, middle-level troop commanders is crucial for the coup's success. It is the infantry and tank battalions stationed in or near the capital city that almost always spearhead the coup. And it is the field grade officers who are in full control of these strategically placed forces.

The uncompromisable principle of obedience to immediate superiors places complete control of these troops in the hands of the highest-ranking officers with whom they are in face-to-face contact. Except in miniscule armies of one or two thousand men, it is the colonels and majors who literally stand at the head of their troops. Captains and lieutenants are rarely in a position to act independently given the on-the-scene presence of colonels and majors, whereas senior officers and middle-level staff officers are not posted amid the troops. Middle-level troop commanders are consequently

---

[28] There have been other Latin American coups of a similar nature. A unified officer corps has openly discussed and decided the issue, then "asking" for the president's resignation and receiving it, without any troops being moved.

[29] These rules also lose some of their significance if almost the entire military and all the crucial civilian targets are concentrated in the capital city. In Freetown, Sierra Leone, for example, "the logistics of coupmaking present virtually no physical obstacles even to the most unsophisticated of strategists" (Cox, pp. 114–15).

the only ones who can order the soldiers to move against the government—orders that are invariably obeyed even if they entail action against the senior officers themselves.

Moreover, once the military is politicized, field-grade officers attain considerable independence. Senior officers cannot simply order them to take part in a coup. They must be persuaded to do so. The troop commanders not only are in a position to refuse to march against the government, they have the means to thwart an attempted coup, or to carry out one of their own against the government and its high-ranking military supporters.

The involvement of senior officers is hardly negligible. They are able to assign activist officers to crucial posts as garrison commanders in or near the capital, transfer governmental supporters to out-of-the-way assignments, and arrange for "authorized" troop movements to the capital. The active support of senior officers is thus highly advantageous. But the participation of strategically situated troop commanders is necessary. Some indirect evidence for this generalization comes from a survey of coup attempts in the Middle East between 1936 and 1969. Those coups that were led by junior and middle-level officers were 25 percent more successful than those organized by senior officers (Perlmutter, 1970, p. 292).

Rule 2 The conspirators must have sufficient troops to seize all the powerful opponents of the coup, along with several critical installations and buildings, almost simultaneously. The number of enlisted men commanded by the conspirators must be large enough to arrest the incumbents and their leading civilian and military supporters in one fell swoop. They must be prevented from resisting, escaping, or warning others who are better situated to organize an opposition. At the same time, radio, television, and telephone installations must be seized to prevent opponents from organizing themselves and rallying support against the praetorians. Road, rail, and air links to the capital city may have to be blocked to prevent the entry of loyalist troops. It is also necessary to occupy those public buildings that symbolize the seat of power—the presidential residence, the legislative assembly, and the military's general headquarters. Unless these buildings are secured, they may serve as the focus of resistance, and without them the praetorians cannot effectively claim to constitute a new government.

Judging from these considerations alone, it would seem that the larger the conspiratorial group, the greater the likelihood of success. Assuming it is possible to recruit additional activists, why not do so in order to make certain that all crucial targets are taken simultaneously? This would make sense except for the problem of maintaining secrecy. The already significant risk of exposure, accidental or otherwise, increases proportionally with the size of the conspiratorial group. A government that learns of the plotters' identities can have them arrested or transferred away from the capital; a government that hears of their plans even an hour ahead of the scheduled coup can avoid capture or organize resistance. The optimum size of the conspiratorial group should therefore be just large enough to provide sufficient troops for nearly simultaneous action against all the crucial targets. And this depends primarily upon the size of possible opposition from other military units, as well as the number and dispersion of power centers.

The first Nigerian coup was only a partial success just because the conspiratorial group was too small to carry out all the necessary tasks simultaneously. The coup was carried out by 30 officers and some 150 enlisted men in an army of over 500 officers and 10,000 men. The majors who led the coup kept their numbers limited in order to preserve the utmost secrecy, and they acted before attaining full strength to take advantage of a propitious moment when most of the battalion commanders were away from their posts. While 30 officers might have carried out the coup successfully, most of the Nigerian plotters held staff and training assignments that placed them in command of only a small number of troops. Thus the majors also ignored Rule 1 by failing to recruit strategically situated troop commanders.

The coup was successfully executed in the northern region, and in the capital of Lagos the conspirators were able to seize army headquarters, police headquarters, and the telephone exchange. The majors managed to assassinate the highest-ranking governmental incumbents, most of the powerful politicians, and many of the senior loyalist officers. But several of the latter escaped the assassination squads. There were too few troops to carry out their tasks simultaneously. In the words of one conspirator, "We were rushing from one assignment to another instead of being able to pull them all off simultaneously."

General Ironsi, the highest-ranking officer, was one of the loyalists who escaped. He managed to reach police headquarters, which was occupied by several enlisted men with orders to shoot whoever tried to enter the building. But since the major who had issued these instructions had to leave the building to carry out his other assignments, they accepted the authority of General Ironsi who, in this most unusual situation, was now their "immediate" superior. Ironsi was then able to use police headquarters to organize an effective military opposition. This was all the easier because the conspirators had neglected Rule 1 in not recruiting any officers of the 2nd Battalion —the main troop concentration in the capital area, stationed only sixteen miles outside of Lagos. While the coup was underway one of the majors drove out to 2nd Battalion headquarters, but by that time Ironsi had already ensured its loyalty. Lagos was secure. And rather than take responsibility for a civil war with the military on opposing sides, the majors in the north surrendered to the new military government headed by Ironsi (Luckham, pp. 20–27, 33; First, pp. 298–99).

Rule 3   Speed and coordination are essential in executing the coup. Those coups that are not executed in a single, well-coordinated stroke have a habit of failing. In order to surprise the government, more is required than sufficient troops to seize all the crucial targets almost simultaneously. Surprise also requires speed and coordination among the various units. Given several units standing at different distances from their targets, and possibly moving toward them at varying speeds depending upon the available mode of transport, exceptional care must be taken to co-ordinate their movements so that they arrive at their targets almost simultaneously.

The problem may become more complicated by the presence of "early warning systems" which can alert the government beforehand. Police, pro-government troops, or civilians who are situated along the line of march could make for early detection of troop movements. Crossing such an early warning line too soon would thus give the loyalists time to react before the units reached their targets. Coordination is further complicated by the need to maintain absolute secrecy. The day and exact time cannot be set beforehand, since the information might leak out. Problems of coordination are magnified when only a small handful of leaders, and perhaps only one of them, knows exactly when the coup is to be carried out, with the orders being issued only hours beforehand (Luttwak, pp. 159–61).

A typical coup situation finds a small number of conspirators facing a large number of neutral, uncommitted officers and a significant number of loyalist officers. If the loyalists decide to resist, the coup is likely to fail; if the loyalists and the uncommitted officers decide to resist, it will certainly fail. To prevent either possibility from arising requires a swiftly executed coup, one whose speed and coordination ensure the immediate seizure of all crucial targets.

The decision of the uncommitted officers—whether to resist the praetorians, to join them, or to remain neutral—is almost always based upon a single consideration: Will the coup succeed or fail? Being little concerned or undecided about the issues at stake, uncommitted officers will react according to the dictates of military unity and individual interests, which means aligning themselves with the side that is most likely to prevail. Ideally, the coup is executed with such swiftness that the uncommitted officers do not have a chance to consider the issue; for delays indicate possible failure.

If the loyalist officers are few it may be possible to arrest them all at the outset. But if they constitute a sizable group, especially if the group includes troop commanders stationed away from the capital, the activists cannot eliminate the threat at the outset. But while opposed to the coup, the loyalists will not necessarily order their troops, tanks, or planes to attack the conspirators' forces. Whether or not opposition is transformed into resistance depends heavily upon the activists' success in immediately capturing the critical personnel, buildings, and installations within the capital. If these are quickly secured, the activists can assume a defensive posture. They have achieved their immediate goals. It is the loyalist officers who must now accept this unhappy outcome or make the highly distasteful and onerous decision of dividing the military and perhaps the country against itself. Whereas the conspirators can call for order, unity, and the peaceful acceptance of their *fait accompli,* the loyalists would have to take responsibility for ordering their troops into fratricidal combat, possibly ushering in a civil war.

The importance of speed and coordination is amply illustrated by the narrow success of the 1966 Ghanaian coup.[30] One of the units inadvertently acted too soon in seizing loyalist officers, and the Signals Regiment was behind schedule in disconnecting the telephone system. A senior general consequently learned of the arrests and was able to call other officers. Having lost the element of surprise, the loyalist commander of the President's Own Guard Regiment was able to leave his quarters (where he was to have been arrested) for the presidential residence, where he met the conspirators with rifle and machine gun fire. Although Nkrumah was out of the country at the time, the praetorians thought it necessary to seize Flagstaff House because of its symbolic significance. And the battle was almost lost by the time delayed reinforcements from outside the capital arrived.[31]

The 1961 South Korean coup illustrates the enormous reluctance of loyalist officers to divide the army against itself by attacking the conspirators, whose swift, well-coordinated actions placed them in complete control of the capital. During the predawn hours some 250 officers and 3,500 troops under the command of General Park were able to capture all the crucial targets within Seoul. The coup was announced as an accomplished fact along with the declaration of martial law. But in actuality the activists had not yet secured their position. For they were confronted with two enormous troop con-

---

[30] The coup also came within a hair's-breadth of failure because insufficient attention had been paid to Rule 1. Only at the last minute did the conspirators realize that they would fail without the 1st Infantry Brigade which was stationed in the capital. The brigade commander went along largely because other troops had already received their orders to move toward Accra (First, p. 372).

[31] Police Commissioner Harlley's cooperation allowed for the rapid, undetected movement of these troops. General Kotoka's 2nd Brigade had to travel four hundred miles from its base to the capital. Although ostensibly on a night-training exercise, its movements would ordinarily have been reported to the army command by police forces stationed along the route of march. The 2nd Brigade's progress toward Accra was reported to police headquarters, but the police commissioner did not pass on the information to the loyalist generals or the government ministers (First, pp. 371–74; Bebler, pp. 63–67).

centrations totaling 600,000 men, with commanding officers who were not at all sympathetic to the conspirators.

The First Field Army, with twenty combat-ready divisions, could easily have destroyed the force within Seoul. Its commanding general denounced the coup, without however taking any decisive action during the next two critical days. His reluctance was largely due to a concern for the thousands of men who would die if he moved against the conspirators. On the third day the Military Revolutionary Council had him arrested. The sizable frontier forces stationed along the North Korean border could also have overwhelmed the praetorians. Their senior commanders also decided not to act out of an unwillingness to take responsibility for the bloodshed that would be required to dislodge the praetorians. For once the capital had been taken, the unpalatable responsibility for dividing army and country lay with the loyalists (Se-Jin Kim, pp. 93–98).

As soon as the conspirators have successfully executed their coup, they invariably issue a fairly standard communiqué, or *pronunciamento*. Praetorianism's public rationale is largely predictable just because it speaks to the problems facing all military governors in the aftermath of the coup—the consolidation of their control, the justification of their actions, and the legitimization of their power.[32]

[32] See pp. 19–21.

OFFICERS AS GOVERNORS 4

The officers now control the government. A military council or junta is formed which exercises all executive and legislative powers until the situation is stabilized. Once that happens we find three types of executive arrangements among military regimes: (1) the predominantly military executive, in which at least 90 percent of the cabinet positions are held by officers, (2) the mixed military-civilian executive, and (3) an exclusively military council along with a mixed cabinet. The first pattern is found in approximately 15 percent of military regimes, the second and third patterns each occur in about 40 percent of military regimes (McKinlay and Cohan, 1974, p. 4).[1] But whatever executive arrangement is adopted, a military officer assumes the position of chief executive as chairman of the council, prime minister, or president. There is considerable variation in the power of the chief executive in relation to the councils and cabinets. In some governments these officers are "first among equals," in other instances they clearly overshadow the other senior officers, but in all instances they clearly predominate in relation to the civilians.[2]

Now that the praetorians are seated in the governmental saddle, what do they do with their newly acquired power? Without in any way detracting from the importance of the coup itself as it closes off important political and economic possibilities, and as it affects the relative power of different political contenders, it should be apparent that what the soldiers do after taking con-

[1] The sometimes grandiloquent and radical-sounding titles of these executive bodies are meant to publicize the praetorians' revitalizing goals: the Revolutionary Command Council (Egypt and the Sudan), the National Reformation Council (Sierra Leone), the National Renovation Committee (Dahomey), the Supreme Council for National Reconstruction (South Korea), the Revolutionary Council (Burma and Syria).

[2] For some African variations, see Bebler, pp. 169–90.

trol of the government is of greater importance than the takeover itself. How a society is governed is more consequential than the identity of the governors and the manner in which they have attained their positions.[3]

In analyzing the characteristic features of officers as governors we shall be concerned with the structure of military regimes, the praetorians' governing style, the frequency with which they are able to legitimize themselves, and the duration of military regimes.

THE AUTHORITARIAN STRUCTURE OF MILITARY REGIMES

In asking the central question of this chapter—What do the soldiers do with their power after the coup? —we begin with regime structure as a highly salient aspect of any polity. Regime structure refers to the distribution of political power between the governors and the governed—the degree to which the latter can influence the selection and decisions of the governors, and the extent to which the governors control the behavior of the governed. There are enormous variations in nonelite "inputs," in the degree to which the governors exercise their power independently of the nonelite. The differences are primarily related to the presence or absence of competition for governmental offices with nonelite participation in electing the winners. The other basic dimension of regime structure—the amount of control that the government exercises over the nonelites—also varies greatly. In some regimes that control is minimal, with the government doing little more than ensuring that taxes are collected, order preserved, and laws obeyed. At the other end of the continuum, governmental control is both extensive and intensive. The population is controlled and society is penetrated from above. The government has an enormous impact upon the political and economic behavior of the population, sometimes even shaping citizen beliefs and values.

These two basic dimensions of regime structure—political competition with nonelite participation, and political control and penetration from above —are brought together in Figure 1 to form a typology of democratic, authoritarian, and mobilization regimes. Democratic (or open) regimes are characterized by a relatively high level of nonelite participation in a fairly open

---

[3] Unfortunately there is much truth in the assertion that writers on the Latin American military have "focused exclusively on the *causes* of military intervention . . . and have neglected almost entirely its *consequences*. They leave us with the generals (or colonels as the case may be) battering down the gates to the presidential palace . . . and tell us very little about what these triumphant groups do with their newly-acquired power" (Schmitter, p. 427). Referring to the non-Western countries as a whole, it has been said that "analysts are primarily interested in explaining why coups occur. The dominant focus is the causes rather than the consequences of military intervention. The effects of the soldiers' intrusion into politics are treated only secondarily" (Mittelman, p. 4).

competition for governmental power, and a low level of political control and penetration from above. Mobilization regimes feature just the reverse characteristics. Authoritarian (or closed) regimes are similar to mobilization regimes in that they provide little or no opportunity for nonelites to influence the selection of the governors or their policies; as in democratic regimes, there is a low level of political control and penetration from above.[4]

4 The "open spaces" between these three types of regimes are meant to signify the existence of regimes that are not pure types featuring different "mixtures" of the two dimensions. The top right-hand corner of Figure 1 is empty because the combination of extensive political control and penetration from above with high competitiveness and participation is not found in any of the contemporary polities. However, control and penetration from above along with genuine mass participation (Rousseauistic democracy) is possible in principle and has been approximated in a few historical cases (e.g., England under Cromwell and Geneva under Calvin). Yet even if instituted, such regimes are highly unstable.

Figure 1   A Typology of Regime Structures

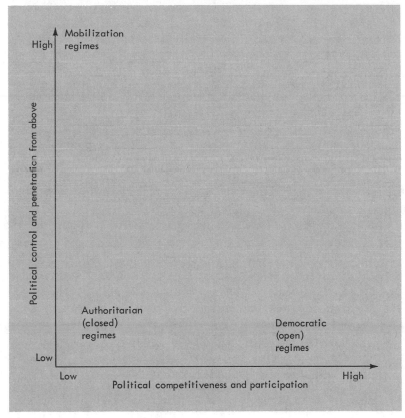

Using this typology as a frame of reference we can make the following generalizations about civilian and military regimes. Civilian regimes are found in each of the three "corners" of the figure; they may feature mobilization, authoritarian, or democratic structures. In contrast, when the military are in power they almost always maintain authoritarian structures. There is little or no political competition and participation, and no more than minimal levels of control and penetration from above. Although a few ruler-type praetorians have attempted to create mobilization regimes, for reasons that will be spelled out in a moment, their efforts have been unsuccessful.

Since the previous civilian regime may have approximated any one of the three types, the onset of military government does not necessarily entail a reduction in nonelite influence or an increase in governmental control. The overthrow of a democratic regime reduces nonelite inputs, but the overthrow of an authoritarian regime would have no appreciable effects in either regard, while the replacement of a mobilization regime decreases the scope of political and economic control from above without altering the nonelite's minimal decisional inputs.

THE ABSENCE OF COMPETITION AND PARTICIPATION

The very first actions taken by the new governors involve the near exclusive concentration of power in their hands. To a greater or lesser degree political rights and liberties are suspended; the authority of the judiciary is curtailed; debilitating restrictions are placed upon the activities of those political parties and politicized associations that are not ordered to dissolve themselves entirely; newspapers are closed or bridled; elections become a thing of the past or the future; and most if not all executive and legislative powers are concentrated in the hands of the military government.[5]

The immediate reasons for the elimination of competition and the clampdown on participation are quite apparent. The soldiers have taken power in order to bring about or prevent certain changes. They are then not about to permit the former incumbents or their supporters to challenge them. Those who threatened the interests of the military, the middle class, or the officers' communal segments may or may not be "punished" for having done so, but they will surely not be allowed to continue to do so. And since the praetorians publicly justified their coups in terms of civilian performance failures, they neutralize the power or restrict the activities of those charged with responsibility for these failures.

[5] Only some 15 percent of military regimes feature legislatures that enjoy a significant amount of power, and only about 15 percent allow more than a single party to operate (McKinlay and Cohan 1974, pp. 4–5).

The praetorians also opt for regime closure because of their character-istic political attitudes. The inordinately high value that they attach to political order biases them against the free expression of political interests, since these might eventuate in a raucous and riotous politics. The negative attitude toward political activity—the belief that political activity is self-serving and unnecessarily divisive—leads directly to the closure option. So also does the apolitical attitude toward the governing of states, which leaves little room for bargaining, competition, participation, and the articulation of nonelite demands. In the words of a retired Peruvian major, "The military man by his intellectual formation does not accept ambiguity; his mentality is not oriented to discussion. His long custom of commanding and obeying in-capacitates him to construct a democratic government" (Villanueva, 1962, p. 180).

While all military regimes are closed, some are more so than others. Guardian types control the government; praetorian rulers dominate the re-gime.[6] Due to differences in their objectives and the expected longevity of their governments, guardian-type praetorians often permit some competition and participation, whereas ruler types generally opt for total regime closure. Given their less than ambitious political and economic goals, the guardians need not destroy all political organizations and eliminate all forms of partici-pation. And since they intend to withdraw to the barracks within a few years, acceptable political parties and leaders must be available to take up the mantle of power. Thus political parties are not destroyed unless they are sharply opposed to the guardians' political and economic goals; elections may be held for legislative positions at the national and local levels, but only candidates and parties that are acceptable to the praetorians are permitted to compete.

Ruler-type praetorians take several further steps in the direction of re-gime closure due to their ambitious political and economic objectives, unmit-igated by the expectation of transferring power to civilians within the near future. Given their intentions of transforming the polity and economy, the actual and potential power of the opposition must be destroyed so that the intended changes can be implemented and their permanence ensured. The heightened governmental capabilities required for the transformation of pol-ity and economy are to be realized by the elimination of independent politi-cal parties, trade unions, and other politicized associations. Only those that can be controlled by the governors are allowed to exist. Competition and nonelite participation through elections are completely absent or virtually meaningless "rubber stamp" affairs, in which upward of 90 percent of the electorate vote for the officially approved candidates. Newspapers are heav-ily censored or published by governmental appointees.

---

[6] See pp. 24–27.

An analysis of the authoritarian structure of military regimes must also account for the low level of political control and penetration. This may be done quite simply for guardian-type praetorians: the maintenance of the basic political and economic status quo, whether accomplished by preventative actions or mild reforms, simply does not necessitate extensive control and intensive penetration. Nor would there be enough time to transform an authoritarian regime into a mobilization type. The vast organizational apparatus needed to mobilize the population would only become fully operative after two or three years, just when the guardians are thinking about their return to the barracks.

The situation is quite different in the case of ruler-type praetorians. The realization of their far-reaching objectives requires high levels of control and penetration, which in turn depend upon the creation of a mass political organization capable of mobilizing the population. Only through a well-organized mass party (or movement) that is securely rooted in the population can the governors uproot existing attachments, neutralize local power brokers, break down "traditional" attitudes, elicit widespread support for their formidable goals, and shape political and economic activity at the grass-roots level.

Yet some ruler-type praetorians fail to recognize the validity of these assertions. Their antipolitical attitudes, managerial-technical assumptions, and political inexperience foster the belief that political and economic transformations can be accomplished without a mass party. They assume that their monopoly of power is sufficient; decisions taken at the top not only will be implemented at the grass-roots level but will have a decided impact upon large swatches of political and economic life. Communication, exhortation, rewards, organization, and penetration are unnecessary, and a mass party thus superfluous.

Other ruler types are (or later become) more aware of the need for a mass party if their objectives are to be achieved. But not sufficiently so to overcome their disinterest and distaste for sustained efforts at political organizing, persuasion, exhortation, and symbol wielding. There is a "fundamental contradiction between military values and radicalism: the military officer must be more than idealistic; he must be willing to pursue his goals by means that are wholly foreign to his professional background. . . . Though military officers often seek broad reforms within their societies . . . they seldom show interest in political as distinct from administrative organization. The thought of actually mobilizing and organizing the masses as a political resource is antithetical to their ingrained contempt for politics" (Welch and

Smith, p. 65; Huntington, 1968, p. 243). Moreover, the praetorians are concerned about challenges to their own rule and policies that might emanate from such parties. The governors are consequently dissuaded from establishing mass parties, and if created, they turn out to be little more than paper organizations or ineffective structures because of their total dependence upon the governors.

Turning to those few praetorian rulers who have tried to build an effective mass party, it must first be said that this is no easy task. There are the formidable problems of rousing people out of political lethargy, overcoming their long-standing distrust and fear of government, and undermining patron-client relationships, communal attachments, and partisan loyalties. The governors must appreciate the enormous difficulties involved and be prepared to act accordingly, such as relying upon indigenous leaders or politicians rather than locally stationed civil servants to organize at the grassroots level. They must also recognize the inherent difficulties involved in generating and retaining popular support for an organization controlled from above. A large, committed following must be accorded some genuine participatory opportunities, provided with material rewards, or inspired by an ideology. These and other problems must be faced squarely and handled skillfully.

Yet the praetorians are not well endowed for the party-building enterprise. Here again their antipolitical and apolitical attitudes, ingrained political incapacities, and political inexperience get in the way. Undoubtedly some officers in praetorian armies deviate from this characterization, but they are usually too few to staff even the upper echelons of a mass party.

Egypt constitutes an especially telling example of the inability of praetorian rulers to build a mass party capable of mobilizing the population. For this particular failure occurred under exceptionally favorable conditions. The officers who took power in 1952 soon recognized the need for a mass party. They have had ample time to create one. Until Nasser's death in 1971, the government was headed by one of the few truly charismatic figures capable of eliciting emotion-charged support, loyalty, and energy at the mass level. Egyptian society is not divided along ethnic, racial, religious, linguistic, or regional lines that would have made the building of a nationwide party a highly problematic undertaking. And the presence of a powerful and much hated neighboring state has given rise to a nationalist fervor that could readily be used to recruit and energize a mass party. Given the failure of the Egyptian praetorians under these exceptionally propitious conditions, how much more problematic is the creation of effective mass parties on the part of less advantageously placed military governments?

At the outset the Egyptian praetorians exhibited the most basic kind of political failing, the unrealistic assumption that mass support can be readily enlisted and organized. The people need only be offered an organizational framework for them to accept the military leaders' invitation to join. Nasser naively believed that united, widespread support would appear immediately after the monarchy was overthrown:

> *I had imagined that the whole nation was ready and prepared, waiting for nothing but a vanguard to lead the charge against the battlements, whereupon it would fall in behind in serried ranks ready for the sacred advance towards the great objective . . . Then suddenly came the reality after [the coup of] July 23rd. The vanguard performed its task and charged the battlements of tyranny. It threw out Farouk and then paused, waiting for the serried ranks to come. For a long time it waited. Crowds did eventually come, and they came in endless droves—but how different is the reality from the dream! The masses that came were disunited, divided groups of stragglers. [Nasser, pp. 32–33]*

Not only did Nasser unrealistically expect the people to come forward immediately, without any prodding, they were to do so in a united manner. The failure to appreciate the distinctive characteristics of politics, the assumption that what applies within the military sphere also applies within the political realm, is evidenced in the constant references to military phenomena in discussing Egyptian politics. Nasser writes of battlements, charges, advances, serried ranks, marching feet, and a command vanguard; he does not mention issues, interests, conflicts, programs, persuasion, or leadership.

Even after getting a better grip on political reality, the Egyptian praetorians were unable to create an effective mass party. The soldiers themselves were displeased with the results. The National Liberation Rally was launched in 1953 to mobilize the people behind the government, by 1957 its deficiencies had become sufficiently apparent to prompt its replacement by the equally ineffective National Union, which in turn gave way to the Arab Socialist Union in 1961. At the time of the latter's creation Nasser openly admitted that its predecessors "had not put out sufficiently deep roots to be able to face the inevitable social change" (Abdel-Malek, p. 343). He charged the Arab Socialist Union with the task of enlisting and organizing "the mass effort of the popular forces," but it too failed to elicit the commitment, interest, and enthusiasm of the masses, and this despite the forced "integration" of additional labor, student, professional, and other interest groups. Although President Sadat initiated an assessment of the ASU in which the organization's ineffectiveness was admitted, his 1974 paper on the evolution of the ASU plainly demonstrated that he was not interested in making major changes.

Unable to stir up any attachments in the villages, urban neighborhoods, and factories, each of the three parties went from political torpor to paralysis. They failed to take hold at the grass-roots level largely because of the politically antiseptic manner in which they were run. Created by officers who visualized Egypt in managerial terms, as an organization instead of a polity, led and staffed by officers and civil servants with minimal political skills who were quite removed from their local "constituents," distributing no political, economic, or symbolic rewards to the membership, it is not surprising that these three parties had little attraction for the masses and little value for those who did join (Feit, pp. 152–57; Be'eri, pp. 448–52; Mayfield, p. 254; Waterbury, pp. 17–18).

Without an effective mass party the praetorians were only partly successful in controlling and penetrating Egyptian society. Apparently even the most advantageously placed and ambitious of ruler-type praetorians are unable to transform authoritarian regimes into mobilization regimes.[7]

THE PRAETORIANS' GOVERNING STYLE: DECISION MAKING WITHOUT POLITICS

To govern is to make authoritative decisions. The characteristic manner in which decisions are made, what may be referred to as the incumbent's governing style, varies markedly along several dimensions: the extent to which the views and interests of those outside the government are accorded serious consideration, the broad criteria that are used in selecting specific decisional options, and beliefs about the greater or lesser impact of governmental decisions upon their "target" areas.

The praetorians tend to adopt a governing style that may be described as decision making without politics—a style that distinguishes them from the majority of civilian incumbents. Many civilian governments exhibit one or another of its three aspects, but it is the praetorians who not only adhere to them more frequently, they alone sometimes make decisions in accordance with all three dimensions. This adherence to a similar governing style grows out of the officers' common socialization experiences within a rigidly hierarchical and bureaucratic environment, their professional training, and political attitudes.

---

[7] During Perón's rule in Argentina between 1946 and 1955 conditions were also auspicious for the creation of an effective mass party: the leader and his wife, Eva, enjoyed a charismatic halo among the urban workers; shortly after coming to power he enjoyed the active support of a majority of Argentinians; there were no communal divisions that could make mass recruitment highly problematic; and the exceptionally high levels of urbanization and literacy were especially propitious for mass politicization. Yet even so, the *Partido Peronista* turned out to be a factionalized, poorly structured, and loosely organized party.

According to the most basic dimension of decision making without politics—the one that gives some shape and reinforcement to the others—the
demands and views of politicians and citizens alike are to be largely ignored.
So far as possible, they are not to be inserted into the decisional calculus.
Janowitz makes this point somewhat more broadly when he writes that "interest in politics goes hand in hand with a negative outlook and even hostility to politicians and political groups. It is the politics of wanting to be above
politics . . . There is no glorification of, or even respect and understanding
for, the creative role of the politician and the political process" (Janowitz,
1964, p. 65). Government is to be "above politics" by being devoid of it.

To view governmental decision making as a political enterprise would
involve the praetorians in the unpalatable task of soliciting popular preferences, appeasing some groups and negotiating with others, resulting in
illogically constructed bargains, ineffectual palliatives, or clearly harmful
policies. Whatever the exact outcome, such decisions would not conform to the
national interest. This apolitical attitude toward the governing of states is
regularly buttressed by the officers' confidence in themselves as well-trained
professionals. Especially in comparison with the (supposedly) incompetent
civilian politicians, the soldiers see themselves as best able to deal with the
country's problems. They have little to learn from politicians and citizens.[8]

The following characterization of the 1958–60 military government in
Burma is equally applicable to the praetorians' governing style from 1962
(when they again took power) to the present:

> *The extraordinary fact was that the Burmese Army, in seeking to realize
> its ideal of government, was in essence seeking to force upon Burmese
> society once again the basic structure and pattern of prewar colonial Burmese
> government. Indeed, the ideals and the goals of the army seemed to be
> quite explicitly those of the old British Burma. In particular, the emphasis
> was on reestablishing administrative rule and restraining all forms of popu-
> lar, agitational politics. Law and order and efficient operation of govern-
> ment became the guiding principles. . . . The government was assumed
> to know what was the best interest of the country. The people had to be
> taught and trained. . . . Above all else, army rule in Burma lacked any
> mechanism for handling conflicting interests within society. The means for*

---

[8] These generalizations are less applicable to Latin American praetorians. Given
the regularity with which the officers and the middle class hold similar views
on the outstanding issues, the praetorians often pay considerable attention to
the views of its leaders, often according them cabinet seats.

adjusting and accommodating the demands of various interests was missing, for it was blandly assumed that the administrative programs of government were inevitably in the best interest of all. [Pye, 1962B, pp. 246–48]

Even in Nigeria, with its intense currents of tribal-regional hostility, the Ironsi government was convinced that the views of citizens and politicians could be safely and advantageously ignored. General Ironsi held to the highly simplistic belief that it was the politicians alone who had brought about Nigeria's communal problems; by depriving them of their power—which he did—the tribal-regional conflict would be eliminated. Nor did the government evidence any concern for information about popular views and feelings. With the proscription of political parties and activities, the abolition of regional governments and legislatures, and the absence of a free press, only the military could channel information from the four regions to the center. And in this it was particularly defective. The near-exclusive responsibility for inserting each region's interests into the decision-making process at the center was left with a single individual—the region's military governor who sat on the Supreme Military Council and the Federal Executive Council. Almost all important decisions were made by a group of half a dozen senior officers, together with a handful of civil servants as advisers. (First, pp. 304–5; Luckham, pp. 253–57).[9] In the following chapter we shall see how this politically antiseptic governing style contributed to the outbreak of civil war.

THE RELIANCE UPON MANAGERIAL AND TECHNICAL CRITERIA

The second dimension of the praetorians' governing style refers to the criteria most frequently utilized in choosing among decisional options. One set of criteria is eminently political, emphasizing considerations of mutual advantage, tradeoffs, the cumulation of political resources, and the attainment of popular support. These are often rejected in favor of managerial and technical criteria, which turn governmental decision making into an apolitical, problem-solving exercise. Societies are to be administered rather than governed. Decisional options are evaluated by invoking the criteria of rationality, efficiency, and sound administration. If these are properly ap-

---

[9] For an example of a Nigerian officer who acted as both a political leader and a member of the Supreme Military Council, see the discussion of Colonel Adebayo as governor of the Western State between 1966 and 1971, in Bienen, forthcoming, Chapters 3 and 5. In contrast, there is the leadership style of Castello Branco, the first president of Brazil's post-1964 military regime, who "often felt that any dialogue or attempt to win the support of the people for his plans was a form of demagoguery." (Stepan, 1971, p. 234)

plied, each problem will usually turn out to have a single, readily determined, "correct" solution.

This kind of intellectual framework is commonly appropriate within the military sphere, but far less so in confronting political and economic problems. Yet the praetorians are not given to making such a distinction. They confidently transfer what has been learned in a bureaucratic organization with its high regard for rationality, efficiency, and sound administration, to the governmental sphere. The transference is buttressed by the officers' image of themselves as more technically proficient and managerially efficient than the politicians.

Few praetorians have evidenced such an exclusive faith in technical solutions to a variety of problems as have the Brazilians. Effective political power clearly resides with the military, but they have depended so heavily upon economists, engineers, agronomists, and urban planners that the Brazilian case has been described as a military-technocratic "alliance." Two civilian economists have wielded extraordinary influence within the highest decision-making circles. Each military government since 1964 has invoked the technocrats' "monopoly of rationality" to achieve its primary goals—those of economic growth and modernization. Economic planning has been based on "the assumption that a technocracy (especially one guided almost solely by economic technicians) which airily ignores the basic stuff of politics can make even technically correct policies work when they are overlaid on a society as underorganized and nonparticipative as the Brazilian. . . . The entire notion of 'inputs' into the political system—the human supports, demands, and mobilization stemming from authentic political parties, interest groups, ideologies and even myths—is virtually ignored in an exclusive concentration on 'correct' policies, 'rational' decisions, and a 'good image' abroad" [10] (Rowe, pp. 3, 21; Schneider, pp. 113–14; Sanders, 1973B, pp. 3–4, 8–9; Stepan, 1971, pp. 232–34).

Brazil is one of the most complex and economically developed of non-Western societies. The technocratic-managerial approach to decision making has also been applied by praetorians in countries that are at the other end of the continuum. The praetorians who overthrew President Keita of Mali have been described as "military technocrats [who] tended to view the two chief goals of economic recovery and national reconciliation as 'nonideological' and 'nonpolitical' ones. They hoped to achieve these goals by streamlining the administration [and] improving its efficiency and rationality." Bebler found that the praetorians of the three other African countries he studied—Dahomey, Sierra Leone, and Ghana—were governing in a similar fashion (Bebler, pp. 92, 200).

---

[10] Given the implicit criticism in this quotation, it should be noted that the economy has been growing at an exceptionally fast rate under military auspices.

If other considerations are not entirely excluded, these managerial-technical criteria are certainly relevant to economic decision making. Yet they have even been applied to the most sensitive and emotion charged of political issues, as in the case of Nigeria's intense regional-tribal conflict. Under the civilian regime the highly inflammable issue of civil service recruitment was dampened by the use of quotas; civil servants were recruited from the northern, western, and eastern regions in proportion to population size. Soon after taking power, the Ironsi government abolished the quota arrangements. Merit criteria alone would be used in the selection of new recruits, which clearly benefited the better-educated eastern Ibos who had consistently received higher grades on the competitive entrance examinations. The government did not recognize the contradictions between the recruitment of the best-qualified people to the civil service and the mitigation of communal hatreds and jealousies. In fact, managerial considerations were naively expected to have a positive political impact in helping to unify the country. The exclusive reliance upon merit criteria was part of the government's misdirected attack upon tribalism (Luckham, pp. 265, 283–84; Dudley, pp. 216–17). As will be seen in the following chapter, this decision triggered the communal rioting that led down the path to civil war.

A corollary to the adoption of managerial-technical criteria is the tendency to accord senior civil servants a prominent place in the decision-making process. It is rare for the influence of higher civil servants to be reduced after the soldiers take power; it either remains at about the precoup level or is enhanced. Over and above their usual role of providing the governors with information and advising them on the technical feasibility of policy options, senior bureaucrats have served as almost equal partners in the decision-making process.[11] The praetorians hold the reins of power, but with a considerable amount of slack and a willingness to be guided.[12]

The considerable decision-making influence of the civil servants is readily understandable given their strong affinities with the praetorians. Both groups have been trained as managers and socialized within a bureaucratic environment. Like the "armed bureaucrats," civil servants are thus given to tackling problems by devising rational, efficient, technical, and organizational solutions. The armed and unarmed bureaucrats perceive the world as "essentially plagued by poor organization, and it is organization that can provide the means by which problems can be overcome" (Feit, p.

---

[11] In Latin America it is the technically trained administrators—economists, lawyers, engineers, professors—who are accorded considerable influence. Several *técnicos* are often placed in the highest positions within the ministries.

[12] Evidence that civilian politicians share these perceptions comes from a survey carried out during the period of military government in Nigeria (Bienen, p. 336; Bienen, forthcoming, Chapter 5).

11; Welch, 1970, p. 48). They also evidence a set of similar antipolitical beliefs: politicians are devoid of expertise, their decisions are the product of a
continuous search for party advantage, they are inherently corrupt, and they
sometimes stir up an unhealthy ideological and emotional fervor. Governments are clearly better off without them (First, p. 113). It is thus not surprising to find the praetorians regularly investigating, disgracing, and often
punishing the politicians of the previous regime, while the bureaucracy seldom suffers a similar fate even if it is thoroughly corrupt (Feit, pp. 70–71).

The African praetorians' reliance upon civil servants has been especially pronounced. They evidence an unusually high measure of respect for
the bureaucrats due to their own relatively low educational attainments, many
uneducated senior officers having been promoted from the ranks after the
rapid departure of the British and French. And the small size of almost all
African armies means that senior officers cannot be spared from their military
responsibilities. There are simply not enough of them to staff the upper
reaches of government ministries and the military.

In Ghana, Dahomey, Sierra Leone, and Mali, military governments
markedly enhanced the autonomy of the bureaucrats by removing or minimizing "political" pressures, without at the same time instituting controls of
their own. The senior civil servants fared exceptionally well under the first
military government in Ghana (1966–69). The officers exercised their authority in a loose, almost superficial manner. "The civil servants were now able
to reverse policies which they had long disliked. Thus the Ministry of Agri-
culture was able to dispose of many unwanted state farms, the Ministry of
Education was able to increase the period of secondary education from four
years to five, and the Ministry of Labour was able to end compulsory trade
union membership." Moreover, the praetorians created specialized committees of bureaucrats whose advice was taken so regularly that they might almost be described as wielding executive power. "The Administrative Committee was able to bring about a drastic reduction in the number of ministries, a recommendation which would have met with far more resistance
from a civilian government wanting to dispense patronage; and the Economic Committee was given virtually a free hand in deciding how the
problems of inflation, budget deficits and foreign debts, inherited from the
previous government, should be tackled" (Bebler, p. 203; Pinkney, pp 62–64;
Kraus, p. 189).

AN EXAGGERATED BELIEF IN THE IMPACT OF GOVERNMENTAL DECISIONS

The third dimension of the praetorians' governing style is an exaggerated
belief in the impact of their decisions. Political, economic, social, cultural,
and institutional patterns are thought to be considerably more malleable,

more easily affected by governmental actions, than they are in reality. At the extreme, some praetorians believe that all problems are resolvable if only the governors select the correct course of action, and then pursue it in a head-on, undeviating, and, if necessary, forceful manner. There are few limits upon what the government can accomplish.[13] Little if any account needs to be taken of popular interests and prejudices, institutional arrangements and roadblocks, or political and economic relationships.

This aspect of their governing style is reinforced by the just mentioned managerial-technocratic orientation to problem solving. "Technocratic thinking" encourages the belief that "any problem is amenable to a direct and simple solution. Leaders are men who can identify the heart of a problem—be it technical, military or social—and who are prepared to drive through to the desired outcome" (Janowitz, 1964, p. 66). Another explanatory factor is the officers' self-confidence as highly capable decision makers. According to Zolberg, it is the "arrogant self-assurance of [African] military officers that they can govern with greater wisdom and skill than civilian countrymen which leads them to come down with a heavy step where angels fear to tread. They hesitate even less than do other authoritarian leaders to destroy the tenuous institutional fabric of African political life" (Zolberg, 1973, p. 319).

Colonel Qassem's actions as head of the Iraqi government provide a sharply etched illustration of the praetorian tendency to ignore political reality in attacking problems in a rapid, direct, inflexible, and forceful manner. Qassem's failure to achieve any of his objectives underscores the generalization because there is reason to think that he would not be susceptible to this kind of basic miscalculation. If any praetorians are able to appreciate the necessity of compromise and conciliation, we might very well expect to find them in a Middle East that is well known for the "Byzantine politics" of intrigue and shifting alliances. If one officer were presumed to be highly skilled in manipulating people and events, it would be Qassem, whose shrewdness helped place him at the head of the conspiratorial group. If there is one country whose antagonistic and complex divisions along ethnic, religious, class, and foreign policy lines made the need for a gradual, indirect, and flexible problem-solving approach highly apparent, it would be Iraq.

The praetorians who overthrew the much despised ruling dynasty in 1958 were enthusiastically welcomed by almost every section of opinion.

---

[13] This is not to suggest that military governments are on the whole more "activist" than civilian ones; they are no more likely to recognize the existence of serious problems for which the government has some responsibility. But when they do, the praetorians more often take direct and inflexible actions in the confident belief that the problems can be solved.

There were widespread expectations that a new start could begin along several previously stagnant fronts. Yet within four weeks the civilian groups who had most strongly supported the coup had begun to fall out with the praetorians. Within four years the process was complete, Qassem's rule ending in "bankruptcy" and his assassination. By then the nationalists, the constitutionalists, and the Communists had withdrawn and gone into opposition, while the Kurdish tribesmen were at war with the central government. Qassem devoted prodigious energies to the realization of his ambitious goals, but he failed to reach any of them because he held a thoroughly "rigid conception of the new Iraq." Each of his goals was somewhat problematic to begin with in the Iraqi context; when pursued simultaneously and inflexibly, they became exceptionally unrealistic. "Qassem's views of an independent, nonaligned, indivisible, socially progressive, secular state, authoritarian under his rule, took no account of the realities of the Iraqi condition and, in sum, were incompatible with the aims of any one of the political forces which had given the revolution its initial welcome" (Dann, p. 376; Be'eri, p. 192).

THE UNSUCCESSFUL QUEST FOR A LEGITIMIZING FORMULA

Whether or not governments are legitimate is certainly among the most important normative standards against which to evaluate them. With the radical critique of democracy coming into its own, the legitimacy factor has taken on greater evaluative and normative significance than the somewhat outmoded dichotomy between "good" democratic governments and "bad" dictatorial ones. Or to put it differently, whether a government is legitimate, nonlegitimate, or illegitimate in the eyes of the politicized stratum of the civilian population is an exceptionally important criterion of governmental performance.[14] It is also related to the frequency with which the governors resort to coercive measures to maintain themselves in office, the scope of political violence, and the degree of national integration.

Are there, then, any major differences between military and civilian governments in attaining and maintaining a moral right to govern? What kinds of legitimizing formulas are available to military governments? Do the praetorians regularly undertake concerted efforts to envelop their power with a legitimizing mantle?

In the immediate postcoup period the praetorians are frequently accorded a good measure of legitimacy. It is regularly forthcoming in the

---

[14] Legitimate governments are accorded a moral right to govern, nonlegitimate governments have no such right, and illegitimate governments are those that are seen as positively immoral by the politically aware stratum of the civilian population.

wake of the first coup. For the military regularly enjoys considerable respect and popularity prior to its first intrusion into the governmental arena. In Pakistan, for example, the officer corps' pre-1958 record as soldiers inspired popular confidence. Its reputation for integrity was intact. It was exempted from the resentments that had built up against previous civilian governments. There were consequently widespread expectations that the officers would be more responsive to popular aspirations and more effective in generating economic growth (von Vorys, pp. 146–47). But in Pakistan as elsewhere, popular respect for the military was implicitly or explicitly premised upon its remaining outside the political arena. After entering that arena· the military's reputation for political impartiality, and consequently one possible basis of legitimacy, is lost.

In the preceding chapter it was said that coups follow in the wake of civilian performance failures and legitimacy deflations. These clearly contribute to the warm welcome that the praetorians often receive.[15] But even the many praetorians who do receive a warm welcome cannot rely upon quickly fading memories of civilian failures for their own legitimacy. Along with those military governments that do not enjoy initial claims to legitimacy, they must turn to other formulas if their moral right to govern is to be widely acknowledged.

Here it will be suggested that only a small fraction of military governments attain and maintain a legitimizing mantle. Certainly a much larger proportion of civilian governments succeed in doing so. The generalization that military governments regularly fail to legitimize themselves, both in absolute terms and relative to the record of civilian governments, will be developed by examining the several legitimizing formulas available to the praetorians. With just a handful of exceptions, none of these formulas has been successfully employed, although some of the reasons for the failure to do so are beyond the praetorians' control.

THE MILITARY VIRTUES

To begin with those legitimizing formulas available to military governments alone, there is the possibility of relying upon the actual or perceived military virtues. The officer corps is commonly seen to embody and value

---

[15] This generalization is subject to some significant modifications with respect to Latin America, where legitimizing welcomes are much less common. There the armed forces are hardly political newcomers. The people have had direct experience or indirect knowledge of previous military governments which has cast greater or lesser doubt upon the supposed virtues of praetorianism. And since Latin American officers often intervene in order to thwart the interests and neutralize the power of the lower classes, they are not about to receive the political blessing of these groups.

bravery, discipline, obedience, self-denial, austerity, honesty, political impartiality, and dedication to the public interest. These perceived virtues often generate considerable respect and sympathy for the armed forces; at times they engender a veritable mystique (Finer, pp. 10–11). It would thus seem likely that the praetorians who are seen to embody these military virtues would have their power legitimized.

Yet it turns out that the praetorians rarely if ever succeed in capitalizing upon these actual or supposed military virtues. Some of these virtues have little relevance for the governing of states; others are not attainable by any government, military or civilian; while those that are both relevant and realizable are not regularly exhibited by the military after they have taken power.

The martial virtues of bravery, discipline, and obedience under fire have little relevance for the governing of states. The soldiers may very well possess them in abundance, but as governors they are evaluated according to quite different criteria, which means that these particular military virtues cannot provide a legitimizing mantle. Even in the war-racked Middle East, and with Islam exalting the martial virtues, the praetorians' legitimacy has been only marginally affected by their courage under fire.

What then of the military virtues of political impartiality, service to the nation, and dedication to the public interest? If the praetorians were seen to embody them, might not their control of the government be legitimized? For better or worse, these virtues represent a Platonic ideal which might begin to be approached, but never realized. Military and civilian governments alike respond to the interests of particular groups, although they may believe themselves to be acting in the public interest. Praetorians most commonly respond to the interests of the military itself, those of the middle class, and those of the communal segments into which they were born. Even if a concerted effort is made to govern in accordance with the Platonic ideal, the attempt will be lacking in credibility. Those who take issue with the government are not about to view it as an executor of the public interest, as a politically neutral servant of the nation as a whole. Governments cannot stand above politics; they are certainly not seen to do so. The praetorians are consequently unable to rely upon this set of military virtues to legitimize themselves.

Most praetorians justify their coups by claiming that their civilian predecessors were dishonest, corrupt, and inordinately self-serving. Given the common validity of such charges, along with the officers' public claim to be honest, incorruptible, and self-denying, military governments sometimes try to use the puritanical virtues to legitimize themselves. However, even when there is a sharp contrast between the behavior of civilians and praetorians, the puritanical virtues do not constitute an effective legitimizing formula. Memories of previous civilian failings are short, and the Augean stables can only be cleaned out once. Equally important, civilians are not prone to give much credit to their governors just because they have clean hands. Widespread corruption may help produce a legitimacy deflation, but honesty and austerity do not have nearly as strong a positive impact upon the legitimization of governments. Civilians who value the honest conduct of government react negatively to incumbents with sticky fingers, without however giving much credit to those with empty hands. They are expected to be honest.

Moreover, military governments are on the whole no less corrupt and self-serving than civilian ones. It has even been said that African praetorians are more corrupt and self-indulgent than their civilian predecessors, and as much so as their Latin American counterparts (Shabtai, pp. 245–47; Bretton, p. 233). Certainly Latin America's praetorians cannot be described as puritanical, although only a few of them—such as Perón in Argentina and Pérez Jiménez in Venezuela—engaged in the public looting of legendary sums. Once they have the opportunity to do so as governors, soldiers are just as likely as civilians to enrich themselves through legal, quasi-legal, and illegal means, which can only detract from their legitimization.[16]

African military governments in particular have tried to project a puritanical public image, at least during the early part of their incumbencies. They regularly claim that the officer corps is the most honest group in society, the only one that is incorruptible (Shabtai, p. 129). And among the officer corps of Africa none had a higher reputation for integrity than Ghana's. It is thus especially significant that its self-denying and incorruptible public image was sharply punctured after taking power.

The National Liberation Council responded to the precarious economic situation that had been brought on by Nkrumah's financial profligacy by making substantial cutbacks in government spending while repeatedly publicizing the seriousness of the problem. Yet at the same time the NLC increased the economically unproductive military budget by 40 percent, put through a sizable pay increase for the officer corps, and used the country's critically depleted foreign reserves to purchase luxury items for themselves, such as Mercedes-Benz cars. Almost twice as many of these expensive status symbols were purchased in the two-year period after the 1966 coup than dur-

---

16 However, actual evidence of military corruption is less readily attainable than that of comparable civilian transgressions. For the praetorians are better able to hide behind the protective walls of their authoritarian regimes, and almost invariably do so. General Mobutu's government in Zaire is one of the rare instances in which military officers were brought to trial for illegal, self-aggrandizing activities. Between 1965 and 1971 dozens of officers, including some high-ranking ones, were sentenced to long prison terms (Willame, p. 34). And it should also be noted that the civilian governments that succeed the praetorians are not about to investigate or prosecute the latter for their corruption. For the civilians are realistically apprehensive of another coup if they were to discredit the military.

ing the previous two years. By 1968 the puritanical image of the military had been sufficiently deflated to account for the appearance of a popular recording entitled "The Cars Are the Same, Only the Drivers Have Changed." It was quickly banned. And at just about the same time General Ankrah resigned as head of the NLC after it became known that he had accepted "unofficial" payments from foreign businessmen (Price, 1971A, pp. 371–72; Price, 1971B, p. 426).

The behavior of the Ghanaian praetorians was sufficient to puncture their puritanical image. That of the Sudanese officers, who were also highly regarded before taking power, was sufficiently corrupt to help bring down General Abboud's government in 1964. Governmental corruption, which was by no means unknown prior to the 1958 coup, reached dramatic proportions under praetorian auspices. Military officers directly or indirectly bought up huge plots of restricted public land. Roads were built to the new homes of senior army officers and their relatives. Several high-ranking officers were charged with taking bribes for the granting of import licenses, prosecuted for scandalous sex and embezzlement crimes, and then accused of manipulating the courts to have themselves absolved. When the government was challenged by student and trade union demonstrators no one came to its defense —not even the army. The governors were despised for their arrogant disregard of public norms, newly acquired wealth, blatant corruption, and manipulation of the judicial process (First, p. 251; Be'eri, p. 219).

Just because corruption has been so prevalent in Indonesia, the government headed by General Suharto since 1965 might have been able to legitimize itself by keeping its own hands clean. Although the praetorians could hardly have eliminated *korupsi*, at least not without critically dislocating the entire economic structure, had they refrained from enriching themselves illegally such a marked deviation from the norm might have contributed to their legitimization. Not only did these praetorians ignore their own precoup calls for a thorough governmental housecleaning, corruption became more widespread since the takeover. It is widely known that officers act as patrons for the wealthy ethnic Chinese entrepreneurs who literally surround them. In return for their influence with governmental agencies, the businessmen handle the details of tapping into lucrative ventures for the officers.[17] Out of these and other corrupt practices, senior officers have managed to acquire large houses, fleets of automobiles, and sizable bank accounts. They pursue the lavish life-style that was supposedly reserved for corrupt civilian politicians and wealthy entrepreneurs (Hanna, pp. 1–6; Crouch).

---

[17] A similar relationship between praetorians and businessmen is characteristic of politics in Thailand.

Turning from the military virtues to those formulas that are potentially available to military and civilian governments alike, there is Weber's well-known typology of charismatic, traditional, and rational-legal legitimacy. Charismatic legitimacy is derived from popular beliefs in the leader's extraordinary achievements and superhuman qualities. However, due to the paucity of truly charismatic (as opposed to highly popular) leaders, this legitimizing formula is rarely available to the praetorians. Given the highly personalistic and idiosyncratic aspects of charisma, it certainly cannot be produced "on order." Only two genuinely charismatic praetorians—Perón and Nasser—have appeared among the more than one hundred non-Western military governments.[18] Indeed, the armed forces are far from being charismatic breeding grounds, given their bureaucratic features and seniority rules. And a praetorian officer corps is often fearful of a charismatic leader just because he will disrupt the military's bureaucratic structure. It is only a partial exaggeration to claim that "any officer with clear political skills and potential for populistic charismatic appeal is vetoed by the military organization" (Linz, p. 241).

Governmental power is legitimized on traditional grounds when there is a widespread belief in the sanctity of tradition—an abiding commitment to time-honored practices—combined with the government's adherence to these traditions. A deep respect for what has actually or allegedly existed in the past is transferred to the government if it is seen to conform to these valued practices. Military governments may have their power acknowledged as rightful on traditional grounds in two ways: praetorianism itself may constitute a long-standing, time-honored practice, or the praetorians may adopt

---

[18] The strength of Perón's charisma may be gauged from the fact that over a third of the Argentine population continued to support him avidly almost twenty years after he was forced into exile. Two million supporters turned out to welcome him as a national savior on his return in 1973. Nasser's charisma was most sharply evidenced after the disastrous Egyptian defeat in the 1967 war with Israel. Unlike the previous two defeats no ready scapegoat or explanation could neutralize the humiliating impact of Israel's lightning victory. But when Nasser publicly offered his resignation, the people of Cairo came out into the streets in a frenzied demonstration of protest. It was this manifestation of their continued dedication and belief in his extraordinary qualities that allowed him to withdraw his resignation and retain power until his death in 1971.

and support traditional practices that were originally unrelated to the military.

With regard to the first possibility, military governments cannot utilize a traditional formula because praetorianism does not constitute an honored and long-standing practice in any of the non-Western areas. It can hardly begin to do so in Africa and much of Asia where national armies were only recently created with the culmination of colonial rule. In contrast, the history of Middle Eastern countries is studded with instances of soldiers seizing power. Yet praetorianism was not transformed into a glorified or even respected tradition. For the soldiers used their power in an extortionist manner, they were usually recruited from among slaves or foreign mercenaries and thus alien to the population, they showed little respect for the Islamic faith, and they often split apart along personal, factional, tribal, and regional lines (Halpern, pp. 19–20). Almost all of the Latin American countries had become independent by the 1820s, with soldiers more or less regularly seizing power since then. But due to the soldiers' actual or perceived predatory qualities, the unexceptional performance of military governments, and their hostility to the lower classes, praetorianism has not been transformed into a time-honored practice. In some Latin American countries the officer corps have been highly regarded as a political force, but their intervention is legitimized only insofar as it is designed to protect the constitution. It does not extend beyond the temporary assumption of power until a new civilian government can be formed, a matter of a few weeks at the most.

The other possibility is for the praetorians to legitimize themselves by supporting, adopting, and conforming to traditional practices and symbols. Yet there are several limitations upon the extent and frequency with which the praetorians can use this kind of legitimizing formula.

Not all societies feature long-standing traditions that are imbued with a good measure of political salience. And where such politically relevant traditions do exist, they are usually subgroup rather than national traditions. Different religious, linguistic, racial, and ethnic groups evidence strong attachments to their time-honored practices and symbols. But these are just that—their particular traditions, which are more or less strongly resented by other groups. Their adoption by the government would do far more to divide the nation than to provide the praetorians with a legitimizing mantle.

It may be possible to resurrect traditions that have died out or to create new myths that speak to the nation as a whole, but this would require the kind of manipulative, symbol-wielding activities that most praetorians disdain. And were they able to overcome their distaste for such activities, the paucity of political skills and sophistication would not augur well for a successful effort.

One other possible stumbling block applies to ruler-type praetorians with progressive, modernizing goals. They find it difficult (though by no means impossible) to espouse traditional ideas that glorify the past and the absence of change. In doing so they provide traditional forces with considerable political leverage in their efforts to preserve the status quo. Their interests and appeals must then be acknowledged as deserving of respect; their political support might have to be bought at too high a price for change-oriented praetorians.

It is this set of limitations and stumbling blocks that explains why only a handful of military governments have tried to legitimize themselves along traditional lines, and why those that made the attempt have rarely succeeded.[19] Even under the uncommonly propitious conditions found in Egypt, and with the praetorians showing an unusual appreciation for the uses of tradition, they were only partly successful. Egyptian society provides an exceptionally auspicious context for the use of a traditional formula: Islam is accepted by the vast majority, no other communal attachment divides the society, Islam itself asserts a close and overlapping relationship between the religious and governmental spheres, and it is identified with historical claims to Egyptian glory.

Capitalizing upon this uncommon set of advantages, the praetorians sought to have themselves identified with Islam. They too were to become defenders of the faith, a role that had previously been the exclusive prerogative of conservative religious leaders. The praetorians created the Islamic Congress to uphold and promote the message of Islam, Islam was adopted as the state religion, civil courts continued to hand down verdicts in accordance with religious law, Islamic ritual was publicly respected by the praetorians who quoted liberally from the Koran, and governmental decisions were announced during the traditional Friday sermon.

These actions had some positive impact upon an Islam-conscious people, but they apparently did not significantly buttress the government's legitimacy. Perhaps the best estimate is this: if the praetorians had not conformed to the political-religious dictates of the Islamic tradition, their legitimacy would have been cast into serious doubt. Moreover, the traditional religious formula created some difficulties for the praetorian rulers. It prevented Nasser from completely neutralizing religion as a political force. The conservative political-religious groups were the only ones that succeeded in organizing antigovernment demonstrations over a ten-year period. The government also had to face some basic contradictions between the population's

---

[19] Thailand is an atypical case in which the king has endowed military governments with their only substantial claim to legitimacy; and this conditional "transfer" of traditional legitimacy has limited the praetorians' power. A major factor behind the fall of the military regime in 1973 was the king's explicit transfer of legitimacy from the praetorians to respected civilians, thereby "punishing" the military governors for their intransigence and brutality in the face of student demonstrations (Morell, pp. 288, 293).

Islamic beliefs and practices and its own modernization programs. The praetorians adopted a dual approach to this problem, confronting the traditional impediments to modernization head-on while trying to adapt Islamic beliefs to notions of social and economic change. Although both strategies were modestly successful, Nasser and the army leadership recognized the impact of Islam in slowing down the pace of modernization (Vatiokitis, pp. 191–99; Feit, p. 154; Be'eri, pp. 283–85).

The presidency of General Mobutu in Zaire (the former Belgian Congo) is especially significant for quite different reasons. It illustrates the possibilities of legitimizing the government by popularizing long-buried traditional practices and symbols. Under colonial rule the Congolese people tended to downgrade their indigenous traditions, denigrate their own civilization, and believe that the best they could aspire to was an assimilation of Belgian or Western values. Starting in 1967 Mobutu led and inspired a "Return to Authenticity" movement. The nation was to identify and resurrect its own traditions, simultaneously rejecting foreign ideas and symbols. The name of the country was changed, as were those of the largest cities, streets, parks, mountains, and other places with European names. The Nationality Law obliged everyone with a foreign-sounding first or family name to change it to a Zairian one. With its endless repetitions on television programs, insinuation into popular music and folklore, Mobutu's frequent and enthralling speeches, and the people's receptivity, the Authenticity campaign came to influence and inspire a wide spectrum of political and economic activities. This blend of political astuteness, public theatre, and an apparently sincere commitment to the resurrection of the nation's authentic traditions have gone a long way in consolidating the president's authority and legitimizing his government (Dubois).

But even this, possibly the most successful case of a military government legitimizing itself on traditional grounds, paradoxically tends to bear out the generalization that praetorians are rarely able to do just that. The astute recognition of the traditional formula's legitimizing potential, a willingness to communicate directly and extensively with the people, the skillful formulation and articulation of popular appeals—these are certainly not typical of praetorian soldiers. And the man who developed and led the Authenticity movement was hardly a typical officer. Mobutu resigned from Belgium's *Force Publique* after serving only six years. He then pursued a dual career in journalism and party politics before being somewhat fortuitously appointed chief of staff shortly after independence in 1960. Mobutu was only marginally affected by his brief military experience, and was likely to behave in a decidedly nonmilitary fashion as a result of his journalistic and political activities.

Governments may also be legitimized—indeed they are most often legitimized —when they are seen to conform to certain highly valued rational-legal principles. Legitimacy derives from the making of decisions in accordance with valued constitutional and procedural principles. In addition, rational-legal legitimization provides for some popular participation in selecting the governors, whose actions are limited by their official positions, the constitutionally defined procedures for the enactment of laws, and the rights, liberties, and equality of citizens as protected by the constitution and the courts. The enactment, substance, and application of governmental decisions do not contravene constitutionally prescribed procedures and guarantees.

At least since 1945, military (and civilian) governments have most often tried to legitimize themselves by relying upon the rational-legal or constitutional formula. Judging from their rhetoric, it would appear that all military governments are respectful of individual liberties and committed to the equal application of the laws; some even go on to claim that the regime is structured democratically. In many instances the rhetoric is reinforced by the promulgation of the appropriate constitutional documents. The utilization of the rational-legal formula is also seen in the publicly stated intention of instituting a democratic regime as soon as the polity is restored to good health.

Yet the praetorians regularly fail to legitimize themselves with a rational-legal formula. One set of reasons relates to the authoritarian structure of military regimes. Governments that close off opportunities for mass participation, political competition, and the public airing of demands are contravening major tenets of the rational-legal formula. They denude the people of basic political liberties and rights, and often that of judicial due process. Military regimes that are partially closed are contravening an additional set of constitutional principles. The procedural laws (or their application) have a sharply differential impact upon various groups and individuals, depending upon the praetorians' definitions of friends, opponents, and enemies. Partially closed regimes do not provide for equal political opportunities, rights, and liberties; laws and rules are arbitrary, discriminatory, and prejudicial in content or application.

There is the possibility of legitimizing the government of an authoritarian regime by fabricating constitutional-democratic structures. Formal arrangements and institutions are created to give the impression that the people are able to articulate and press their demands upon the government, perhaps even electing the chief executive and the legislature. There are various ways in which the praetorians have provided themselves with a constitutional-democratic facade: a national legislature that can do little more than discuss and approve legislation introduced by the government; elections for national, state, and local offices that are restricted to officially approved candidates; elections for the presidency featuring a single candidate; plebiscites in which the government asks for and "receives" the approval of more than 90 percent of those who cast their ballots; and the "civilianization" of the regime, whereby the head of government sheds his uniform in order to look more like a constitutional president or prime minister. But whatever form it takes, such a facade does not provide a legitimizing mantle. The formal structure quickly comes to be seen for what it is—a constitutional-democratic fiction.

The Pakistani case underscores these points because it constitutes the most ambitious attempt of any praetorian government to clothe itself in a constitutional-democratic facade. The vast and complex structure known as the Basic Democracies was designed to legitimize the "civilianized" presidency of Ayub Khan, simultaneously defusing the grievances of the masses by giving them a sense of participation. Yet the attempt was only marginally successful.

The overall structure comprised five levels. All citizens elected the Basic Democrats (some 80,000 of them) at the district level, who in turn elected the second tier of representatives, and so on, with each level in the pyramid supposedly being representative of the ones below. But even this highly indirect structure of representation was not thought sufficient to defuse genuine mass participation, for the government appointed half of the representatives at all levels but the first, most of whom were civil servants. Moreover, the first tier of Basic Democrats were chosen in such a way as to practically ensure the election of a majority of prosperous farmers, who then used public resources at the local level exclusively on their own behalf, unresponsive to the millions of rural poor. And it was these supposedly representative Basic Democrats, themselves the targets of mass discontent and highly susceptible to governmental influence, who elected the president, as well as the virtually powerless national and provincial legislatures. It is then little wonder that this massive structure contributed little to the legitimization of the government in its first years and none whatsoever in its last years (Jahan, pp. 287–89; Heitoweit, pp. 24–27; von Vorys, pp. 230–90). Ayub Khan portrayed the Basic Democracies as a democracy that "people can understand and work." They apparently understood only too well, and thus concluded that it could not be made to work. [20]

---

[20] Much the same thing may be said about Nasser's "Presidential Democracy," which included formally representative regime and party structures, without however allowing for genuine participation within them or according them a significant place in governmental decision making.

There is another reason why military governments fail to utilize the rational-legal formula. It requires a consistent conformity to the constitution and the laws even when disadvantageous to do so. The governors do not manipulate the procedural rules or enact arbitrary laws in order to attain their goals. Yet military governments have frequently been unwilling to abide by the constitutional rules, including those that they themselves have promulgated. Given their usually unassailable positions of power, inability to accept criticism, unwillingness to tolerate opposition, and an action orientation with its nearly exclusive concern for results, military governments tend to attack problems and opponents arbitrarily and illegally when this is thought to be advantageous. Not only are the ends more important than the rules but the latter may have little normative importance to begin with.

The Brazilian case persuasively bears out these generalizations. From 1945 to the 1964 coup the officer corps had on the whole demonstrated an unusually high regard for constitutional rules and practices. The new incumbents intended to govern legally, which was thought to be eminently possible after dissolving all existing parties, proscribing the political rights of former President Goulart's influential supporters, and promulgating a constitution that assigned abundant authority to the government. But even in this case, instead of conforming to the legal rules and their own constitution, these were continually violated as succeeding governments gave in to the "hard-liners" within the officer corps.

Brazil's praetorians undertook repeated purges of all those who dared to criticize or offend them. Politicians who were among the earliest supporters of the military government, politicians who occupied the center and right side of the political spectrum, congressmen who belonged to the political party formed by the government itself, and even military officers by the score lost their positions and political rights. Criticism of the government was defined as "subversion." Statements that were thought to discredit the armed forces became punishable offenses, tried by military courts. Despite the near impotence of national, state, and municipal legislatures, elections were often rigged, and the legislatures were occasionally suspended when some members voiced their disagreement with the government. And when the critics turned to the courts to protect their constitutional rights, uncooperative members of the supreme court were forced into retirement, the court was "packed," and the constitution was unilaterally amended to exclude all governmental actions from judicial review (Schneider, pp. 270–98; Stepan, 1971, pp. 221–62). Since 1968 the police and local military commanders have regularly tortured suspects and their relatives to extort information and confessions.

The praetorians in South Korea derived a good measure of legitimacy from the rational-legal formula. Yet paradoxically, this case supports the generalization that military governments rarely succeed in doing so. For despite their success, not only did the praetorians lose their moral right to govern after choosing to act in a highly unconstitutional, illegal, and arbitrary manner, the choice was made in the absence of a threat to their power.

Shortly after the 1961 coup the Supreme Council for National Reconstruction, with General Park at its head, decided that the military would retain power for the foreseeable future. And in doing so, they would try to legitimize their rule with a rational-legal formula. The regime was to appear, and to a large extent actually to be, an open one, featuring genuinely competitive elections and respect for the rights of governmental opponents. The 1963 elections saw a "civilianized" General Park win the presidency by a close vote, while the Democratic-Republican party, which had been created and sponsored by the military, won two-thirds of the legislative seats. Had the election results turned out differently they would probably have been annulled, since the military was intent upon retaining power. But what is important here is that relatively honest and competitive elections were held, the results were favorable to the praetorians, and the government was thereby legitimized.

Its immediate and subsequent legitimacy was also buttressed by the Democratic-Republican party, which was conceived almost single-handedly by one of the leading praetorians. Here is an instance of an officer acting in an untypical military manner in being particularly astute and quick in learning some crucial political lessons. Secretly financed by the "appropriation" of treasury funds, and shaped by a group of politically untainted university professors, journalists, and politicians, the party framework was unveiled shortly before the 1963 elections to the surprise of all, including the generals. And what is especially remarkable, this party turned out to be quite unlike its civilian competitors—parties characterized by extreme factionalism at their upper reaches and without grass-roots organization. The Democratic-Republican party combined grass-roots support, an open structure, extensive organization, and central control. At its base stood freely elected district committees, which nominated the party's legislative candidates, and at a national convention they freely ratified the military's choice of General Park as the party's presidential candidate. Several features were adopted that were new to South Korean parties: an organization department, a publicity section, and a party secretariat manned by paid cadres extending down to the district level (C. I. Eugene Kim, 1971, pp. 371–77).

The praetorian-led and -sponsored Democratic-Republican party was again successful in the 1967 and 1971 elections. No effective political opposition had appeared and none was discernible on the horizon. The "civilianized" military government had been legitimized. But despite the absence of any significant threat to its power, its enjoyment of widespread popular support, and the continuation of an exceptionally high economic growth rate, by 1972 the government was no longer willing to abide by the dictates of the rational-legal formula. Martial law was declared. The government undertook a series of arbitrary, illegal, and unconstitutional acts which undermined its legitimacy.

With three years still left to him in his last term of office, President Park unilaterally deleted the constitutional provision that prevented the chief executive from succeeding himself after having served three terms—a deletion approved by 90 percent of those who took part in a somewhat less than genuine national referendum. Park then had himself reelected for a six-year term by a newly created National Council for Unification. It is not clear how its 2,357 members were elected, but the fact that every one of them voted for Park makes his election suspect. By 1974 the regime was totally closed and repressive. Using the bogeyman of possible Communist subversion, "emergency decrees" were issued banning any criticism of the custom-tailored constitution—a constitution that gives Park virtually unlimited powers, including the so-called death decree which threatens political demonstrators with execution after trial by a military court. Regime closure turned into active repression with the mysterious disappearance of scores of politicians, academics, and religious leaders, and the police regularly torturing those suspected of political misdeeds.

The South Korean case suggests that even those few military governments that succeed in using constitutionalism to legitimize themselves are unwilling to pay the smallest costs to retain this legitimizing mantle.

We thus come to the conclusion that the overwhelming majority of military governments are unwilling or unable to avail themselves of a legitimizing formula.[21] They are either nonlegitimate or illegitimate. And most of the legitimate ones enjoy only a temporary moral right to govern, based on civilian expectations and military pronouncements that they will soon return power to the civilians—that praetorianism is a temporary expedient to allow for a new period of civilian rule based on the rational-legal formula.

---

[21] Although they are not strictly speaking legitimizing formulas, there are two additional factors that could affect the legitimacy of military governments. One of these is a mass party capable of generating grass-roots support for the praetorians, but for reasons discussed on pp. 114–17, such parties are rarely found among military regimes. The other possible factor is the successful promotion of economic change, with rapid economic growth making for expanded mobility opportunities and progressive policies providing greater economic rewards to larger numbers of people. But rapid economic growth is not a common phenomenon, and sustained growth is decidedly uncommon, given the non-Western countries' dependence upon the vagaries of nature as they affect crop production and upon fluctuations in international trade as they determine the prices received. Moreover, in the short run, economic growth requires a reduction in current expenditures in order to provide investment capital. And as will be seen on pp. 171–89, there are very few military governments that bring about progressive economic changes.

	There are enormous variations in the longevity of
THE	regimes. Some regimes are stable fixtures over a
INSTABILITY	period of generations; they endure without any fun-
OF	damental alterations in their structural or elite
MILITARY	characteristics. Others are highly unstable, lasting
REGIMES	only a few years as democratic structures give way

to authoritarian structures, or as civilian elites are
replaced by military officers, and so on.[22]

Civilian regimes are found along the entire expanse of the stability-instability continuum. Knowing only that the civilians are in power does not allow us to generalize about (or predict) their actual (or probable) longevity. In contrast, military regimes cluster toward the unstable end of the continuum. They tend to be inherently unstable—a generalization that the present section is designed to underscore and develop.

To demonstrate that the average life span of military regimes is far shorter than that of their civilian counterparts, and to make the further point that praetorian regimes are even unstable in an "absolute" sense, we first need to specify the minimal number of years that a regime must endure in order to qualify as stable. While all definitions are more or less arbitrary, it would seem that a life span of twenty years is an appropriate minimum standard to use in characterizing a regime as stable. Such a regime should have endured for a sufficiently long time to allow for five or six possible changes of government, and with individual governments holding power for several years, this leads us toward the figure of twenty years. The definitional criterion should also provide adequate time to permit a possible transition of power from one political generation to another, which also points to the appropriateness of the twenty-year standard. Regime stability requires sufficient time for several governments to be able to succeed each other, and for the younger generation of leaders to replace the "old guard," without major alterations in regime structure and elite characteristics.

With the twenty-year benchmark as our criterion of minimum regime stability, it turns out that only three of the approximately one hundred military regimes that have sprung up in the non-Western countries since 1945 fulfill this requirement. The Egyptian praetorians who seized power in 1952 are still in control today, as is Paraguay's General Stroessner, who took control in 1954, and the Thai military sat in the governmental saddle from 1947 to 1968. [23] In contrast, among the non-Western countries there are some two

---

[22] Note that we are concerned with the duration of military regimes, not governments; that is, the length of time that officers retain power, not the longevity of any one chief executive or any single group of incumbents.

[23] If Nicaragua is classified as a military regime under the Somoza family since 1936, it would qualify as a fourth instance of a stable military regime.

dozen civilian regimes that have met the minimum stability criterion, retaining their open, authoritarian, or mobilization structures for at least twenty years.[24] Even when our minimal criterion of regime stability is halved, it turns out that only a handful of military regimes have survived for ten or more years, Argentina (1945–55), Pakistan (1958–70), South Korea (1961–), Burma (1962–), Syria (1963–), Brazil (1964–), Zaire (1965–), Indonesia (1965–), and Nigeria (1966–)—these are the only ones that have met even this exceptionally loose criterion of regime stability.

Military regimes have an average life span of approximately five years. And as such, it can be said that they are inherently unstable.[25]

We can analyze their instability by looking at the three possible paths by which military regimes give way to civilian regimes:

1. The praetorians are forced to relinquish their power by extensive civilian opposition.
2. The military incumbents are overthrown by officers outside the government who then turn the reins of power over to civilians.
3. With or without considerable pressure from civilians or officers, the praetorian governors "voluntarily" disengage.

CIVILIAN PRESSURE

The first possibility is not only the least likely of the three, it has rarely if ever occurred in its pure form. The only close approximation of civilian pressures, demonstrations, strikes, and riots forcing out a military government in favor of a civilian one occurred in the Sudan (1964) and Thailand (1973). Yet even in these two instances the military leaders relinquished their power only after other officers refused their support. There has not been a single instance in which civilians alone demonstrated the strength to overthrow a military regime backed by a unified officer corps intent upon retaining power. They simply do not have sufficient numbers, organization, and weapons to defeat the military. And while this possibility is not entirely remote, before the civilian opposition has developed the means to topple a

---

[24] These include the open regimes of the Philippines, Japan, India, Malaysia, Israel, Lebanon, Ceylon, Uruguay, and Costa Rica; the authoritarian regimes of Afghanistan, South Africa, Liberia, Ethiopia, Jordan, Saudi Arabia, Iran, Tunisia, Morocco, Haiti, and Mexico; and the mobilization regimes of Communist China, North Vietnam, and North Korea.

[25] It is, of course, possible for military regimes to be unstable without being replaced by civilian regimes. The praetorians would retain power while regime structures undergo fundamental transformations. However, this is a rare occurrence, since the praetorians almost invariably establish and maintain authoritarian structures.

military regime, the governors themselves, a section of the officer corps, or both, will probably opt for a return to the barracks.

The second possible path toward disengagement, with officers outside the government staging a successful countercoup and then handing power over to the civilians, has occurred in several instances. The Argentine military overthrew Perón in 1955, Colombian officers ousted Rojas Pinilla in 1957, Pérez Jiménez was unseated by Venezuelan officers in 1958, and General Soglo of Dahomey was removed in 1967, with civilian governments then being seated in each instance.[26] Yet the transition from military to civilian rule has only occasionally been brought about through the medium of the countercoup. Although countercoups are quite common—between 1945 and 1972 the average number of coup attempts was two times higher in military than in civilian regimes (Kennedy, pp. 25–26)—the vast majority have involved the overthrow of one military government and its replacement by another, rather than the transition from a military to a civilian regime.[27]

[26] With regard to the motivations behind these contercoups, the overthrow of Perón is somewhat unusual because few praetorian governors markedly impinge upon the military's corporate interests. The Argentine military acted primarily because of his interference with promotions and command assignments which came to be based upon the officers' personal allegiances to Perón, and his attempt to create working-class militias to serve as a rival power base to the military. The officer corps was thus not only to be divided and dominated by Perón, it was to suffer a decline in its political power. The 1955 countercoup was also inspired by Perón's strenuous efforts to build up support for himself among the urban workers, and then playing them off against the middle class, the industrialists, and the church (Beltrán, p. 332). Rojas Pinilla was overthrown due to his inept attempt to create a mass following for himself, which only succeeded in antagonizing the middle class, the landed elite, and the church (Dix, p. 120). The motivations behind the countercoups in Venezuela and Dahomey are discussed on p. 145.

[27] With regard to the soldiers' motivations in overthrowing military governments, these include personal ambition, policy disagreements, communal resentments, the governors' assumption of excessive power, their divisive politicization of the officer corps, and the use of the army as a police force. Motives are translated into actions by four facilitating conditions, which encourage and allow for the common phenomenon of the countercoup: (1) The officers' self-imposed constraints upon the illegal utilization of military power against governmental superiors, be they civilian or military, can only be lowered after witnessing or taking part in the original coup against the civilians, especially if it was led by officers other than the service commanders. It is only part hyperbole to write that after the first coup the "sanction against a military seizure is broken forever. A major-general or brigadier who usurps state power must expect to be emulated by a colonel; and what one colonel can do, another can copy, improve upon, or undo" (First, p. 437). (2) The likelihood of a countercoup

There are two reasons for the small number of countercoups that are intended to restore civilian rule. First, the circumstances that make a return to the barracks an increasingly attractive alternative often affect the praetorian governors as well as the officer corps. Under certain conditions—which will be discussed in a moment—both groups of officers are likely to favor disengagement, thereby eliminating the need for officers outside the government to stage a countercoup. And second, even if the leading praetorians want to retain power contrary to the wishes of a significant number of officers, they sometimes disengage in order to preserve the unity of the officer corps or to forestall a countercoup. The withdrawal of support by a sizable section of the officer corps, a small number of senior officers, or strategically placed troop commanders may be sufficient to prompt a withdrawal.

"VOLUNTARY" DISENGAGEMENT

This brings us to the third and by far the most often trod path back to the barracks: the military "voluntarily" withdraw to the governmental sidelines. There may be considerable civilian pressure for them to do so, with the soldiers then finding their position untenable and the country ungovernable. But disengagement is "voluntary," since a military government with a unified officer corps behind it almost invariably has ample coercive force to retain control of the government. Why then are the praetorians—the governors, the officers outside the government, or both—not impelled to retain power for more than a few years on the average? What factors motivate them to withdraw as soon as an acceptable transition to civilian rule can be arranged? Under what circumstances are these disengagement motives likely to emerge? It is the answers to these questions that explain the short life span of most military regimes, in absolute terms and relative to the duration of civilian regimes.

It is undoubtedly true that many praetorian governors find themselves

---

is also heightened by the success of the original coup as it enhances the confidence of potential conspirators. Confidence does not necessarily breed success, but it does increase the probability of attempts to seize power. (3) With the senior officers' time and energies being primarily taken up by governmental matters, their day-to-day control over potential conspirators among the strategically situated troop commanders is less than it was prior to their assumption of power. (4) Lastly, there is the government's loss of legitimacy. Just as interventionist-minded officers rarely (if ever) overthrow legitimate civilian governments, for the same reasons that were discussed in the preceding chapter, a legitimacy deflation must usually set before praetorian officers will attempt a countercoup. And we have just seen that military governments rarely legitimize themselves in the eyes of the civilian population.

enjoying the exercise of power ("power for power's sake"), as well as the high status and material rewards that go along with it (Welch, 1970, p. 50). [28] They are consequently reluctant to give up the privileges of high governmental office by returning to the barracks. But on the whole, they are much less averse to doing so than civilians. It is most unusual for civilian incumbents willingly to vacate the seats of power. Civilians do so when required by the "rules of the game," when they lose the necessary backing of other civilian leaders or supporters, or when they are forced out by those with greater power, including of course the military.

Using the language of Max Weber, we can account for this difference by pointing out that politics is a full-time "vocation" for the great majority of civilians who reach high governmental positions. They live "for" politics, "off" of politics, or both. They entered the political arena in the hope of attaining the direct or indirect rewards of governmental office. Politics for military men, on the other hand, is generally far more of a part-time "avocation." Only a small proportion originally entered the military in the hope of attaining governmental offices. Many praetorians took up the reins of government with little enthusiasm. Most of them would probably have much preferred to remain in the barracks if their objectives, particularly the defense or enhancement of the military's corporate interests, could have been realized from that vantage point. A public statement by a member of Nigeria's first military government can be taken at close to face value: "No soldier wants to rule. Our normal function is not to govern but to protect the integrity and safety of the nation. We should be much happier doing that than governing" (Luckham, p. 276).

Moreover, the praetorians more often than the civilian incumbents have alternative sources of power, prestige, and material rewards. These can be derived from their professional activities as "managers of force," "experts in violence," and "armed bureaucrats." The former governors also continue to be prominent members of the political, social, and economic elites after returning to the barracks. The officers continue to exercise considerable power from the governmental sidelines as moderator-type praetorians, while their military ranks, expertise, and responsibilities provide high status and material rewards. Disengagement consequently does not constitute a drastic "fall" in the stratification pyramid. The short duration of military regimes relative to civilian ones is thus partly due to the soldiers' less intense desire to retain governmental power and its related privileges.

The praetorians' governing objectives are also relevant. Guardian types are concerned with the relatively unambitious goals of preserving the status quo (possibly through the introduction of some limited reforms), preventing lower-class parties from attaining power, restoring political order, and revital-

---

[28] General Amin of Uganda is probably the most flagrantly obvious example.

izing sluggish economies. They consequently intend to retain power for only a few years. The ruler type's far-reaching objectives of political regeneration, and possibly major socioeconomic transformations, require a long period in office. But as pointed out in Chapter 1, guardian types greatly outnumber ruler-type praetorians, which then helps account for the low average life span of military regimes.

Whatever their interventionist and governing goals, a return to the barracks is facilitated by the belief that these are unlikely to be contravened or undone by the civilian successors. The new incumbents have been clearly warned that the military can and may take power again, and perhaps rather quickly, since future coups require a lower "flash" point than the first. With both officers and civilians aware of this possibility, a return to the barracks is abetted by the belief that the successor governments will not ignore the interests and policy preferences of the military.[29]

The praetorians are also impelled to disengage due to the unexpected difficulties they encounter as governors. To govern is hardly as simple and straightforward as the officers had imagined prior to the coup, and certainly not as easy as they would have liked. Their preferred style of governing—that of decision making without politics—generally turns out to be untenable. This leaves them with two choices. They can continue to govern in an apolitical manner, without however achieving many of their objectives; or they can adapt their preferred style to the requisites of political reality, but then governing in a distasteful fashion. In either case, after two or three years it is not uncommon to find the practorians increasingly frustrated, disillusioned with government and with themselves as governors. There is a dissipation of the will to govern. Their self-confidence as exceptionally capable governors is eroded; their positive self-image becomes tarnished.

The less demanding, complex, and seemingly more honorable role of the soldiers as military men consequently comes to look increasingly attractive. Their negative governing experiences can best be dispelled by vacating the seat of power. Any further political "contamination" can be avoided by returning to the less frustrating and more honorable life of parade grounds, military exercises, hierarchy, bureaucracy, and technical training.

That the praetorians sometimes do so for just these reasons is exemplified by the first Ne Win government, which returned power to the civilians after two years in office:

The Burmese Army had believed in 1958 that the country's problems could readily be solved if only the government displayed determination and a willingness to call for self-sacrifices. It saw the spirit and ethos of the politi-

[29] On the other hand, withdrawal is sometimes seen as overly dangerous, if not impossible. The soldiers have created too many enemies, while their "friends" have insufficient support to govern, as in Brazil since the late 1960s.

cians as little more than uncontrolled cravings for corruption and compromise. As soldiers they believed all could be resolved through the purifying influences of action and honor. Within six months the leading army officers were beginning to learn that government was an extremely complicated and intractable business. The solutions were not quite as easy as they had assumed. After a year in power army officers came to realize that they were beginning to compromise their original standards. They could see themselves losing the status of military men and taking on some of the aspects of the politicians, whom they had always held in contempt. [Pye, 1962B, p. 232]

It was these considerations, along with criticisms from the junior officers that the governors were becoming "just like the politicians," that led to an early withdrawal. [30]

Praetorians occasionally disengage in order to preserve the public reputation of the military—an institution to which they are dedicated and which helps provide them with a positive self-image. After one or two years in power the military's standing regularly suffers a decline. For the performance of military governments is infrequently better than that of their civilian predecessors, often less satisfactory, and sometimes far worse.[31] And we have already seen that only a few military governments succeed in legitimizing themselves.[32] Closely identified with and serving to maintain the government, the reputation of the officer corps can only suffer at the hands of unpopular, ineffective, and less than legitimate military governments. Withdrawal may help preserve or enhance the military's public standing.

This consideration was another factor in the Burmese army's decision to disengage after only two years. By 1960 there was widespread concern within the officer corps that under continuing military government the communally divided country might become united, but only in its opposition to the army. A return to the barracks was thus called for while the military could still make something of a claim for its integrity. And with popular dis-

---

[30] In Brazil, President Costa e Silva (1967–69) was also criticized from within the military for "playing the game" of politics with politicians and for betraying the apolitical ideals of the "revolution." But in this instance withdrawal was seen as impractical, given the considerable opposition engendered by the military as governors. The praetorians thus opted to remain in power *and* to purge the regime of its "political" coloring. "This restructuring was seen as simultaneously *less* political and *more* revolutionary" (Stepan, 1971, p. 259).

[31] See Chapter 6.

[32] We have also seen that the military virtues that engender public esteem are usually not exhibited by the officers as governors. Those of political impartiality, service to the nation, and dedication to the public interest turn out to be unattainable by any government, military or civilian. And the puritanical virtues—soldiers as especially honest, self-denying, and self-sacrificing—frequently give way to the temptations of power.

satisfaction being directed at the army, senior officers saw the advantages of having civilian governors and politicians to deflect it (Pye, 1962B, pp. 233, 248). [33]

Lastly, praetorians have sometimes accelerated the transition to civilian rule in order to restore the highly valued cohesiveness and hierarchical structure of the military. Unity is a matter of pride; hierarchy is normatively exalted. A divided military is without an *esprit de corps*, disadvantaged as a politicized institution. And it is when the military controls the government that sharp intramilitary divisions most often develop—divisions that can best be healed by a return to the barracks.[34] In Ghana, for example, the National Liberation Council accelerated the transition to civilian government due to its concern with the deleterious effect of "politics" upon the internal cohesion of the army. The praetorian governors responded to an abortive countercoup, a near mutiny, and rumors of a tribally based countercoup (Bebler, pp. 53, 221).

There are two major explanations for the tendency of praetorian armies to become factionalized. They also suggest why unit and hierarchy can commonly be best restored by turning governmental offices over to civilians. First, the vast majority of coups against civilians are executed by officers with only vague ideas about their governing objectives and the means for attaining them.[35] Intramilitary divisions develop in the absence of prior thinking

---

[33] This factor also helped motivate two of the previously mentioned countercoups. When demonstrations and riots broke out against Colonel Pérez Jiménez's repressive rule, Venezuelan officers overthrew him and allowed national elections to be held within a year. The officers had become incensed with the military's sharp decline in popular esteem, which dropped even further when they had to put down violent disturbances to maintain him in power (Finer, pp. 184–85). And in Dahomey, a group of junior officers carried out a disengagement countercoup when the army's prestige was being eroded because Colonel Soglo's government was unable to mitigate the tribal-regional conflict and promote economic growth. The junior officers' pride in their army was sharply affected by the vocal and widespread criticism which called into doubt the military's ability to run the country. As they put it in the proclamation of their countercoup: "The army was accused. It was said that the army had failed" (Skurnik, pp. 104–5).

[34] The divisions could also be overcome if the praetorian governors are powerful enough to purge the dissident officers, as happened in Turkey and Brazil. Those officers who did not support the governors' decisions were forced to retire or encouraged to do so by refusals to promote them (Stepan, 1971, pp. 223–24; Yalman, p. 140). However, this method of restoring unity and hierarchy is rarely used because it contradicts the high value placed upon unity while publicizing its absence. It also makes it more difficult for the military to disengage after having generated intense opposition.

[35] The absence of developed policy ideas is attributable to the overriding importance of corporate interests in motivating the coup, the conspirators' attempts to win broad support within an officer corps that could divide along policy lines, and the lack of time and opportunity to formulate a set of policy goals.

and agreement on the specific goals that are to be pursued, the priorities assigned to them, and the strategies and policies through which they are to be realized. These issues not having been settled beforehand, there is the distinct possibility that they will jeopardize military unity after the takeover.

The probability of their doing so is heightened by a second factor: a praetorian officer corps is a highly politicized officer corps. When officers are governors, the officer corps as a whole is closely identified with the government. It is also the government's primary supporter. Officers are bound to react to the decisions of "their" government, and possibly hold quite different views about what the praetorian governors should be doing. Particularly in the absence of a well-developed governing program, a highly politicized officer corps is then likely to become factionalized, with middle-level officers possibly questioning the decisions of their superiors within the government.

In some instances intramilitary divisions revolve around the issue of disengagement itself. Having taken power without much thought or agreement on the length of time in which they will remain in office, the praetorians disagree about the appropriate time for returning power to the civilians. The issue of disengagement most commonly divides those Latin American armies that intervened to prevent the leaders of labor and peasant parties from attaining governmental power. There are divergent estimates of the time that it will take to neutralize the threat from below (Huntington, 1968, p. 231).

It is in Argentina, with its exceptionally powerful labor movement, that the praetorians have most often disagreed about the manner in which the lower-class opposition is to be handled. We have already seen that President Frondizi was overthrown because he allowed legislative and municipal elections to be held in which the *peronistas*—to the surprise and chagrin of both Frondizi and the military—won a considerable number of seats. After the 1962 coup the *gorila* faction strongly favored a prolongation of military rule as the most efficacious way of preventing the *peronistas* from attaining power through the electoral process. Yet many other officers opposed the idea. They foresaw its deleterious consequences for military cohesiveness. These *legalistas* overcame the *gorilas*, the military then disengaging after the 1963 elections in order to preserve its cohesiveness (O'Donnell, pp. 157–58).

Both unity and hierarchy can best be restored by a return to the barracks. When military officers are not sitting in the governmental saddle, the absence of an agreed-upon set of governing objectives is clearly less likely to generate sharp divisions within the officer corps. And being less closely identified and involved with the government, the probability of intramilitary divisions decreases further as the level of politicization declines. There may still be divisions after disengagement, especially since the military continues to "oversee" the government as moderator-type praetorians. But these are rarely as intense as when the military is in power, while the hierarchical imperative can be reasserted as the soldiers attribute greater importance to their purely military activities.

In summary, the most important factors behind the praetorians' "voluntary" decision to withdraw, and thus the major reasons for the short duration of military regimes, include the following: the desire to retain governmental power and its related privileges is less strongly felt by military than by civilian incumbents; most military governments are headed by guardian-type praetorians whose limited governing objectives can be realized within a short time span; the praetorians can usually disengage in the expectation that the successor governments will be reluctant to contravene their interests and views; some officers want to return to the more attractive life of the "professional" soldier after encountering unexpected difficulties as governors; a return to the barracks is intended to preserve the armed forces' declining reputation; and disengagement may best restore military unity and hierarchy.

NATIONAL INTEGRATION AND ECONOMIC CHANGE

5

Of the numerous problems and challenges facing the non-Western states those of national integration and economic change are acutely pressing and common. Approximately half of these societies are divided along communal lines; religious, racial, linguistic, tribal, and regional divisions give rise to more or less severe communal conflicts. Where these divisions have not already become inflamed, they are potentially inflammable. Where they have already developed into intense conflicts, they commonly eventuate in civil wars, insurgencies, riotous bloodlettings, and government-sponsored violence against one communal segment.[1] National disintegration along communal lines is thus not only a distinct possibility, its occurrence entails disastrous consequences.

Almost all non-Western societies are afflicted with serious economic scarcities and inequities. Their populations harbor unrealized aspirations for greater material well-being, economic security, and mobility opportunities. At least a third of the population is impoverished, with perhaps another third eking out a bare subsistence. When measured in terms of morbidity alone, economic problems may be even more acute than communal violence; for the death rate spirals upward in years of natural adversity, and the average life span remains low every year due to dietary deficiencies and sorely inadequate medical services.

Although the challenges of avoiding widespread communal violence and promoting economic change are clearly distinct, they do overlap in one basic respect. They both relate to political conflict, whether it be between communal segments or classes. Communal groups come into conflict over

---

[1] In the post-1945 period there has been at least some communal violence in twenty-two African states, fourteen Asian states, nine Middle Eastern and North African states, and two Latin American states (von der Mehden, p. 8).

such issues as the adoption of a state religion, the selection of the language(s) to be used in government and taught in the schools, and the allocation of jobs in the public sector, as well as more general issues involving the distribution of political power and governmental expenditures. The promotion of economic growth raises the issue of which class is to bear the major costs involved. The possible redistribution of liquid and landed wealth obviously brings the different classes into conflict, as do questions of public investment in education, social welfare programs, agricultural reform, and so on. This chapter may therefore be read as an analysis of the manner in which military governments deal with political conflicts, whether these involve communal segments or classes.[2]

More specifically, are these two common and decidedly pressing problems generally ameliorated, left unaffected, or exacerbated under military auspices? How can we account for the performance of military governments in preventing communal violence and bringing about economic change?

TOWARD THE DISINTEGRATION OF COMMUNALLY DIVIDED SOCIETIES

Many non-Western societies are so deeply divided along communal lines that their total or partial disintegration through widespread violence—from civil wars to "officially" sanctioned violence against the members of one communal group—is a real possibility. The communal groups are well aware of the incompatibility between their interests and values and those of other communal segments. The issues at stake revolve around the groups' most-sought-after material rewards, most-cherished cultural and symbolic values, and inalienable rights. The communal segments also tend to exhibit emotion-charged antagonisms toward each other, these being based upon highly unflattering stereotypes, deep-seated prejudices, and long-standing jealousies.

Despite the intensity of these conflicts and their attendant centrifugal forces, the outcome has not always been widespread violence. Some conflicts have been regulated. While their intensity has not been markedly reduced (at least in the short run), they have not eventuated in greater or lesser degrees of national disintegration. In other instances the conflicts not

---

[2] In geographic terms there is considerable variation between these two types of conflicts. Severe communal conflicts are rare in Latin America, and it is in these societies that class conflicts have taken on their greatest intensity. The relatively high levels of socioeconomic modernization in Latin America have activated latent class interests and politicized the lower classes. Class conflicts are found in the other non-Western areas, but they are not nearly as severe. Rather, communal divisions are quite common, often giving rise to intense conflicts. And whether class and communal conflicts are cross-cutting or superimposed upon each other, the communal conflicts are almost invariably far more salient.

only have been further exacerbated but have sometimes resulted in civil wars costing hundreds of thousands of lives.

According to the praetorians themselves and most political scientists who have addressed themselves to the problem, military governments are especially well suited for the task of national integration.[3] In actuality, however, the praetorians' record in preventing the disintegration of their societies along communal lines is a poor one. Military governments that have come to power in societies that are deeply divided along communal lines have usually been unwilling or unable to contain the severity of these conflicts. They have generally exacerbated them, sometimes bringing about an explosive outcome. Their poor performance has been exceptionally evident in Iraq, the Sudan, Nigeria, Indonesia, Burma, and Pakistan. Several million people died in these countries while the praetorians were in power, their actions fomenting civil wars, insurgencies, bloody rioting, and government-sanctioned slaughters. Of the many instances of communal violence since 1945, the death toll reached its highest levels under military auspices, in the Nigerian and Pakistani civil wars.

The successful regulation of intense communal conflicts is explained by the actions of the political elites. Nonelite actions and characteristics, as well as various political, social, and economic patterns, go a long way in accounting for the emergence of severe communal conflicts. But once the conflict has become intense, the actions of the political elites—in the case of authoritarian military regimes this means the praetorians themselves—are most important in accounting for the absence of widespread violence. And whether the elites act in ways that minimize the likelihood of national disintegration largely depends upon certain motivations and attitudes (Nordlinger, 1972). After identifying these motivations and attitudes and showing that they are not characteristic of military governments, we shall illustrate the hypotheses with the praetorians' failures in the Sudan, Pakistan, and Nigeria.

BELIEFS ABOUT THE NATURE OF INTENSE COMMUNAL CONFLICTS

If widespread violence is to be avoided, the governors must have a good grasp of political reality. They must recognize that the communal divisions, based upon strong subgroup loyalties and basic economic, social, and cultural differences, are so deep-seated as to negate the possibility of markedly diminishing them within a few years. They must also realize that the intense communal conflicts that grow out of these divisions involve such salient and emotion-charged issues that their severity cannot be significantly reduced in the short run. They certainly cannot be eliminated. Political reality dictates that the governors accept the continuing existence of severe com-

[3] See pp. 37–39.

munal conflict, with a good measure of political turbulence and perhaps minor violence. They might then succeed in preventing national disintegration, which is surely no easy or small accomplishment in deeply divided societies.

Any attempt to bring about a significantly greater measure of national unity is not only bound to fail in deeply divided societies. Far more importantly, it will further escalate the conflict and quite possibly lead to total disintegration. With the antagonistic groups finding it extremely difficult to "live together" in the first place, their nonviolent "cohabitation" becomes all the more problematic when compelled to live even "closer" to each other. The government's issuance of some type of unification decree is thus not about to have a positive effect. Rather, it would stir up even greater communal animosities and fears of domination. Nor can national unity be achieved from above by giving the traditions, beliefs, and symbols of one communal segment a "national" label, and then imposing them upon the other segment(s). The latter are not about to accept the loss of their own strongly held values, nor the "elevation" of opposing ones to national status —something that would be sorely degrading given existing jealousies, antagonisms, and prejudices. Such attempts at national unification would most certainly further intensify the conflict, probably foster widespread violence, and (almost by definition) entail national disintegration if done coercively.

Thus if widespread violence is to be averted, the governors must recognize the dictates of political reality: neither the depth of the communal divisions nor the intensity of the conflicts can be mitigated in the short run. Their continuation must be accepted, along with the related turbulence. An appreciation of the nature of political reality would lead to the adoption of a limited but crucial objective—the avoidance of widespread violence, rather than the highly ambitious, but unrealistic and ill-fated goal of achieving a "higher" level of national unity.

According to our analysis of the soldiers' governing style, they tend to be deficient in appreciating the nature of political reality. They believe that political, economic, social, and cultural patterns are considerably more malleable than they actually are, that governmental decrees have a decided if not decisive impact upon the population, and that major problems can be readily overcome if dealt with in a head-on, undeviating manner. Severe communal conflicts and other political problems are similar to military and technical ones. They can be quickly solved if "attacked" directly, unswervingly, and, if necessary, forcefully.

The praetorians' proclivities to do just that are reinforced by their inordinate sensitivity to political disorder.[4] Rather than accept the inexorable

---

[4] These proclivities might also be strengthened by the officers' nationalistic self-image, nationalism becoming somewhat incorrectly identified with a high level of national unity.

continuation of severe communal conflicts, greater or lesser political disturbances, and possibly some violence, military governments regularly opt for complete calm. It is one thing to place a high value upon political order; it is quite another to believe that it can be attained in deeply divided societies by somehow doing away with the conflicts themselves. The manner in which this is to be accomplished—from the issuance of governmental decrees, to the imposition of one communal group's values upon another, to the outright use of force—varies enormously, as will be seen in our subsequent discussion of the Sudanese, Nigerian, and Pakistani cases. But whatever strategy is chosen, the objectives are the unattainable ones of considerably greater national integration and total political calm, rather than the far more realistic and important one of averting widespread violence. Indeed, to pursue the former is to promote violence—violence by the government, against the government, between communal groups, or all three.

CONCILIATORY ATTITUDES

To claim that the governors cannot possibly eradicate the communal divisions or eliminate the conflict's severity does not mean that they cannot have a positive effect on its outcome. Indeed, their role is exceptionally important as it relates to the divisive issues themselves. It is their actions (or inactions) that largely determine whether compromise agreements emerge that are acceptable to the opposing segments. If such agreements can be worked out—in which the opposing segments are not anywhere near fully satisfied, yet neither do they find the agreements lacking in benefits to themselves—the likelihood of a violent outcome is significantly reduced.[5]

Whether the political elites attempt to work out agreements that represent a roughly equitable balance of interests is partly dependent upon the presence or absence of conciliatory attitudes. There are great variations in the extent to which political elites view compromise as respectable, bargaining as acceptable or necessary, and the accommodation of opposing groups as advantageous if not essential.

Military officers tend to cluster at one end of this attitudinal continuum. As part of their apolitical governing style they view compromise, bargaining, and the accommodation of opposing groups in a decidedly negative manner. Such conciliatory actions are thought to be unnecessary, ineffective, and positively harmful. They are also personally unpalatable to the

---

[5] Compromise agreements involve the conflict issues themselves: the choice of a national language or languages, the possible adoption of a state religion, communal representation within the national government, the relative power of federal and regional governments, the distribution of public funds among the regions, and the criteria for recruitment to the civil service.

officers. Conciliatory behavior is generally seen as less than honorable and is interpreted as a sign of weakness, a lack of resolve, and a failure of nerve. And since the praetorians came to power by force and are trained in its application, they "more readily turn to violence than to palaver, to repression rather than to compromise. Bargaining and compromise are not familiar techniques to military leaders. In scorning politics, they may scorn the techniques well known to politicians, such as the artful ethnic balance" (Welch, 1970, p. 47).

Thus the praetorians are not disposed to undertake the arduous task of working out "political" settlements that are acceptable to the opposing communal segments. Nor are they given to making concessions to communal groups that are opposed to the praetorians' own goals and policies. They are far more likely to issue unilaterally formulated decrees, impose their own views, or repress one segment with force, 'than they are to elicit differing views and negotiate outstanding differences between the segments, or between themselves and one segment or another.

CONFLICT-REGULATING MOTIVES

Turning from the relevant political attitudes to the governors' motivations, it is obvious that a relatively peaceful, nonrepressive outcome is far likelier when the governors are strongly motivated to act as impartial mediators or arbiters, working toward a roughly equitable settlement of the outstanding conflict issues. It has already been said that this Platonic ideal of political neutrality is just that—an ideal that cannot be realized by military or civilian governments. Yet governments do differ greatly in the degree to which they approach or depart from it.

There is reason to think that the praetorians act as relatively impartial mediators and arbiters. Several writers have suggested that military recruitment, training, socialization, and promotional patterns have broken down the officers' communal loyalties.[6] The armed forces are said to serve as something of a communal melting pot where officers develop common national identities and a secular outlook which replace subgroup attachments. As secular-nationalizing soldiers they are thought to be strongly motivated toward moderating extremist behavior, concomitantly promoting roughly equitable, mutually acceptable agreements.

Yet in Chapter 2 the model of the secular-nationalizing soldier was found unacceptable; its two underlying assumptions were called into question. One of these assumptions—that the officer corps is commonly recruited from the various communal groups in rough proportion to their population size—is commonly incorrect. Rather than the officer corps being representa-

[6] See pp. 37–39.

tive of the major communal groups, it is far more often recruited exclusively or predominantly from certain segments. The likelihood of military governors being motivated to take up the mantle of impartial mediator or arbiter is thereby sharply reduced. As the more or less exclusive preserve of a particular communal segment, the officer corps is strongly inclined to act on behalf of its interests.

The second assumption—that various aspects of the military experience break down communal attachments and substitute secular-national ones—was also found wanting. Even when communal segments are proportionately represented within the military, subgroup identities and loyalties continue to be highly salient. Communal identities and loyalties are so deeply embedded that the military experience cannot eradicate and replace them with secular-national values. The latter are developed, without however overshadowing the former. The two sets of values "coexist," and perhaps quite comfortably where communal divisions have not given rise to intense conflicts. But in the midst of a severe communal conflict the contradictions between the praetorians' two sets of values come to the surface. And it is their communal loyalties that regularly prevail. They are not then about to act as impartial governors, trying to work out mutually acceptable agreements on the issues that divide their own communal segments from the others. Even where the praetorians are attempting to govern in something of a politically neutral fashion, they would not be seen to be doing so by the communal activists, partly because the soldiers do not have the will or skills to convince the latter of their "good" intentions.

Thus rather than accept the model of the secular-nationalizing soldier and its positive consequences for the integration of deeply divided societies, it would be far more accurate to portray the praetorians as being primarily motivated by their communal attachments. They tend to act according to subgroup interests, thereby further intensifying the conflict, ushering in widespread violence, or directly producing a disintegrative "solution" when force is used to repress the opposing segments.

THREE CASES OF NATIONAL DISINTEGRATION: THE SUDAN, PAKISTAN, AND NIGERIA   When taken together, the characteristics of military governments hardly suggest that they perform well in preventing widespread violence within communally divided societies. The unrealistic and ill-fated belief that communal divisions and conflicts can be eliminated and that this can be accomplished in a direct, head-on manner, the dismissal of conciliatory efforts as ineffective and less than honorable, the generally unrepresentative communal makeup of the officer corps, and the predominance of communal loyalties—the presence of these attributes and their consequences are strikingly illustrated by the egregious failures of military governments in the Sudan, Pakistan, and Nigeria.

When General Abboud took control of the Sudanese government in 1958, the country's overlapping racial-religious-regional divisions had already given rise to a severe conflict. On one side stood the light-skinned, Muslim northerners, making up approximately 70 percent of the population; on the other, the dark-skinned southerners, a mixture of Christians and tradition-directed pagans. The northerners enjoyed a highly disproportionate share of the country's wealth and political power, and the most-sought-after jobs in the civil service and the modern sector of the economy. The Arabs regularly exhibited their distinct disdain for the less "civilized" southerners eking out a bare agricultural and pastoral existence.

Southern resentment became inflamed in the 1950s when the northern-dominated government assigned Arabs to civil service positions in the south, refused to allocate a proportionate share of development and educational funds to the south, and turned down southern demands for proportional representation within the government (i.e., a third of the cabinet positions). In the last years of civilian rule the racial-religious-regional conflict had become sharply intensified. There were sporadic outbreaks of violence against northern officials stationed in the south, and a mutiny of southern sergeants against their northern officers.

However, it was the military government that transformed this smoldering conflict into a civil war. An officer corps almost exclusively made up of northerners absolutely refused to accommodate southern demands. Even more so than the previous civilian government, the praetorians acted solely on behalf of the already politically and economically dominant north. A larger number of Arabs were assigned to the south as provincial governors, civil servants, and policemen. Developmental and educational investments were limited solely to the north. And quite unlike their civilian predecessors, the military government attempted to eliminate the communal divisions and impose "national unity." The south's indigenous cultures—deriving from African and Christian sources—were to be eradicated and replaced by the Arab culture and Islamic religion of the north. This effort was given the nationalizing label of "Sudanization." Christian schools and missions were closed, the foreign missionaries expelled. Mosques and institutes of Islamic education were built in the south, with the Department of Religious Affairs concomitantly disseminating Muslim propaganda. Arabic was decreed the single language of education and administration. Friday, the Muslim day of prayer, replaced Saturday and Sunday as holidays throughout the country.

These heavy-handed, exceedingly one-sided efforts to impose "national unity" had just the reverse effect. Two years after the military took power, southerners were emigrating to neighboring countries. In the next few years the smoldering conflict was transformed into a rebellion, and then into a civil war when the praetorians decided that the only "solution" to the integration problem was one of further repression and military action. With military efforts stalemated or defeated by southern guerrilla forces, and as forceful repression provoked more resistance, the government sent additional troops to the south and heightened the level of repression by restricting thousands of villagers to guarded camps. When the military government collapsed in 1964, the total political disintegration of the Sudan was within sight.[7] (Collins, pp. 397–401; Be'eri, p. 216; First, p. 252; Beshir, p. 81).

PAKISTAN

From the time of its creation in 1947 Pakistan was confronted with a serious integration problem. Its two halves were separated by one thousand miles of Indian territory. An ethnically and linguistically diverse West Pakistan faced a slightly more populous East Pakistan made up almost entirely of Bengalis. Despite the enormous-potential for their intensification, the overlapping regional-linguistic-ethnic divisions did not become inflamed under the open civilian regime between 1947 and 1958, partly because high governmental positions were shared equally between West and East. In contrast, between 1958 and 1971 the praetorians transformed the communal divisions into an intense conflict and unleashed a barbarous bloodletting upon the East, which turned into a civil war that culminated in the East's secession as the independent state of Bangladesh.

Neither before nor during the period of military rule were the armed forces of Pakistan anywhere near representative of the two regions. Pakistan's army was formed from the British colonial forces which had been recruited solely from the "martial races" living in what was later to become West Pakistan, and thus not a single Bengali held a rank above that of colonel at independence. East Pakistani representation in the officer corps of the politically dominant army, which constituted nearly 90 percent of the armed forces, did not exceed 5 percent before or after the military takeover.[8] As the linchpin

---

[7] The second military government which took control in 1969 apparently learned some lessons from the failures of the first. It adopted a far more conciliatory, and thus effective, approach to the integration problem. The south was offered a somewhat vague federal alternative to the previous concentration of power in the northern capital, some developmental funds, a significant number of civil service jobs, and a few military and governmental positions. The fighting ended after the conclusion of secret negotiations with southern guerrilla leaders in 1972, although some southern leaders remain in self-imposed exile.

[8] Bengalis never constituted more than 17 percent and 10 percent of the air force and navy, respectively.

of the regime, the army was to remain a cohesive and thus an exclusive West Pakistani preserve, despite numerous and vociferous Bengali calls for greater representation[9] (Sayeed, pp. 275–76; Jahan, pp. 279–83).

Just as the army was maintained as a nearly exclusive West Pakistani preserve, the regime was also to remain just that, and for almost identical reasons. Ayub Khan stated publicly that his goal was to see the country as well organized as the military; centralized concentration of power was deemed essential for national integration. The cohesiveness of the army was premised upon hierarchy and the exclusion of East Pakistanis; national integration was to be achieved by structuring the regime along similar lines. Whereas Bengalis held half of the powerful legislative and executive positions under the previous democratic regime, under military rule power was concentrated in the hands of the president-general, senior officers, and civilian bureaucrats, the great majority of whom were West Pakistanis.[10] It was this extreme centralization of power in non-Bengali hands that exacerbated the conflict as the Bengalis vociferously demanded a federal regime, and when these calls went unheeded, they were escalated to demands for a semiautonomous regional government.

The severity of the conflict was further heightened by economic policies that penalized the East. The praetorians may have felt some concern for the more equitable regional distribution of economic rewards, but if they did, the goal of rapid industrialization took precedence. The industrialization strategy assigned the West a disproportionate amount of public investment, while the East paid far more than its share of the necessary costs. The West was allotted double the East's share of investment funds because that is where existing industries were located. The East's agricultural exports paid for the importation of the industrial infrastructure and most raw materials. The low domestic prices that the Bengali farmers received for their produce allowed the wages of industrial workers to be kept low, thereby generating greater profits and investment capital. During the last five years of military rule the disparity between the incomes of the two regions was consequently widened. The per capita income of the already poorer East was increasing at only half the rate of the West. It is then hardly surprising that the Bengalis

9 However, unlike the Sudanese case, deliberate efforts were made to increase the proportion of Bengalis in the civil service. In 1947 there were virtually no Bengalis in the civil bureaucracy. The reservation of 40 percent of the new positions for East Pakistanis provided them with 24 percent representation by 1958, with a further increase to 34 percent by 1966, after eight years of military rule (Jahan, pp. 282–83).

10 Half of the representation in the Basic Democracies and the National Assembly was allotted to the East. But as already noted in discussing the unsuccessful effort to legitimize the regime with a democratic-constitutional format, these bodies were readily detectable facades which could not hide the realities of Ayub's centralized control.

came to view themselves as an exploited "colony." Their unfulfilled demands for the redress of economic imbalances were escalated to calls for semiautonomy (Heitoweit, pp. 9–20).

After seven years of continued praetorian intransigence with respect to the mitigation of Bengali grievances, spontaneous rioting broke out in 1965. From that time on the East was placed under emergency rule. By 1969, demands for semiautonomy had grown into talk of secession, which convinced Ayub Khan and the senior generals that the situation was sufficiently serious to warrant his resignation. He ceded his authority to General Yahya Khan, the army commander in chief. But even the declaration of martial law, an army-patrolled curfew, and continued rule by emergency decree did not prevent the murder of regime officials, rioting, looting, and burning. The generals were then impelled to announce their willingness to transfer power to the civilians. However, the praetorians would only return to the barracks on condition that the East was not to become semiautonomous and civilians whose "national loyalties" were suspect were to be kept out of the government.

Free elections were held in 1970 for a national constitutional assembly; the seats were divided equally between East and West based upon their relative population size. The vote was a surprise to all. The Bengalis rallied around the Awami League, which captured all but two of the East's 169 seats, while the vote in the West was split among several parties. Not only did the election turn the Awami League into by far the single most powerful party with a clear majority of assembly seats, it heavily underscored the East's demand for greater regional autonomy. General Yahya Khan did not allow the constitutional assembly to meet. The transition to civilian rule was put off because he opposed any autonomy for the East that did not have the full endorsement of all the major political leaders, which was obviously meant to negate the basic demand of the country's majority party (LaPorte, p. 98–101).

While negotiations between the government and the Awami League were still continuing in early 1971, the decision was made to preserve "national unity" by forceful means. In General Yahya Khan's words, "I have ordered the armed forces to do their job and fully restore the authority of the Government." An army of West Pakistanis did far more than arrest and kill the leaders of the Awami League. It unleashed a veritable reign of terror and destruction upon the East—one of the twentieth century's most ruthless attempts at political genocide. It used modern weaponry against the virtually unarmed, defenseless Bengalis, killing close to 1 million people within a few months and forcing more than 5 million to take refuge in India.[11] Nor did the bloodbath of forced "integration" succeed. Within the year

---

[11] Recall that the officers' aversion to the use of force against unarmed nationals does not apply in the midst of an emotion-charged communal (or class) conflict.

Bengali guerrillas turned this attempt at political genocide into a civil war, and then with the help of the Indian army, they won their independence as the new state of Bangladesh (LaPorte, pp. 101–8; Heitoweit, pp. 2–3).

In the end, the praetorians had transformed the overlapping regional-linguistic-ethnic divisions into an intense conflict and ordered and executed a debacle of deathly repression and terror, culminating in one of the bloodiest civil wars of the post-1945 period, mass starvation, economic ruin, and the dismemberment of the Pakistan that they had set out to preserve.

NIGERIA

The political disintegration of Nigeria is directly attributable to the praetorians' adoption of well-intentioned, but sorely misguided and mal-adroitly applied, unification policies. In the aftermath of only six months of military government over a million Nigerians were murdered in communal rioting, killed in the Eastern Region's attempted secession as the independent state of Biafra, or died from disease and starvation during two years of civil war.

Under the open civilian regime Nigeria was already sharply divided along regional-tribal lines, the major conflict having developed between the Hausa-Fulani of the Northern Region and the Ibos of the Eastern Region.[12] Constituting almost one-third of the total population, and being concentrated in the northern half of the country, the Hausa-Fulani controlled the Regional Government of the North and predominated within the federal government. Making up nearly one-fifth of the population, the far better educated Ibos managed to secure a disproportionate share of the much-sought-after positions within the officer corps, the civil service, and the commercial sector of the economy. The Hausa-Fulani were consequently resentful, jealous, and suspicious of the ambitious Ibos; the sizable number of Ibo officials and entrepreneurs living in northern cities were seen as un-welcome intruders. For their part, the Ibos looked down upon the poor, barely educated northerners. Both segments were fearful that the other's political and governmental positions would allow them to dominate the federation.

The January 1966 coup further inflamed the smoldering conflict, bringing more of these suspicions, fears, and antagonisms to the surface. Although not intended as such, it was widely rumored that the coup was an Ibo con-

---

[12] The regional-tribal conflict before and after the military takeover also involved other communal segments, in particular the Yoruba of the Western Region. But since the sharpest antagonisms were exhibited between the Hausa-Fulani and the Ibos, the following analysis is not thought to be flawed by omitting the other segments' interests and actions.

spiracy to take control of the entire country. For it was led by Ibo majors whose bullets were almost all reserved for high-ranking northern politicians and officers; due to the assassination of senior northern officers the Ibos became even more conspicuous in the upper ranks of the officer corps; and an Ibo (General Ironsi) became head of the Federal Military Government. Although General Ironsi was to have been assassinated by the conspirators, he was instrumental in defeating them. He came to power with the consent of the civilian leadership due to his position as commander in chief of the military (Luckham, pp. 17–50).

Under these highly inflammable circumstances a considerable measure of political acumen and skill was required to prevent the further ignition of communal animosities and fears. The Ironsi government was aware of the need to placate the North and took some steps to do so, such as promoting a Hausa-Fulani officer and then appointing him military governor of the North. Yet a basic failure to appreciate the nature of political reality led to the adoption of disastrous policies. The governors adhered to the highly simplistic and naive belief that the severe conflict was due solely to the shortcomings and self-serving manipulations of the politicians. Hostile expressions of tribalism and regionalism would be averted by denuding the politicians of their power, by refusing to consult with them or the country's "natural" political leaders, the chiefs and emirs. National unity was to be achieved, not by consultation, bargaining, and accommodation, but by banning all political activities and organizations; and then within this presumed political vacuum, by issuing a unification decree. Decree 34 was to eliminate regionalism and tribalism by centralizing the regime and abolishing the quota system for recruitment to the civil service. Yet it had just the reverse effect. In the North it was widely, and quite plausibly, interpreted as the government's chosen instrument for consolidating the Ibo minority's power throughout Nigeria, although this was not its intention.

Decree 34 abolished the four tribally centered regions and their regional governments. Nigeria ceased to be a federation. It was announced that this action was designed to "remove the last vestiges of the intense regionalism of the recent past and to produce that cohesion in the governmental structure which is so necessary in achieving and maintaining the paramount objective of national unity." The unofficial explanation was in accord with the praetorians' actual intentions, but hardly with political reality. The dissolution of federalism was a superfluous, ill-timed act of political ineptitude. It did not strengthen central control in any important respect because the Federal Military Government had already been vested with more authority than that of the previous federal and regional governments. The praetorians assumed that the elimination of the formal-legal trappings of regionalism would eradicate its discordant political expressions. According to a communiqué issued by the Supreme Military Council, the unification decree would allow the soldiers "to run the government as a military government under a unified command."

The decree was also meant as a public gesture, as evidence of the governors' commitment to national unity. This decidedly inept effort at impression management was even accepted by high-ranking northern officers as an appropriate gesture to underscore the desire for national unity, without appreciating its impact in the North where it sparked an immediate outcry. There it was seen to be—and could reasonably be interpreted as—the further accumulation of power in the hands of senior Ibo officers and civil servants in the capital (Luckham, pp. 265–66; Welch, 1970, p. 46).

This overly simplistic, direct "attack" upon the national integration problem also characterized the other part of Decree 34. The previously employed quota system, which had reserved half of the new civil service openings for northerners, was abolished. It had been adopted on behalf of the less well educated northerners, who would otherwise have consistently lost out in the competitive examinations to Ibos and Yorubas, who already held a greatly disproportionate number of bureaucratic places. Not only did this previous arrangement please northern aspirants for these much-sought-after positions; it also helped mollify the Hausa-Fulani by placing more of their own people in positions of authority in the Northern Region and the capital. The praetorians abolished the quota system at a stroke in the naive belief that its continuation would maintain regional tribal attachments. These were to be severely weakened, if not eradicated, by having the applicants compete on a purely individual achievement basis. The exclusive use of merit criteria would somehow break down communal attachments and assuage communal resentments and fears.[13]

The praetorians were extraordinarily unrealistic in thinking that the elimination of the quota system would be interpreted as evidence of their commitment to national unity. The consequences of the decree were immediately recognized in the North. The Ibos would gain most of the scarce, highly valued positions in a civil service in which they were already disproportionately represented. It was widely believed that the Ibos were about to "colonize" the North, migrating northward in droves to take over all the competitive posts, and then give undue preference to fellow tribesmen in entrepreneurial ventures. These expectations were given further credence by the precipitate announcement of Decree 34. It was issued before the several investigatory and advisory commissions dealing with various aspects of the integration issue had completed their deliberations. Quite understandably, the

---

[13] A secondary reason for doing away with proportional recruitment relates to the praetorians' apolitical conception of government. Recruitment based upon merit criteria alone—the applicants' performance on the competitive examinations—would make for a more effective civil service (Luckham, pp. 283–84).

government was thought to be acting in accordance with some preconceived plan for the consolidation of Ibo control, when there was no such plan at all (Luckham, p. 265; Dudley, pp. 216–17). [14]

The violent reaction to Decree 34 occurred five days after its announcement. In light of what was just said about the elimination of quotas as this would affect northern aspirants for bureaucratic positions, it is significant that the reaction began with a demonstration of northern students preparing for civil service careers at the Institute of Public Administration. That demonstration was immediately followed by communal rioting, arson, and fierce mob killing and wounding of several hundred Ibos who were living in northern cities. The military government was taken by complete surprise. And even then, when confronted with the outraged reaction of the North, the praetorians did not reconsider their unification strategy. In fact, it was expanded and accelerated in the inordinately naive belief that once the government had presented its case, reason would prevail and the opposition would somehow evaporate. Nor could the unification effort be softened or slowed down, since that would be publicly interpreted as a sign of weakness. Governmental authority and public order had to be preserved without temporizing.

Even northern commanders stressed the importance of maintaining public discipline rather than compromising with the opponents of the unification policy. And those few northern officers who now recognized the great risks involved did not make their views known to the governors. They saw themselves solely as military men within a hierarchical structure. Their job was to take orders from the supreme command, not to express regional interests or to persuade the government to take them into account. As the military governor of the North announced at the time—he himself being a Hausa-Fulani—"We have got a unified command and it is the method we are used to" (Luckham, pp. 275–76, 288–89; Miners, pp. 203–4, 207–8).

In July 1966, two months after the decree was issued, amid continuing furor and with the encouragement of some northern politicians, a group of Hausa-Fulani lieutenants and sergeants carried out a revenge coup. It was purposefully and unabashedly executed to stave off the apparent Ibo quest for national domination. General Ironsi and a score of other Ibo officers were killed. The army split apart. As the most senior northerner, and a well-respected officer, Colonel Gowon took command of the entire army outside the East from his position in the capital. The other chain of command was headed by Colonel Ojukwu, an Ibo who had been serving as military gover-

---

[14] For other instances of inept governmental actions and inactions that furthered the belief that the praetorians were purposefully promoting Ibo interests and domination, see Luckham, pp. 52–53, 266–70, 274; and Miners, pp. 207–8, 210–11, 218–20.

nor of the East. In the three months after the countercoup one and a half million Ibos emigrated to the East. Some seven thousand were slaughtered before reaching their destination.

The two military commanders and their delegations tried to negotiate a mutually acceptable settlement for almost a year. They failed to resolve their differences on two crucial issues—the structure of the regime and the army. Was the country to be divided into four or twelve regions, and how much or how little authority was to be vested in the central government? How was the army to be hierarchically constituted at the very highest level (i.e., should Colonel Ojukwu in the East take orders from Colonel Gowon in the capital), and what powers were to be reserved for the military governors of the separate regions? With the negotiations stalemated and the Ibos no longer feeling safe in a northern-dominated Nigeria, the East seceded in May 1967, declaring itself the independent Republic of Biafra. The ensuing civil war lasted more than two years, with combat deaths alone running into the hundreds of thousands, until a thoroughly depleted and defeated Biafra surrendered in January 1970 (Luckham, pp. 298–340).

Thus within a few months after taking power the praetorians' overly ambitious, ill-conceived, and poorly executed unification strategy moved the country down the path to total disintegration. Given the severity of the tribal-regional conflict prior to the military takeover, it is of course possible that a similar outcome would have occurred under continued civilian rule. Perhaps. The issue cannot be resolved with certainty. But in the judgment of First and others, while

> Nigeria might have gone to war with itself under a civilian government, [it] surely would not have done so with such deadly swiftness. The parties and the politicians used tribalism for their own ends; but the very existence of the parties insulated the country to some extent from its most explosive forms. Communal conflicts were in part processed through the party, to emerge amended somewhat and more subdued; communal tensions might be dissipated or absorbed in prolonged political maneuvering. Perhaps this is where Nigerians got their reputation for riding to the brink, and then reining back. The [praetorians] have ridden at a full gallop; and, in their bravado, did so without the reins. [First, pp. 352–53; for similar assessments, see Luckham, pp. 287–88; and Chick and Mazrui, pp. 290–91] [15]

[15] Yet it must also be said that between the end of the civil war and the 1975 countercoup in which he was overthrown, General Gowon performed exceptionally well in reintegrating the country. Despite enormous pressures to take revenge upon the Ibos, making them "pay for the civil war," Cowon adopted policies of some magnimity and equity. He provided greater security for the smaller tribes by creating twelve regions in place of the four that had given the North a politically predominant position, "reinducted" many Ibo enlisted men and officers into the Nigerian army, and was politically astute in choosing two former Biafran officers as his personal pilots.

Taking these three cases together, they clearly illustrate the double-barreled generalization that was put forward in the previous section: the presence of three elite attributes is crucial for the political integration of deeply divided communal societies; they are unlikely to be exhibited by military governors. First, the officers have a poor grasp upon political reality in believing that national unity can be heightened by the imposition of one segment's values upon another (the Sudan), by the use of coercive force (the Sudan, Pakistan), or by the issuance of governmental decrees (Nigeria). Second, the praetorians are negatively disposed toward conciliating mutually hostile segments (the Sudan, Pakistan, Nigeria). Third, rather than evidencing strong regulatory motives, they tend to act in accordance with the interests of their own communal groups to the decided detriment of other segments (the Sudan, Pakistan, and Nigeria during and after the revenge coup).

TOWARD THE PRESERVATION OF THE ECONOMIC STATUS QUO

Given their political and economic leverage, all governments have a potentially marked effect upon economic growth and the pace of modernization. The impact of non-Western governments also derives from the absence of a developed private sector, the commonly high ratio of public to private investment expenditures, and the scarcity of investment funds which multiplies the effects of those amounts that are available. And it is, of course, governments alone that can bring about progressive socioeconomic changes, from increases in social expenditures to the redistribution of landed wealth.

The first part of this section deals with the performance of military governments in promoting economic growth and modernization, as indicated principally by increases in the gross national product (GNP), the level of industrialization, and agricultural output. Contrary to the claims of the praetorians themselves at the time of the coup, and of those political scientists who have developed the model of the progressive-modernizing soldier,[16] the overall record is not a positive one. More specifically, it is no better than that of their civilian counterparts, although the underlying reasons differ significantly.

The second part deals with economic changes of a progressive variety, the more equitable redistribution of personal, industrial, and landed wealth, and the expansion of social service and welfare programs. Again, contrary to the claims of many praetorians and the model of the progressive-moderniz-

16 See pp. 34–38.

ing soldier, only a small proportion of military governments evidence a genuine concern for progressive economic changes, and of these, only a few have actually implemented them. The praetorians' record in this regard is a poor one, both in absolute terms and relative to that of civilian governments. Thus the title of this section—"Toward the Preservation of the Economic Status Quo."

ECONOMIC GROWTH AND MODERNIZATION

Like virtually all governments, military governments are concerned with economic growth and modernization. The praetorians' interest in economic expansion is commonly related to their nationalism, since a country's industrial base and its growth rate are commonly equated with international prestige, power, and independence; their "modern" values and self-image as effective economic decision makers and capable managers; their desire to avoid the political hardships of dealing with unfulfilled economic expectations and insistent demands for greater economic goods; and their wish to better the material well-being of all or some societal strata.

Both military and civilian governments favor economic expansion. But are they equally willing to bear the costs that it entails? For there are possible conflicts between the interests of the governors and the allocation of public funds for the expansion of industry, the building of transportation and communications networks, and the improvement of agricultural productivity. In the case of the praetorians, are public funds to be invested in these growth projects or allotted to the armed forces? Given the scarcity of capital and the enormous amounts required to generate annual GNP increases of 5 percent or more, it becomes difficult to finance both simultaneously. That defense budgets may hinder the rate of economic growth can be appreciated by citing two figures. Among the non-Western countries an average of 16 percent of GNP is devoted to capital formation (i.e., the purchase and construction of new fixed assets). At the same time an average of 4 percent of GNP is allotted to the armed forces.[17] Military expenditures represent fully one-fourth of the total amount of capital, public and private, that is invested in the economy.

Given this partial conflict between the satisfaction of corporate interests and economic growth, the praetorians consistently attribute greater importance to the former. Economic growth is desired, but not at the military's expense. For as was seen in Chapter 3, after the coup there is a regular increase in the proportion of total governmental expenditures and GNP that is

[17] These figures for the year 1965 have been calculated from Taylor and Hudson, pp. 34–36, 341–42.

allotted to the armed forces. On the average, these amounts are between 50 and 75 percent higher under military governments.[18]

Economic growth can be achieved through industrialization, agricultural modernization, or a combination of the two.[19] Although civilian governments have been overly enamored of the former strategy as the single quickest way to achieve a high growth rate, military governments have been even more so. The praetorians' exceptional emphasis upon industrialization is based upon additional considerations: industrialization allows for the domestic production of some military hardware and infrastructure, provides greater military power in the event of (an improbable) war, and heightens international prestige. Yet industrialization efforts are hardly an economic panacea given the inordinately high costs involved and the possibility of severe economic dislocations if undertaken in an overly rapid manner. In some instances the praetorians' hasty industrialization efforts have exacerbated economic difficulties rather than providing for economic expansion. In other instances they probably could have generated a higher growth rate by making larger investments in the rural areas since agricultural modernization often constitutes a more efficacious growth strategy (Nordlinger, 1970, p. 1136).

Given the praetorians' concern with economic expansion, at least after their corporate interests have been satisfied, we need to consider their strengths and weaknesses as economic decision makers. The formulation and execution of successful policies obviously requires considerable knowledge and expertise. It has been said—by some political scientists and the praetorians themselves—that military officers possess greater technical skills and managerial talent than do the civilian governors. And in discussing military professionalism we noted the fairly recent emergence of military managers and technologists, both in number and rank, alongside the heroic-martial-

---

[18] Although some military expenditures have a positive economic impact—the building of roads to the country's borders, the installation of a communication network, and especially the training of officers and enlisted men in skills that prove occupationally useful after their discharge—by far the greatest proportion is economically unproductive. The purchase of unnecessarily sophisticated and powerful weapons, the superfluous expansion of the armed forces, and the raising of salaries within an already well paid officer corps—such expenditures hardly contribute to economic growth. Moreover, the purchase of expensive equipment and weapons retards growth, since these are almost invariably bought abroad; foreign exchange reserves which could be used to buy economically productive equipment and supplies (e.g., tractors and fertilizers) are diverted if not depleted.

[19] Growth is, of course, also related to the international terms of trade. However, this issue is not discussed here for two reasons. First, the great majority of non-Western governments have little control over the price of exports or imports. Second, there are no discernible patterns in the policies of military governments, nor any apparent differences between military and civilian ones, with regard to international trade.

type officers. But whether the officers can transfer their technical-managerial skills from the military to the economic sphere is an open question at best, especially since these usually derive from the handling of military organization, logistics, and equipment of World War II vintage. They may very well be able to do so with regard to routine administrative matters, but it is doubtful that transferability occurs with regard to the far more complex, specialized, and demanding sphere of economic and financial decision making. It is one thing to manage military installations, to lead relatively uncomplex infantry battalions, and to develop military strategies. It is quite another to learn to use sophisticated fiscal concepts and tools, to assess the multiple consequences of alternative growth and modernization strategies, and to direct broad sectors of the economy. There is consequently little reason to presume that military officers are more capable than civilian incumbents as economic managers.

The praetorians' characteristic governing style has both positive and negative consequences for their effectiveness as economic decision makers. The heavy reliance upon managerial and technical criteria is advantageous when applied to economic problems; the tendency to accord similarly oriented civil servants considerable influence brings valuable expertise into the center of the decision-making process; and the neglect of public opinion allows for the adoption of unpopular policies such as wage freezes. In these respects military governments are perhaps better equipped than civilian ones for the formulation of effective growth and modernization strategies.

On the other hand, an exclusive reliance upon managerial-technical criteria may lead to the adoption of "rational" policies which turn out to be quite inappropriate in a given context. Technically "correct" decisions can produce undesired economic consequences if other important considerations are not taken into account, including the level of social mobilization, the cultural roadblocks to modernization, and the ability of economic interests to derail governmental policies. The tendency to adopt the most "rational" policies, without paying due regard to the societal, organizational, cultural, and political factors that regularly impede economic change, may be reinforced by the belief that all problems can be overcome if only correct policies are unswervingly applied. Inappropriate (and thus less than effective) economic policies are more likely to be adopted when the governors have an exaggerated belief in the impact of their decisions and when it is assumed that the roadblocks to sustained growth can easily be overcome.

Taking these considerations together, there is little reason for thinking that military governments are especially successful in promoting economic growth and modernization. This generalization is supported by a comparison of non-Western regimes in terms of per capita GNP growth rates and the expansion of primary education in the 1951–70 period. Military regimes were compared with civilian regimes in the same countries at different time periods; they were also compared with civilian regimes in those countries in which the soldiers had not occupied the seat of government. In neither comparison did a significant difference appear in their per capita GNP growth rates. The data also indicate that primary school enrollments grew more slowly under military auspices, in comparison with both civilian regimes in the same countries and civilian regimes in those countries where the soldiers did not take up the reins of government (McKinlay and Cohan, 1975, pp. 19–20).

The generalization is also supported by systematically generated data for seventy-four non-Western countries. No significant correlations (statistical associations) appeared between the level of military intervention and several crucial economic indicators during the 1957–62 period (Nordlinger, 1970, pp. 1138–41). The seventy-four countries were placed into one of three categories according to the "political strength of the military": those countries in which the military accepted civilian control, those in which the officers intervened as moderator types, and those in which the soldiers occupied the seat of government as guardian or ruler types. The economic indicators measure the extent to which economic growth and modernization have occurred in these countries roughly between 1957 and 1962, as well as the likelihood of economic change in the following years.

If the praetorians were successful in promoting economic growth and modernization, we should find strong positive correlations between the political strength of the military and the economic indicators. Yet the data in Table 2 show no such pattern, with a virtually nonexistent average correlation of .04. Compared with their civilian counterparts, the praetorians do not generate significant increases in per capita GNP, improve agricultural productivity, or increase enrollments in high schools, technical institutes, and universities. Nor do they enlarge public investments that would contribute to future economic growth. And there is a mild negative correlation ($r = -.22$) between the level of intervention and the "governors' commitment to economical development," which also does not bode well for future growth and

Table 2   Correlations Between The Political Strength of the Military and Economic Growth and Modernization

Rate of increase in per capita GNP	.13
Improvement in agricultural productivity	.07
Level of economic investment	—.11
Increased enrollments in post-primary schools	.08
Governors' commitment to economic development	—.22
Rate of change in the level of industrialization	.29

Nordlinger, 1970, p. 1139. For possible weaknesses in the validity and interpretation of the correlations, see pp. 1138–40. Since these data were collected, there have been two countries that have attained and sustained exceptionally high growth rates under military auspices. In South Korea and Brazil GNP increases have remained at 8 and 10 percent annually.

modernization. Only with regard to the rate of industrialization ($r = .29$) do the praetorians have an appreciable positive impact upon economic change, which is understandable given the previously mentioned reasons for their exceptionally strong interest in industrial expansion.

Taken together, these data suggest that the praetorians are interested in economic change, but they are not usually willing or able to make strenuous and effective efforts on its behalf.[20] The praetorians' economic record is not an enviable one. Presumably the paramount importance of their corporate interests, and the absence of any special economic and managerial skills, "prevents" them from making a determined and effective effort.

There is, however, a significant difference in the economic performance of military and civilian governments depending upon the societal context. Both of the quantitative studies just cited came up with the following finding. In the relatively modernized non-Western countries (as measured by per capita GNP), civilian governments promote somewhat faster rates of growth and modernization than do military governments, whereas military governments outperform their civilian counterparts in the least modernized countries (McKinlay and Cohan, 1975, p. 21; Nordlinger, 1970, p. 1142). [21]

The explanations for this pattern are developed in our analysis of progressive socioeconomic change. Here we may briefly note that the level of modernization is closely associated with the politicization of the lower classes, and thus the extent to which they are seen to threaten military and middle-class interests. That threat is substantially greater in the more modernized societies, the praetorians then being more strongly impelled to preserve the status quo.

[20] This interpretation is supported by controlling for two factors which affect economic growth, but over which the incumbents may have little or no control. One of these is the well-developed technical expertise and administrative capacities of the civil servants who advise the governors and execute their policies. The other is the absence of severe conflict and violence, which allows for the formulation of well-thought-out economic policies and enough certainty to encourage investments in the private and public sectors. When the political strength of the military was related to the economic indicators in those countries featuring the most conducive conditions for growth and modernization, the correlations were still of a zero-order variety. These findings suggest that the economic record of military governments is largely due to certain characteristics of the praetorians themselves, rather than to the quality of the civil service and the severity of political conflict over which they may have little control (Nordlinger, 1970, p. 1141).

[21] Roughly two-thirds of the non-Western countries fall into the "relatively modernized" category.

PROGRESSIVE SOCIOECONOMIC CHANGE

Turning to the other basic dimension of economic change, we want to analyze the frequency and degree to which military governments bring about progressive changes—reformist and radical changes providing markedly greater material benefits and opportunities to the lower classes. Given the praetorians' motivations, political attitudes, and regime capabilities, they infrequently effect such changes, and those that they do implement are usually of a limited variety. Military governors are not generally motivated to adopt progressive socioeconomic policies, although they are more inclined to do so under certain conditions relating to the class structure and the level of mass politicization. Of those praetorians who do harbor progressive inclinations, their characteristic political attitudes militate against the transformation of motives into policies. And in those few instances in which progressive policies have been adopted, the regimes' limited capabilities largely negate the realization of fundamental (i.e., radical or structural) changes.

Some persuasive evidence for the assertion that only a small proportion of praetorians are motivated in progressive directions comes from the survey of 229 attempted coups and countercoups that occurred between 1946 and 1970. Although soldiers may be motivated to overthrow civilian and military governments for reasons having nothing to do with economic change and yet pursue this goal once in power, the reasons for undertaking this risky enterprise are certainly not irrelevant to their policies as governors. And it turns out that "strikingly reformist" motivations were present in only 19 of the 229 cases.[22] A mere 8 percent of the coups were significantly motivated to correct injustices and abuses of an economic, social, or political variety (Thompson, pp. 44–45).[23]

The practorians' motivations as economic decision makers are primarily affected by their corporate interests. The regularity with which military governments increase defense expenditures not only hampers the rate of growth, it also decreases the likelihood of progressive-type changes, and for the very same reason: increased allocations to one program or group entail

---

[22] Recall that this finding was used in Chapter 3 to help substantiate the point that the coup makers are rarely motivated by the goal of improving governmental performance *per se*.

[23] Thompson goes on to say that this finding should not be interpreted to mean that aspiring reformers were not involved in the other 210 coups. "Military coups involve diverse coalitions with equally diverse goals. Some segments of the coalition may well be intensely reform oriented, but it would appear that they tend either to be neutralized by more pragmatic coalition partners or to be peripheral to the coup-leadership circle. But even if [this finding] understates the 'genuine' reform dimension, it still would be necessary to triple the 19 for strikingly reformist motivations to pertain to even a quarter of the coups examined" (Thompson, pp. 44–45).

a loss of funds for others, especially in situations of economic scarcity. Most progressive economic changes require considerable public expenditures. The building of hospitals, the training of doctors, nurses, and teachers, the construction of schools and low-cost housing, broader coverage and increased payments to the unemployed, sick, and aged, loans to small farmers and landless laborers, the redistribution of agricultural lands—all these progressive changes are expensive propositions. And when it comes down to deciding whether to finance such efforts or to increase the defense budget, the soldiers' conception of adequate budgetary support is overriding. Even Colonel Qaddafi's radical military government doubled the salaries of the Libyan military (now possibly the highest in the world) after the 1970 coup.

The military's corporate interests do not detract from the possibilities of progressive change solely because of the zero-sum choice between guns and butter. In societies with moderate to high levels of politicization the praetorians generally view the lower classes as a threat to their corporate interests. They are consequently less than enthusiastic about satisfying the demands of urban squatters, workers, poor peasants, and landless laborers. For a politically active and organized lower class constitutes an additional contender for power and scarce resources, and it may have developed a strong antipathy to the praetorians due to their previous acts of repression. As pointed out in Chapter 3, it is in Latin America, where the lower classes are most extensively politicized, that the conflicts between them and the military are most severe. The military governments of Latin America are the most reluctant to move in progressive directions.[24]

Then there are those motivations growing out of the officers' identification with the middle class. Having been largely recruited from that class, currently holding "membership" in it by virtue of their commissions and salaries, and being socially and sometimes economically connected with other middle-class individuals, praetorians tend to act in accordance with its interests. This generalization was used to help explain the intervention of Latin American officers. It also helps account for their less than progressive policies once in power. In Latin America (circa 1960) military governments relied more heavily upon regressive forms of taxation which penalize the lower-class majority than did civilian governments. The higher the levels of military intervention, the greater the proportion that workers and peasants paid in taxes compared with the middle class (Schmitter, p. 437).

There is, however, some variation in the military's policies due to the nature of middle-class interests. The middle class is fairly well established or predominant in approximately two-thirds of the non-Western countries, with at least 10 percent of the active male population engaged in commercial,

[24] Some evidence for this point is found in Nordlinger, 1970, pp. 1146–47.

banking, professional, technological, managerial, administrative, and clerical employments. In these societies the size and economically privileged position of the middle class gives a conservative cast to its interests. Its considerable "stake in society" dictates a preservation of the economic status quo. Moreover, given the almost ineluctable interconnections among the various dimensions of economic modernization, where an established middle class is present a politicized lower class of workers and perhaps peasants is also present. Lower-class demands for the redistribution of landed, industrial, and liquid wealth, increased welfare benefits, expansion of social services, and higher wages clearly conflict with middle-class interests. And given the political power of numbers and organization, these demands constitute a real challenge to the middle class. The threat to their privileged position comes from below.

The soldiers who have taken power in countries with an established middle class—indeed, they have occasionally done so partly to protect its interests—act as more or less ardent defenders of the economic status quo. They may make some halting efforts to expand social services and improve their delivery, but they do not adopt policies that would alter the class structure. Their actions (and inactions) are conservative in intent.[25] And with the politicized lower classes challenging the prevailing distribution of economic rewards and opportunities, the praetorians, the middle class, or both may think it necessary to apply stringent repressive measures. Exceptionally harsh and extensive repression is exemplified by the current military governments in Brazil and Chile, which have resorted to the execution, torture, and imprisonment of thousands of lower-class radicals and suspected leftists. Actions against worker and peasant movements are also undertaken on behalf of the military's corporate interests, since these too are seen to be challenged by a politicized lower class.

The situation confronting the praetorians—and thus the interests deriving from their middle-class identities—is quite different in societies with only a miniscule middle class, its members constituting less than 10 percent of the employable male population. In these countries it is the traditional elites who

[25] This point even applies to the praetorians in Pakistan who undertook what appeared to be a major land reform program. The Ayub Khan government did appropriate 2 million acres of land from the large estates; however, not only was much of it unsuitable for cultivation but the land was redistributed in such a way as to benefit the established middle class. It was sold at public auctions which allowed the former owners and prosperous farmers to buy it, while other lands were reserved for civilian and military officials. Although peasants were given the right to farm some of the acreage with the promise that they would receive preferential treatment at the time of its sale, they cultivated the land only to be frustrated when their claims were later ignored. They were ejected from their "own" land (von Vorys, pp. 63–64; Dupree, pp. 5–6; Feit, pp. 81–82).

regularly enjoy positions of political and economic predominance based upon landed wealth, inherited status, and lower-class deference and quiescence. The miniscule middle class is not well established economically, most of its members commonly being employed in the public sector. Neither the small urban working class nor the peasantry is politicized beyond a minimal threshold.[26]

In these societies, constituting roughly one-third of the non-Western countries, the political and economic context gives a progressive cast to middle-class interests. The desire for greater wealth and mobility opportunities is to be realized at the expense of the traditional elites. For it is they who own and control a grossly disproportionate share of economic rewards, while the lower classes' low level of politicization rules out a threat from below. The middle class's interests include the reordering of economic rewards according to proven achievement rather than inherited status, the expansion of the public sector to provide greater mobility opportunities, increases in the number of secondary schools and universities, and the redistribution of the traditional elite's landed wealth to middle-class individuals.

The officers who come to power in these societies are often inclined to act on behalf of the interests of the miniscule middle class, especially since their corporate interests are not being challenged from below. Their motivations may approximate those of the progressive soldier, as illustrated by three of the most radical military governments—those of Egypt, Burma, and Peru, which are examined in the following section. However, two caveats circumscribe the significance and applicability of this generalization.

First, although the praetorians' motivations may be described as reformist and sometimes even as radical, they do not commonly include an abiding concern for the interests of the lower classes who constitute a majority of the population. Attacks upon the traditional elites on behalf of the miniscule middle class, the military, or both rarely provide any direct or short-run economic benefits to workers and peasants. Second, the progressive motivations derived from the praetorians' identification with the middle class often have little impact upon economic policies. They are neutralized by the officers' communal attachments. For more than half of those countries featuring a miniscule middle class are more or less sharply divided along communal lines.[27] Especially in these, the least modernized of non-Western societies, communal divisions are much more salient than class divisions. The

---

[26] Where the level of politicization has risen beyond this threshold, it grows out of communal rather than class divisions. We will return to the importance of communal divisions in a moment.

[27] This estimate is based upon a calculation of the quantitative-judgmental data for seventy-four non-Western countries generated by Adelman and Morris, pp. 30–33, 41–44.

far more severe communal conflicts eclipse class conflicts, or absorb and transform them into communal ones (Nordlinger, 1972, p. 98). Which is to say that the progressive inclinations deriving from the praetorians' identification with a miniscule middle class tend to be overshadowed by a stronger attachment to communal interests. And these are not generally reformist or radical.

With regard to those praetorians who are inclined to introduce progressive economic changes, their characteristic attitudes toward political activity and political order militate against the translation of motives into policy "outputs." Mass political activity tends to be viewed as excessively self-serving, harmful in its exacerbation of societal differences, and normatively unjustified insofar as it calls into question the regime's hierarchical structure. The praetorians are then not about to react positively to lower-class demands and pressures on behalf of their own interests; they are not given to stimulating lower-class politicization by accepting their more or less stridently asserted demands for progressive economic policies. Rather, the negative attitude toward political activity encourages one or more of four reactions to mass demands: neglect, the adoption of distinctly unprogressive policies, the imposition of further restrictions upon political activity, or forceful repression.

These reactions are made all the more probable by the inordinately high value that the officers place upon the maintenance of political order. Even minor disturbances are unacceptable. Yet given the restrictions of an authoritarian regime, the only political resources available to workers and peasants are disorderly ones. Unable to compete for power or publicize and express their interests in a peaceful manner, they can only press them upon the praetorians by engaging in illegal demonstrations, marches, strikes, land seizures, riots, and sporadic protests. If they do so, military governments come down particularly hard on them, the disorderly actions further reinforcing the reluctance to sponsor reforms that benefit the lower classes.

The pervasive commitment to political order further reduces the likelihood of progressive economic change since its introduction could usher in a period of political turbulence. Where there is a politicized lower class, it may push hard for more extensive reforms; the opponents of change may try to protect their interests by fomenting disturbances; and the implementation of any important economic changes contains the potential for unexpected political outbursts once their impact is felt. Even the foremost interpreter of the Latin American officer corps as reformist in inclination would apparently agree with this point. Johnson claims that Latin American praetorians might be willing to sanction land reform, but only if it can proceed in an orderly manner (and, parenthetically, as long as the cost to the military is not too high) (Johnson, p. 147). What Johnson does not say is that neither in the estimates of the military nor in actuality does land reform commonly proceed under stringently orderly circumstances. Thus even those praetorians who favor progressive economic change may hold back. Order comes first in the soldiers' hierarchy of values.

Lastly, the capabilities of military regimes become relevant with respect to that small proportion of praetorians with progressive motivations that are not neutralized by their political attitudes. All governments are able to carry out minor reforms, such as a small increase in educational expenditures, but there are enormous variations in their capabilities for implementing major reforms and structural alterations. At a minimum, such fundamental changes require considerable regime stability. They cannot be designed, executed, and securely rooted within two or three years. Yet we have underscored the almost inherent instability of military regimes. The overwhelming majority do not have a sufficiently long life span to undertake and secure major economic changes.

If the praetorians are to effect basic economic changes, especially the radical redistribution of landed wealth, they usually must control the population and penetrate the society to ensure their implementation. And this requires the creation of a well-organized mass party extending down to the grass-roots level. Only with such an "organizational weapon" can radically inclined praetorians effectively energize the masses, control their political and economic behavior, and overcome the well-entrenched opponents of change. Yet as was seen in the preceding chapter, military men are rarely interested or able to create political organizations capable of mobilizing the population. Which is to say that very few military regimes have the requisite capabilities for the implementation of fundamental economic changes.

To conclude this discussion of the possibilities of major economic reform under military auspices, we can make some rough comparisons between military and civilian governments. Unlike the praetorians who evidence few progressive motivations, civilian governors may or may not be so inclined. They are so inclined when dependent upon, or in search of, lower-class support. The praetorians are far less concerned with attaining such support given their monopoly of force and the conflicts between military and lower-class interests. With regard to political attitudes, any generalizations about civilian attitudes would be most problematic. We can therefore presume that their attitudes do not consistently militate against the adoption of progressive policies. In contrast, none of the officers' characteristic political attitudes are hospitable toward major economic change. Then there are the greater capabilities of civilian regimes due to their longer duration and the governors' more developed talents for the creation of effective mass parties. Civilian incumbents consequently have more frequent opportunities to implement ambitious reformist and radical policies.

In short, military governments perform poorly in bringing about progressive economic change in absolute terms and relative to their civilian counterparts.[28]

THREE
PROGRESSIVE
MODERNIZING
CASES:
PERU,
BURMA,
AND
EGYPT

In the first half of this chapter it was argued that the praetorians are regularly unsuccessful in dealing with severe communal conflicts. This proposition and its underlying reasoning were illustrated in a discussion of three demonstrable failures (the Sudan, Pakistan, and Nigeria). Here we will be taking a different tack in the selection of cases relating praetorianism to economic change. Rather than choosing those that clearly exemplify the major thrust of the argument, that the great majority of military governments do not promote major economic changes, we will examine three instances in which the praetorians have done just that. Instead of looking at cases that are clearly illustrative, representative, and thus directly supportive of our generalizations, we shall focus on three that are most unrepresentative of the economic policies of military governments. All students of praetorianism would presumably agree that the military governments of Velasco in Peru (1968–75), Ne Win in Burma (1962–), and Nasser in Egypt (1952–71) are among those that have undertaken concerted efforts to bring about fundamental progressive and modernizing changes. Indeed, these are just about the only ones that have done so.[29]

There are several reasons for selecting three highly unrepresentative cases in illustrating, developing, and supporting our generalizations. First, it was said that some praetorians are motivated to bring about major economic changes in societies with certain economic, social, and political contours. Since these conditions obtain in our three cases, they serve to illustrate one part of the argument. Second, by looking at the most ambitious of military governments we can gauge the extent to which the praetorians have actually brought about major progressive, modernizing changes. These cases constitute the outer limits of praetorian efforts and accomplishments in this regard.

---

[28] That military governments perform more poorly than civilian ones in this regard may be underscored by listing those countries in which civilians have implemented major progressive changes at some point in the post-1945 period. These include Communist China, North Korea, North Vietnam, India, Burma, Guinea, Mali, Tanzania, Cuba, Jamaica, Venezuela, Bolivia, Guatemala, Mexico, and Chile. As will be seen in the following section, the number of military governments that have done so is less than half as large.

[29] The only other praetorians that might be included are those that held power in Argentina, Syria, Iraq, Libya, and Algeria at one time or another in the post-1945 period.

Third, to the extent that these changes turn out to be less than fundamental ones, we may be able to account for such "shortcomings" with just those variables that explain why so few military governments bring about major economic changes. And lastly, insofar as our generalizations are unable to account for these unrepresentative cases, we should take note of the weaknesses in their explanatory power. Rather than trying to "save the hypothesis" by ignoring or "explaining away" deviations as being due to "special" circumstances, we should estimate what our generalizations leave unexplained.

Between 1968 and 1975, when he was overthrown by more conservative officers, the government of General Velasco promoted progressive, modernizing programs that are unprecedented in Peruvian history. They are also the most ambitious ones undertaken by any of Latin America's praetorians, past or present. Already prior to the 1968 coup the soldiers were contemplating major transformations in the state's role in the economy, labor-management relations, the agricultural sector, and the distribution of property and income. In 1972 the Velasco government announced its intention of transforming the capitalist economy into one in which the "social property" sector would predominate. Property relations have been markedly altered through the nationalization of the largest domestic and foreign-owned companies, state regulation of the larger private enterprises, and the formation of worker cooperatives. These actions, along with legislation calling for profit-sharing arrangements and a prolabor bias in the settlement of wage disputes, were intended to improve worker-management relations and increase industrial productivity.

Agricultural laborers, sharecroppers, and tenant farmers have benefited from a land reform program which placed meaningful limitations upon the size of privately owned farming and grazing lands. The huge coastal plantations have been converted into worker cooperatives or broken up into small landholdings. Since the land redistribution left many new owners with holdings that are too small for efficient farming, organizers have been sent in to help the peasants form economically viable cooperatives. Peru now has a mixed economy of private, cooperative, and state-owned enterprises, which the praetorians have described as the "non-Communist, non-capitalist revolution of the armed forces" (Jaquette, pp. 650–58; Lowenthal, pp. 147–48; Welch and Smith, p. 156).

Having said that the Velasco government constitutes the most ambitiously progressive and modernizing of Latin America's military governments, we can use this case to gauge the outer limits of such efforts among the praetorians in this part of the non-Western world. It turns out that the government's economic policies are neither revolutionary nor extremely radical. Its socioeconomic goals may more accurately be described as highly ambitious reformist ones. Property, income, and mobility opportunities have been markedly redistributed, yet the material well-being of the great majority of workers and peasants has not been notably improved.

The landed oligarchy has been denuded of its political power and dispossessed of its huge estates. Yet it has received payment for its lands (in the form of government bonds), as well as financial inducements to preserve its wealth by investing in government-approved industrial firms. More importantly, the proportion of the rural poor that has benefited from land reform is quite small. The beneficiaries have been largely limited to the relatively small number of former workers on the huge commercial sugar estates in the coastal region. And the economic position of the urban workers has barely improved. They have had to bear much of the costs of industrialization due to the government's maintenance of relatively low wages. No more than 10 percent of the workers (those in the modern sector) have been affected by the law requiring private companies to give their employees a fixed percentage of profits, or by the prolabor settlements that have usually been approved by the government where wage disputes have arisen.[30] The benefits accruing to the lower class have been primarily symbolic. The majority of workers and peasants—and thus the majority of the total population—have not realized any significant gains in their economic positions (Quijano; Welch and Smith, pp. 168–69; Lowenthal, pp. 149–50).

The reform efforts undertaken by Peru's ruler-type praetorians illustrate the generalization that if the progressive-modernizing soldier is to appear at all, he will do so in societies with a political and economically predominant traditional elite. The Velasco government acted against the powerful landed oligarchy whose economic position prior to the coup is sharply underscored by two figures: 2 percent of all landowners held 76 percent of the farming and grazing land; 1 percent of the population enjoyed almost one-third of the nation's income. The oligarchy's enormous wealth was derived from an agricultural sector whose land tenure arrangements and labor relations were nearly feudal in nature. Its domination of the pre-1968 civilian cabinets and legislatures provided more than adequate political power to preserve its economic privileges. Comprehensive reform programs did not get off the political ground, and those halting efforts that did were either diluted prior to their enactment or ineffectively implemented afterward (Lowenthal, pp. 152–55).

At the time of the military takeover the middle class was no longer

---

[30] However, the urban squatters have been given legal title to the land. Peru is the only Latin American country in which a military government has done so. See Stepan, forthcoming, Chapter 5.

miniscule. A fairly rapid rate of economic modernization in the 1950s and 1960s increased the size of the middle class to slightly more than 10 percent of the active male population. But even in 1968 it was still a small one, with a weak economic base, very much dependent upon the oligarchy and foreign-owned companies. As the country's "preeminent middle-class institution" the officer corps shared that class's interest in breaking the economic and political predominance of the landed oligarchy. The military did just that immediately after taking power. And the conversion of the oligarchy's landed wealth into state-controlled or government-approved industries was to benefit the middle class by promoting economic growth and heightening mobility opportunities. In these and other ways, it is the middle-class professionals, technocrats, and administrators who gained the most under military rule (Lowenthal, pp. 149, 157; Welch and Smith, p. 169).

The Peruvian case diverges from the class-oriented hypothesis in at least one respect. The government's progressive actions have outdistanced the middle class's own perceptions of its interests. There has been considerable restlessness and grumbling among teachers, engineers, doctors, lawyers, and businessmen. The reform program definitely goes beyond what most members of the middle class support, since it aims to bring about marked improvements in the economic position of workers and peasants. Our class-oriented interpretation can account for the praetorians' attacks upon the landed oligarchy and the promotion of middle-class interests, but not for attempts to improve the economic conditions of the lower classes, which is what the Velasco government tried to do despite middle-class displeasure. But having recognized the explanatory gap in the hypothesis, it turns out not to be quite as wide as it first appears.

For the military actually believes itself to be acting on behalf of middle-class interests. The differences between the two groups do not relate to their objectives, but to their perceptions of political realities as these lead to divergent conclusions about the most effective means for realizing their shared interests. Already prior to 1968 the officer corps perceived a potentially serious threat to middle-class (and corporate) interests stemming from downtrodden workers and peasants; the middle class does not share this perception of a latent political crisis. Perceiving a "subversive potential" that could be exploited by Communists and other radical elements, the military concluded that the most effective strategy for defusing the likely threat from below is a reformist program which will also benefit workers and peasants (Welch and Smith, p. 170).

The Peruvian case both conforms to and diverges from our hypothesis regarding the impact of corporate interests upon economic policies. It illustrates the generalization that the soldiers place the utmost importance upon their corporate interests, including the point that military expenditures are not reduced to pay for progressive, modernizing policies. Defense budgets have increased steadily since 1968. Peru diverges from the generalization that the soldiers perceive a conflict between corporate interests and the redistribution of economic rewards to the lower classes. Although the Velasco government's economic policies were primarily shaped by a concern for the protection of corporate interests, what is highly unusual about the Peruvian case is the adoption of an overall strategy that seeks to protect these interests *indirectly* through the introduction of modernizing and progressive economic changes.

The development of an indirect, preventive, sophisticated strategy in defense of corporate interests was triggered by the perception of a growing "subversive potential." The widespread urban and rural land seizures, the political terrorism, and the guerrilla movements of the early 1960s were seen as the top of a massive iceberg of growing economic and political pressures that could engulf the military and the middle class. The rural-based guerrillas were defeated within six months. Nevertheless, the soldiers realized that if a handful of radicalized urban intellectuals could keep thousands of troops occupied for months, the situation would be quite different if peasants and workers participated in future insurgencies. They concluded that Peru had entered a period of "latent insurgency," which could turn into an acute political crisis if economic inequities were maintained by the oligarchy.

To protect their corporate interests the officers opted for intervention —what they referred to as "survival through leadership of change." The soldiers themselves would have to implement major reforms, given their realization that "many of the existing social and economic structures seemed so inefficient or unjust as to create the conditions for, and give legitimacy to, revolutionary protest and hence constitute a security threat. Even conservative officers came to feel that these conditions could ultimately become a threat to the military itself. . . . Peruvian officers increasingly saw their society as caught up in a fundamental, long-term crisis that threatened them both as military men, and personally as often hard-pressed members of the middle class" (Einaudi, pp. 72–73, 79–80).

This kind of thinking was first developed in the early 1960s by instructors and students at the influential Center for Higher Military Studies (CAEM) and in the Intelligence Services. At the CAEM, middle-level officers helped work out the doctrine of "development as a counter-insurgency tactic" at the same time that they were exposed to an exceptionally broad two-year advanced training program, including courses on fiscal policy, land reform, and the methodology of the social sciences. According to this doctrine the best way to handle the latent political crisis was to attack its social and economic roots. Only the alleviation of economic suffering, inequities, and degradation in the agricultural sector would prevent Communists and radicals from exploiting these deep-seated grievances. The absentee landowners and their local henchmen should no longer be able to oppress the rural laborers whose marginal living conditions and degradations could turn them into recruits for future insurgencies. Thus even before taking power the military intended to adopt highly progressive programs in the belief that these would best serve their corporate interests by defusing the threat from below (Einaudi and Stepan, pp. 21, 27, 36; Astiz and García, pp. 677–78; Villaneuva, 1972; Stepan, forthcoming, Chapter 4).

In short, the Velasco government's economic policies were undertaken on behalf of military and middle-class interests. That they took on an ambitious reformist cast is explicable in terms of the contextual conditions of a preindustrial class structure with a landed oligarchy at its pinnacle, the "stimulus" provided by the illegal actions and violence of the early 1960s, and the educational experience at the CAEM which was attended by two-thirds of Velasco's cabinet.

BURMA

Burma constitutes the rare instance of a military government undertaking thoroughly socialist and egalitarian policies. The pre-1962 civilian governments had already taken large strides toward socialism. The Revolutionary Council headed by General Ne Win went beyond them in its first major domestic policy declaration, "The Burmese Way to Socialism." Capitalism was condemned as exploitation. The "revolution for workers and peasants" was to be completed. Nationalization of the means of production was to substitute economic equality for exploitation. And the combination of socialism and Burmanization (the elimination of foreign and non-Burmese ownership) would promote national unity and economic growth.

Within two years of the takeover the ruler-type praetorians had nationalized virtually all industrial, communications, transportation, and commercial enterprises. The state swallowed up the entire modern sector of the economy, including companies that produced and distributed consumer goods. The praetorians also took control of the all-important rice industry, taking responsibility for processing, distribution, and pricing. A highly egalitarian socialism was actively pursued in the countryside. Given the equation of capitalism with exploitation, all rental payments to landowners were abolished. The government also decreed that peasants who were unable to pay existing debts could not have their land or personal property taken away as payment; loans were provided to hard-pressed farmers; local Land Committees were given control over some privately owned lands; and the peasants were given inducements to cooperate with each other (e.g., sharing their few tools and animals) during the planting and harvesting seasons (Trager, pp. 160–61; Silverstein, p. 96; Hoadley, pp. 49, 61).

These exceptionally ambitious radical policies are partly explicable in terms of the country's economic and political contours. Neither the military nor the miniscule middle class had anything to fear from a peasantry featuring one of the lowest levels of politicization in the world, and a virtually nonexistent urban working class. Although there was no predominant, traditional elite whose economic interests could be attacked, almost all privately owned enterprises and much of the farmland was in the hands of foreign companies and foreign nationals (i.e., Indians and Chinese who had settled in Burma). The ethnically Burmese praetorians acted against the economically privileged positions of the nonindigenous communal segments. The nationalization laws benefited the ethnically Burmese middle class by creating mobility opportunities within the rapidly expanded public sector at the expense of the Chinese and Indians who had controlled the private sector of the modern economy. And in the countryside it was the Indians, who owned a third of the cultivated land, who lost out with the abolition of rental payments (Badgley, p. 104; Silverstein, p. 96).

Although the country's economic, political, and communal characteristics go a long way in accounting for the adoption of exceedingly ambitious progressive policies, they do not fully explain the energetic pursuit of exceptionally egalitarian goals. The Burmese praetorians' strenuous efforts to better the material well-being of peasants and workers run counter to several of our generalizations regarding the attitudes and behavior of military officers trained and socialized within a hierarchical, bureaucratically structured institution. Yet these generalizations can quite easily "survive" this deviant case because the Burmese praetorians' backgrounds are hardly typical of the overwhelming majority of military officers. Ne Win and most of the other senior officers were armed nationalists and politicians before becoming military officers; their political attitudes and behavior were not shaped by the typical training and socializing experiences of military officers. In fact, since we would not expect the generalizations to hold in those rare instances in which their underlying assumptions are not satisfied, this deviant case lends them some indirect support.[31]

What then constitutes the notably uncharacteristic backgrounds of the Burmese praetorians that help explain their pursuit of highly egalitarian economic policies? Ne Win and most of the other leading praetorians gained their first military and political experiences during and immediately after

---

[31] The Burmese officers' highly untypical backgrounds also help account for their deviation from another generalization, that the praetorians are regularly unwilling to regulate severe communal conflicts because of their political attitudes and ingrained political incapacities. The post-1962 government defused the religious conflict by dropping the idea of a Buddhist state religion, entered into negotiations with fiercely hostile regional-ethnic minorities, and granted generous amnesties to the armed insurgents (Trager, pp. 202–4, 208–11). However, the central government is still virtually at war with the non-Burmese minorities, despite the loss of much of their popular support.

World War II as leaders of the nationalist Burma Independence Army and the Anti-Fascist People's Freedom League. They joined the Independence Army and brought it over to the Japanese in the hope of ridding the country of British colonialism. Then when it appeared that Japan would be defeated, they fought with the British in pursuit of the same goal. These armed nationalists were also influential members of the Anti-Fascist People's Freedom League—a group of dedicated and exceptionally successful Socialist politicians. The AFPFL was a solidly Marxist party from its formation, the Communists only being excluded in 1948 when the party formed its first government. The AFPFL politicians exhibited considerable adroitness and tactical competence in waging a successful independence campaign against the British, most notably by alternating between a negotiating posture and threats of violence. And having attained independence, the AFPFL wrote its socialist and egalitarian principles into the constitution. It was only in 1948 that the men who were to rule Burma after 1962 created and commanded the country's regular armed forces. In fact, they were assigned to army careers in an almost random fashion once it became necessary for the nationalist politicians to staff all the institutions of the new state (Trager, pp. 68–69, 75, 133–34, 151–52; Pye, 1962B, p. 234).

Turning to the impact of their modernizing and growth-inducing efforts, the Burmese military staggering failures sharply underscore the doubts raised about the officers' ability to serve as economic managers and decision makers. Their record illustrates the difficulties military men experience in designing and administering effective policies due to their overly simplistic assumptions about economic problems, and the questionable transference of their technical and organizational skills to the far more complex fiscal and economic spheres. The Burmese praetorians "have proved unable to cope with the myriad and intricate tasks of central management and planning. Their reputed enthusiasm and devotion to developmental programs have not compensated for the lack of specialized administrative skills needed to manage a whole nation's economic affairs" (Hoadley, p. 59).

It is not just that the economy has stagnated under fourteen years of military rule. It has actually been losing ground since several hundred army officers assumed sole responsibility for economic decision making and administration, including the management of individual enterprises. In 1965 Ne Win publicly admitted as much in describing the economic situation as a "mess." Despite the adoption of a Four Year Plan (1966–70) the state of economic paralysis continues. The economy is still characterized by mismanagement, inflation, consumer goods shortages, distribution blockages, balance-of-payments deficits, and, most importantly, a decline in per capita GNP. The economic performance failures are most evident with regard to what is by far the country's most important product. Prior to the 1962 takeover sufficient rice was produced for both domestic consumption and foreign export. This highly favorable situation was drastically altered after the military took on the sole responsibility for purchasing, milling, distributing, and setting the price of rice. Production declined sharply, and real (i.e., black market) prices increased significantly due to the operation's poor planning and monumental inefficiency. The peasants grew less rice due to the artificially low prices set by the government; wastage occurred because the planners failed to provide for sufficient storage and distribution facilities. Exports plummeted from 1.8 million tons in 1961–62 to 0.3 million tons in 1967–68. Once the world's leading rice exporter, in the near future Burma may have to import rice for domestic consumption, which would be especially problematic since almost all of the country's imports have been financed by rice exports.[32] (Guyot, pp. 311, 317; Badgley, pp. 104, 111; Feit, p. 103; Hoadley, pp. 59–61).

Burma thus constitutes that rare case of a military government undertaking exceedingly ambitious egalitarian policies. This is explicable in terms of the country's social, economic, and political context, as well as the praetorians' highly atypical backgrounds. The radical goals have been only partially realized because of the praetorians' inadequacies as economic decision makers and managers. The determined pursuit of socialist objectives has decreased economic inequalities, but this achievement obviously loses much (or most) of its significance when set alongside the fact that the living standard of almost the entire population has actually declined under military rule.[33]

EGYPT

Egypt under Nasser has been described as the most radical of military regimes. Nasser's revolutionary rhetoric and the virulent ideology of "Arab Socialism" helps make the Egyptian case appear to be just that. It thus becomes important to gauge the extent to which progressive and modernizing policies have been implemented, concomitantly relating their adoption to the hypothesis that the praetorians only do so in a certain type of society.

Egypt was a semifeudal society at the time of the 1952 military takeover. The peasantry was in a centuries-long state of political torpor, there

---

[32] Indeed, plummeting rice exports required a curtailment of imports, including replacements for worn parts in the rice-milling plants, which further reduced rice production.

[33] Even the industrial workers, a relatively privileged minority in all non-Western countries, have lost ground. Their average monthly wages of $40 have only been raised once since 1948, while inflation has long been running at about 30 percent annually. Their dissatisfaction led to a strike in 1974 in which fifty workers were killed by the army.

was hardly an urban working class to speak of, the miniscule middle class was politically impotent and economically weak, and the small modern sector of the economy was in the hands of a tiny group of wealthy entrepreneurs. The large landowners, and King Farouk, the largest among them, dominated the economy and controlled the regime. Eleven thousand landowners held one-third of all the cultivable land. The vast majority of the population lived on a thin margin of survival as nearly landless peasants and tenant farmers, three-quarters of whose earnings went for rental payments. Political power was in the hands of the king and the large landowners, who together controlled the cabinet, legislature, and bureaucracy. Their oligarchical rule was supported by conservative Moslem leaders. Given this economic and political context, it is not surprising that the praetorians' single most important accomplishment was the destruction of the oligarchy. The monarchy was eliminated, and the large landowners and their allies were denuded of their political and economic power, both in government and in the rural periphery (Be'eri, pp. 412, 424; Welch and Smith, p. 190).

The praetorians used the 1952 agrarian reform law as the primary instrument to attack the political and economic predominance of the semi-feudal oligarchy. Holdings were limited to two hundred acres, which led to a transfer of almost one-fifth of the arable land. But as "predicted" by our hypothesis, it was the rural middle class who were the major or sole beneficiaries rather than the poor peasants and landless farmers. Neither the 1952 nor the 1961 agrarian reform laws significantly increased the holdings of the poor peasants or turned tenant farmers into landowners. Only some one hundred thousand acres were distributed to the poor peasants owning less than five acres, which in itself is hardly enough to sustain a family. Their average holdings barely increased from a tiny 0.8 acres to 1.1 acres. Part of the expropriated land was redistributed to farmers who already owned more than five acres. The rest was sold on the open market where it was purchased by financially solvent farmers. In fact it could only be bought by them, since the government did not provide loans to the rural poor with which to acquire these lands. A comparison of land distribution figures for 1952 and 1964 indicates that the rural middle class not only retained its holdings, some strata within this class were able to increase their acreage. The agrarian reform laws thus stabilized the economic position of the well-to-do farmers, simultaneously allowing these so-called village strongmen to continue to exploit the landless tenant farmers[34] (Be'eri, pp. 435–37; Perlmutter, 1974, pp. 118–21).

---

[34] The adoption of these policies is in accord with that part of the hypothesis that relates economic decision making to the praetorians' middle-class backgrounds. For the Egyptian praetorians are "closely bound" to the rural middle class. "In examining the social origins of the officers it became clear that many of them are the sons and nephews of village men of substance. . . . Strong ties

During its first decade Nasser's government did not take any actions that were detrimental to the interests of the wealthy financiers, industrialists, and commercial entrepreneurs. Indeed, it promoted their interests by eliminating the traditional oligarchy, silencing the political left, and destroying the unions. During the 1950s the large financial, industrial, and business firms enjoyed an unprecedented prosperity. Only in the second decade, with the 1961 nationalization laws, did the ruler-type praetorians eliminate the economic power base of the wealthy urban stratum. And they did so to achieve more rapid economic growth and greater power for themselves, not to bring about a progressive redistribution of economic resources.[35] The public sector came to embrace those heights from which the economy could be directed (banks, insurance companies, and export firms) and those fields requiring considerable investment if economic growth was to occur (heavy and light industry). Yet even after the adoption of state socialism within the modern economy's key sectors, the praetorians left the wealthy entrepreneurs with considerable opportunities. Private capital continues to predominate in those fields that provide both fairly certain and quick profits: building construction, real estate, hotels, medium-size industry (especially textiles), and wholesale and retail firms. And with more than a third of public investment being "farmed out" to private firms, state socialism contributed to the emergence and expansion of an entrepreneurial middle class (Abdel-Malek, pp. 115, 134–35, 150–57; Be'eri, pp. 416–18; Waterbury, pp. 10–12).

The economic position of the miniscule middle class, especially the salaried administrators, engineers, technicians, economists, and clerical workers, improved significantly under military rule. The 1961 nationalization of private companies opened up the top positions to men who had previously held middle-management positions; the rapid expansion of the public sector —between 1962 and 1965 the payroll for government employees doubled— provided additional mobility opportunities. New positions were filled and promotions determined on the basis of education and training rather than inherited wealth and status. The praetorians purposefully set out to create a relatively large, well-trained managerial class in order to promote economic growth and modernization. Mobility opportunities were markedly heightened as enrollments in high schools, trade schools, and technical institutes increased tenfold under praetorian auspices. The military shared the middle

---

of social origin connect a certain class whose position improved and property increased . . . with the officers in power. The officers are loyal to the Arab tradition of powerful family solidarity" (Be'eri, p. 437).

35 It might be added that half of the owners of the large firms were Greeks, Maltese, and Copts (all Christian sects in an overwhelmingly Moslem country), the praetorians thus being less reluctant to nationalize their property (Issawi, pp. 89–90).

class's interest in economic growth and modernization, providing that class with the opportunities to contribute toward and benefit from these goals (Abdel-Malek, pp. 174–77; Halpern, pp. 51–60). [36]

Turning to the lower classes, the praetorians have provided them with better medical care, more education, and greater social security benefits. The peasantry has benefited from laws that provide for public assistance at times of crop failure, fairer treatment at the hands of landowners and bureaucrats, ceilings on land rentals, and greater security of tenure on rented plots. The urban workers were accorded minimum wage guarantees, some profit sharing, protection against unjust dismissals, improved working conditions, and shorter hours. Although there have been numerous failures to implement some of these laws, the provision of greater material benefits, security, and social services have won considerable lower-class support for Egypt's praetorians (Abdel-Malek, pp. 72–82, 150–66; Be'eri, p. 417).

The Egyptian case was selected because it has been seen as the most radical of military regimes; it certainly constitutes one of the most ambitious instances of progressive and modernizing policies being undertaken by praetorian soldiers. We can therefore use it to assess the assertion that even those few praetorians who fit the model of the progressive-modernizing soldier do not bring about radical economic changes, with the lower classes as the major beneficiaries.

When the Free Officers took power in 1952, their socioeconomic ideas, to the extent that they were developed at all, did not feature anything bordering on socialism. There were some socialists among them, but all senior leftist officers were dismissed within two years of the coup. During the first decade of military rule there was virtually no mention of socialism in governmental declarations, in the 1956 constitution, or in Nasser's *Philosophy of the Revolution*. It was only ten years after taking power that the praetorians developed the ideology of Arab Socialism with its radical and revolutionary rhetoric. Nor did it emerge out of a genuine interest in progressive egalitarianism; Arab Socialism originally evolved out of a virulent rightist nationalism. The praetorians' major aspirations were those of international prestige and power, regime dominance and political order at home, and the realization of corporate and middle-class interests. Economic policies were designed to serve these ends, with only secondary importance at best attaching to the realization of progressive change *per se* (Be'eri, pp. 122, 391–92, 398; Abdel-Malek, *passim;* Welch and Smith, p. 256).

Of the actual economic changes that the praetorians brought about, only those that struck at the predominance and privileges of the large land-

---

[36] For the argument that the Egyptian case parallels developments and motivations among other Middle Eastern countries governed by "radical-socialist" soldiers, Syria and Iraq in particular, see Be'eri, pp. 465–70 and *passim*.

owners and wealthy entrepreneurs could be called radical. Even then it must be recognized that these changes were in accord with corporate[37] and middle-class interests, without being of any direct benefit to the lower classes. Other actions notably improved the economic position of the lower class, but when seen in a larger context—i.e., the Egyptians being among the most ambitious of progressive-modernizing praetorians, and given the absence of a politicized lower class—this case bears out our major proposition. For if this is about the most that a military government has accomplished, there being very few others that approach the Egyptians in this regard, this case supports the generalization that soldiers rarely bring about major economic changes.[38]

[37] Recall the motivations behind the monarchy's overthrow that were discussed on pp. 71–72.

[38] With regard to the Egyptian praetorians' abilities as economic decision makers, there does not appear to be evidence of any financial or administrative bungling or of the adoption of any especially effective policies for the promotion of economic change. During the 1960s the governors worked to upgrade the skills of those officers who had been appointed to decision-making and managerial positions by encouraging them to take university courses and degrees in economics and business administration. This recognition of the inadequacies of military training and skills for economic decision making and management is quite uncharacteristic of the praetorians. It presumably helps account for the average 6 percent annual growth in GNP.

AN ASSESSMENT OF PRAETORIANISM AND ITS AFTERMATH

6

In this, the concluding chapter, we shall be considering three partly overlapping issues. First, it offers an overall assessment of praetorianism. We want to evaluate the impact of coups and the motivations behind them, the performance of military governments, as well as the (yet to be discussed) inheritance that military governments bequeath to their civilian successors. Such an evaluation serves as a convenient framework for summarizing much of this book. An assessment is also called for because praetorianism is an exceptionally important political phenomenon. More than two-thirds of the non-Western states have experienced military intervention since 1945, and others will surely do so in the near future. Military governments, like all types of governments, have a decided if not decisive impact upon numerous political and economic outcomes. Praetorianism raises basic normative issues about the governing of states insofar as it runs squarely up against liberalism's unqualified preference for regimes that are both civilian and democratic. And given an American foreign policy that features a continuing concern and varying levels of interference in the domestic politics of non-Western states that is often activated by military coups, we want to gauge the extent to which praetorianism is desirable from the vantage point of American interests.

This chapter also offers an analysis of the more or less beneficial legacy of military government. Praetorianism does not derive its importance solely from the seizure and exercise of governmental power. It also has important consequences for the polity after the soldiers withdraw to the barracks. Before doing so, military governors attempt to establish a certain type of civilian regime, while their actions and inactions as governors affect the problems, capabilities, and performance of the successor regimes. We shall be describing and accounting for some of the general political patterns that are often found in the aftermath of military government, then going on to utilize these as another basis for evaluating the phenomenon of praetorianism.

The third issue deals with the military itself after its withdrawal to the barracks. We want to characterize and account for the behavior of the officers under the successor regimes. Is the most frequent sequel to military government the acceptance of civilian control, the exercise of political power from the governmental sidelines as moderator-type praetorians, or a recurrence of military coups and governments? In what ways does the first coup and the subsequent governing experience affect the likelihood of future takeovers?

THE COUP D'ETAT: AN ASSESSMENT

The term praetorianism was adopted partly because it conveys an implicit message. The Praetorian Guards of the Roman Empire were one of the first and most famous military units to intrude into a clearly differentiated civilian political arena. They did so by overthrowing emperors and choosing their successors, who might be civilians or soldiers. And according to Gibbon's classic study, the intervention of the Praetorian Guards "was the first symptom and cause of the decline of the Roman Empire" (Gibbon, Vol. I, p. 91). In estimating the degree to which this negative judgment is also applicable to the coups of contemporary non-Western officers, our first reaction would probably be one of agreement. At first glance it may be quite easy to condemn military officers for overthrowing civilian governments.

A decidedly negative evaluation may be readily forthcoming since the coup contravenes the principles of legality, constitutionalism, and civility. The conspirators are almost invariably acting illegally, usually repudiating the government's constitutionally endowed authority, and always using less than civil means in threatening or employing force. The flouting of these principles becomes easier to condemn when the coup involves the overthrow of freely elected governments and eventuates in some measure of violence.

The condemnation of the coup on these grounds is buttressed by one of our major conclusions: coups are motivated by the defense or enhancement of the soldiers' corporate interests. Despite the praetorians' assertions to the contrary—despite their claims that they acted for public-spirited reasons on behalf of constitution and nation—almost all coups are at least partly, and usually primarily, inspired by the military's own interests. And while these interests pertain to the institution as a whole, it is clear that many individual officers derive special benefits from the realization of corporate interests in the way of rapid promotions, salary increases, and greater power and prestige, as well as opportunities to enrich themselves. We are thus back almost two thousand years to the Praetorian Guards whose decisions to support a particular emperor or to unseat him, to choose one man rather than another as emperor, were almost entirely the product of self-interested considerations. "Even the firmest and best established [emperors] were obliged to mix blandishments with commands, rewards with punishments, to flatter the pride of the Praetorians, indulge their pleasures, connive at their irregularities, and to purchase their precarious faith by a liberal donative, which . . . was exacted as a legal claim on the accession of every new emperor" (Gibbon, Vol. I, p. 92).

Yet these negative assessments cannot stand alone. There is another side to the balance sheet, which, when set against the first, does not necessarily warrant a negative assessment of the coup. When the coup is placed in its larger context and other considerations are introduced, it becomes difficult to criticize the military indiscriminately for the overthrow of civilian governments.

To begin with, it was seen that the military usually act against civilian governments that have evidenced one or more performance failures. If the praetorians are to be censured for their illegal, unconstitutional, and uncivil intervention, it must also be recognized that many of the civilian governments that they have overthrown are subject to comparable charges. These include blatant corruption at all levels of government, the unconstitutional extension of the government's powers and longevity, the excessively arbitrary application of the laws, and a reliance upon coercive measures to maintain themselves in power. It becomes easier to justify the overthrow of governments whose performance failures have lost them the respect of soldiers and civilians alike. As Gibbon tells us, after the Praetorian Guards were moved from the provinces to Rome, they came "to view the vices of their masters with familiar contempt, and to lay aside [their] reverential awe" (Gibbon, Vol. I, p. 92).

Then there is the crucial point that the military only act against less than legitimate governments. They do not attempt to overthrow governments to whom politicized civilians accord a moral right to govern, even when strongly motivated to do so on behalf of their corporate interests. Since the legitimacy factor is clearly one of the most important standards against which to evaluate all governments, it becomes difficult to condemn the praetorians for the overthrow of illegitimate and nonlegitimate governments.

These last observations may be broadened somewhat by saying that in many (perhaps most) instances a large proportion of politicized citizens are not offended by the government's demise, if not positively delighted with its overthrow. The praetorians may even be acting in accordance with the wishes of a majority of civilians. Indeed, in discussing the effect of the legitimacy factor upon their actions, we have seen that the soldiers attribute some importance to civilian opinion. They are reluctant to cross the "moral barrier" set up by the civilians.

Thus liberalism's condemnation of the coup, based upon the high value assigned to legality, constitutionalism, civility, and popular preferences, is largely neutralized by the less than "liberal" attributes of many or most of the civilian governments that have been overthrown. These observations also parallel Gibbon's statement that whatever its negative consequences, the intervention of the Praetorian Guards also constituted a "*symptom*" of the Roman Empire's decline. Or to use the language of Chapter 3, civilian performance failures and legitimacy deflations *facilitate* the coup by allowing or encouraging the transformation of interventionist motives into actions.

The other kind of criticism that can be leveled at the praetorians—that they intervene largely or purely for self-serving reasons—also encounters some difficulties. For if the soldiers are to be condemned for acting on behalf of their corporate interests, it should be shown that their behavior is generally more self-interested than that of the civilians whom they overthrew. Yet it is a basic fact of political life that most men pursue their own interests most of the time. There is little or no reason to suppose that officers are motivationally more self-serving than civilian elites—whether these be in executive, legislative, bureaucratic, or judicial institutions. Indeed, the interests of the military are no different from those of any other public institution, namely, adequate budgetary support, noninterference in its internal affairs, the absence of functional rivals, and the survival of the institution itself. The major variation is not in the basic motivations themselves, but in the presence or absence of the means for realizing them. It just so happens that soldiers have the guns to protect or enhance their interests. When civilian elites have the means to act in accordance with their interests they are just as prone to do so as the military, as seen in the numerous instances in which civilian governors have eliminated their institutional, partisan, and individual rivals.

And it is sometimes the self-serving actions of the civilians that prompt what might be called a defensively inspired coup. In order to enhance their own power positions and extend their incumbencies, civilian chief executives have challenged the autonomy and political neutrality of an officer corps which then reacted by force of arms. By granting promotions on the basis of personal and political loyalties, by injecting political ideas into the military, by appealing for the support of enlisted men, and by using the army against their political opponents, some incumbents not only acted in a highly self-serving manner. They also flouted military regulations, challenged the hierarchical imperative, and contravened the explicit or implicit constitutional basis of civilian supremacy. They shattered the liberal model of civilian control in which the officers acknowledge their subordinate position while the incumbents respect the autonomy and political neutrality of the military. Self-interested attempts by civilians to enhance the scope of their power at the expense of the army sparked self-interested but defensive actions by the army.

When evaluating political behavior in motivational terms it may be appropriate to go beyond the observer's interpretation of those motives to include the actors' self-perceptions as well. Whereas an outside observer may conclude that the behavior was prompted by self-serving goals, the political actors may view themselves quite differently. If they genuinely believe that their behavior is not exclusively or inordinately self-serving, then it may be somewhat more difficult to condemn them for their actions.

This evaluative perspective is particularly applicable to the coup makers. For they often believe themselves to be more effective governors than the civilians and regularly equate military interests with those of the nation-state, which allows for an easy self-justification of their actions. As suggested in Chapter 3, even blatantly self-serving interventionist actions are rarely seen as such by the praetorians themselves. The coup makers know that they are acting on behalf of their corporate interests, but they commonly equate these with those of the nation-state. It is only a partial exaggeration to say that in the minds of the coup makers their actions necessarily promote the national interest because they identify with the nation as sincere patriots, while the nation is identified with the military as the symbol and upholder of national honor, sovereignty, and power. This dual belief is deeply imbued in the minds of the officers from the moment they enter the military academy. They can thus easily interpret their actions positively, as beneficial for the nation. Although no conclusion is readily discernible, we can at least raise the real possibility that civilian leaders are less often able to justify their self-serving actions to themselves, since they have not consistently been socialized into this kind of thinking.

The praetorians are also able to interpret their actions as public spirited given the perceived contrast between themselves and the incumbents whom they have overthrown. On the one hand, there are the poorly performing and less than legitimate governments, which are seen to be staffed by inordinately self-serving, extremely partisan, amateurish politicians. On the other hand, the soldiers see themselves as highly competent, dedicated professionals, whose superior training and technical skills would make them far more competent governors than the incumbents. Believing themselves to possess these special abilities and virtues—both in absolute terms and relative to the incumbents—the praetorians can pursue their corporate interests in the expectation that intervention will redound to the public interest.

Indeed it is not unusual for the officers to believe that they are the only group that possesses the requisite governing qualities. Before succeeding to the presidency after Nasser's death in 1971, Sadat justified the Free Officers' coup which he helped lead in just these terms. "In 1952, the Egyptian revolution was in need of a new leadership . . . and where could the popular leadership of the Egyptian revolution have revealed itself? From where among the millions of enslaved Egyptians could have come the leaders who would turn their faces to the people and their backs to imperialism and the court? These were only the armed forces" (Be'eri, p. 472). This belief in the exclusive virtues and abilities of the military again takes us back to the Praetorian Guards. Their defenders also asked: "Where was the Roman people to be found . . . [whose] ancient and undoubted right" to select their governors had recently been usurped by the Roman Senate? "Not surely amongst the mixed multitude of slaves and strangers that filled the streets of Rome; a servile populace as devoid of spirit as destitute of property. The defenders of the state, selected from the flower of Italian youth, and trained in the exercise of arms and virtue, were the genuine representatives of the people, and the best entitled to elect the chief of the republic" (Gibbon, Vol. I, p. 92).

It is no easy matter to weigh up the two sides of the balance sheet in arriving at a firm positive or negative assessment of the coup itself. To do so requires not only a counting of the pros and cons. An evaluation also very much depends upon the relative importance assigned to them. Yet this discussion does allow for one fairly firm conclusion. Liberalism's outright and sweeping condemnation of the coup itself is not warranted. When placed in its total context, with the inclusion of additional factors, the praetorians' actions become defensible. However, this does not lead to the conclusion that coups are fully and consistently justifiable. Nor does an evaluation of praetorianism hinge solely, or indeed most importantly, upon the coup itself. The performance of military governments and the legacy that they leave to their civilian successors must also be taken into account.

GOVERNMENTAL PERFORMANCE: AN ASSESSMENT

The performance of governments refers to the extent to which they attain those goals and exhibit those operating features that are much desired by the populations themselves and seen as intrinsically desirable by outside observers. The performance dimensions along which we shall be comparing military and civilian governments are thought to be both highly desired and desirable. They were selected with several questions in mind: To what extent do the governors accept the most widely desired and desirable goals as their own responsibility? How successful are they in realizing them? Do they utilize accepted and acceptable means in attempting to do so? These questions "generated" five dimensions of governmental performance. We now want to compare the performance of military and civilian governments in terms of their legitimization, noncoercive rule, the

minimization of violence, responsiveness to popular wishes, and the generation of economic change.[1]

To state our conclusions at the outset, whereas civilian governments
are known·(or presumed) to be scattered along the entire length of each
of these performance dimensions, military governments tend to cluster at
the lower ends of the continua. In other words, it is not possible to generalize about the performance of the total universe of civilian governments—
which is hardly surprising given their enormous diversity—except to say
that varying proportions have attained high, medium, or low ratings on
each of the performance dimensions. In contrast, military governments
share a sufficient number of attitudinal, motivational, behavioral, and institutional features to permit some rough generalizations about their performance
characteristics. It then turns out that their performance is significantly and
almost consistently poorer than that of civilian governments.[2]

Governmental Legitimacy   Civilian governments
are found along the entire length of this continuum, some being legitimate,
nonlegitimate, and illegitimate. Those that have attained a legitimizing
mantle have relied upon rational-legal means, a traditional formula, or an
ideological appeal of a modernizing, egalitarian variety. In contrast, only a
small proportion of military governments have successfully utilized any of
the legitimizing formulas that are available to them. Almost the only formula
that is sometimes successfully employed by the praetorians portrays them
as temporary governors working toward the speedy restoration of civilian
rule. When the praetorians state their intention to withdraw in the very
near future, concomitantly making these statements credible by their actions, politicized civilians may accord them the moral right to govern, and
then only temporarily.

Noncoercive Rule   Both military and civilian gov-
ernments frequently use coercive measures against their critics, rivals, and
opponents in order to maintain themselves in power. But the praetorians do
so more often. Whereas a significant number of non-Western governments
allow for the expression of grievances in the press, demonstrations, and
strikes, the complete or partial closure of all military regimes means that

[1] With regard to each of these, it is thought that governments can have at least
a partial impact upon them, if they choose to make the effort. A sixth commonly
accepted performance criterion, that of regime stability, is not included here because the longevity of regimes *per se* is not thought to be highly desired or
desirable. If it had been included, the conclusions that follow would have been
strengthened since military regimes are far less stable than civilian ones.

[2] Having already explicitly or implicitly analyzed military governments in terms
of our five performance dimensions, the following comparisons with their civilian
counterparts may be offered in a summary fashion.

the praetorians more frequently utilize negative sanctions against those critics and opponents who attempt to express their grievances. Moreover, we may confidently infer that governments without a legitimizing mantle regularly resort to coercive measures to maintain their power against those politicized individuals, groups, and organizations who oppose them. Given the regularity with which the praetorians fail to legitimize their power, both in absolute terms and relative to civilian governments, they more often rely upon forceful measures as a substitute for the voluntary acceptance of their authority.

The Minimization of Violence   Political violence most commonly stems from communal conflicts, class conflicts, and coercive rule. With regard to the outcome of severe communal conflicts, the record of civilian governments is not an especially enviable one. Yet we have seen that the praetorians are even less successful in averting the translation of conflict situations into violent outcomes. In fact, the deadliest communal violence of the post-1945 period occurred under the auspices of military governments. Among the non-Western countries class-based violence is most often found in Latin America, and it increases steadily as the military exercises greater political power. The twenty Latin American countries have been classified according to the level of military intervention for each year between 1951 and 1965, and from another source we have data on the number of persons who died in domestic political clashes in each of these years (Putnam, p. 109; Taylor and Hudson, pp. 110–15). In bringing these two variables together we find that an average of 71 Latin Americans were killed annually in each of those countries in which the civilians were in control. This average death rate increases to 84 in those years and countries where the military played a moderator-type role. It then jumps further to 122 for those years in which the soldiers controlled the governments of their countries. In short, the average number of deaths, many or most of them relating to class-based conflicts, is 70 percent greater during those years in which Latin American officers were sitting in the governmental saddle than when they remained under civilian control. The third major determinant of the level of violence is the governments' application of coercive measures (e.g., press censorship and restrictions upon political activities). Indeed, there is an extraordinarily strong relationship between the two variables—a path coefficient of .82, which also happens to be nearly twice as high as that of some dozen other factors that could plausibly account for the incidence of violence (Hibbs, pp. 180–95).[3] And we have just noted that mili-

---

[3] This statistic represents a valid empirical relationship even after Hibbs has taken into account the other part of the relationship in which violence occurs first, which then impels the governors to employ negative sanctions. Since

tary governments more often resort to these coercive measures that promote violence than their civilian counterparts.

Popular Responsiveness   Civilian governments are scattered along the entire continuum in terms of their responsiveness to popular aspirations and demands. No generalization is possible about the proportion of civilian governments found at the high, medium, and low points of this continuum. But whatever the performance of civilian governments in this regard, that of military governments is less adequate. And this for two reasons. By no means do all people want to participate in politics. Even a distinct majority may not value the opportunity to play some part in selecting their governors and influencing governmental policies. But for those who want to do so—be they a smaller or larger proportion of the population—military governments are more often unresponsive to these wishes or demands than civilian governments. Whereas a significant number of non-Western civilian regimes allow for mass participation and open competition for high offices,[4] the authoritarian (or closed) structure of all military regimes obviates their responsiveness to popular desires for political participation. Second, civilian governments vary considerably in the extent to which their policies are responsive to the interests of majorities or minorities. There is less variation among military governments. For the praetorians tend to act in accordance with the interests of the middle class—a class that constitutes a miniscule or small minority in almost all non-Western societies.

Economic Change   There are no significant differences in the success of military and civilian governments in promoting economic growth, as measured primarily by the rate of increase in per capita GNP. But they do vary in both the frequency and the extent to which they have brought about economic changes of a modernizing and progressive kind. Whereas a significant number of civilian governments have done so, only a handful of military governments even attempted to bring about such changes. And these changes have rarely been of a radical or structural variety.

Thus, unlike our assessment of the coup, which did not eventuate in a conclusive evaluation, on the whole military governments "score" sig-

---

Hibbs's data include both Western and non-Western states, the analysis was redone using only the seventy-nine non-Western ones, for which the path coefficient rises slightly to .86.

[4] Fifteen non-Western civilian regimes were identified that permitted mass participation and opposition circa 1969 (Dahl, p. 248).

nificantly lower than their civilian counterparts on each of the five performance dimensions.

THE
LEGACY:
PATTERNS,
EXPLANATIONS,
AND
ASSESSMENTS

Having turned power over to the civilians, how have the former military governors helped shape the contours of the successor regimes? This question may be conveniently divided into two parts. The first deals with the praetorians' purposeful decisions to shape the successor regime's structure. These almost always involve the establishment of more or less open regimes. The second aspect of the legacy that military governments have bequeathed to their successors is more general. It includes the military governments' impact upon the various problems with which the civilian governors are subsequently faced and their capabilities for handling them effectively. In this section we shall then be describing, explaining, and evaluating the characteristic legacy of military governments, the inheritance they have left behind them.

THE ESTABLISHMENT OF OPEN REGIMES

In the great majority of cases authoritarian military regimes are replaced by more or less open (or democratic) civilian regimes. While still in power the officers regularly opt for the establishment of successor regimes that allow for considerable political competition and popular electoral participation in choosing among the competitors, be they political parties or individual politicians. Prior to their withdrawal the praetorians sometimes appoint a commission, or arrange for the election of a convention, to draft a democratic constitution. National elections for executive and legislative offices are held just before or immediately after the soldiers disengage.

At first glance this may very well appear to be a curious pattern. Do not the officers' attitudes toward political order, political activity, and the governing of states, as well as their concern for the protection of corporate and middle-class interests, run counter to the creation of open regimes featuring mass participation in the competitive struggle for public office? Would these attitudinal preferences and interests not be better realized within the framework of an authoritarian or a mobilization regime? Perhaps so. Yet there are several considerations that account for the regularity with which the praetorians allow, encourage, or work for the creation of more or less open regimes.

To begin with the military's corporate interests, these may of course be threatened by the elected chief executives of open regimes. But the possibility is somewhat greater with regard to the leaders of authoritarian and mobilization regimes. They are more prone to challenge military interests because of the greater scope and more exclusive concentration of power in their hands, which is to remain uncircumscribed and will perhaps be expanded. The officer corps tends to be seen as a rival. All the more so since the officers almost invariably act as moderator-type praetorians after their disengagement.[5] A military that asserts its right to influence or check governmental decisions constitutes an undesired contender for power—power that the leaders of authoritarian and mobilization regimes in particular intend to exercise in an exclusive manner. They consequently have an incentive to try to undermine the political position of the military, which at a minimum constitutes an indirect challenge to its corporate interests.

Even if the leaders of authoritarian and mobilization regimes are no more inclined to act against the military than those of open regimes, they are better situated to do so. Given the fewer limitations upon their power, they are better able to politicize the officer corps by promoting their partisan or personal supporters. Due to the greater concentration of power in their hands they are better placed to penetrate the military with political ideas and personnel.[6] And the leaders of authoritarian and mobilization regimes more often control political parties or movements that can be transformed into functional rivals to the military. These can serve as the organizational basis for the formation or expansion of civilian militias which would infringe upon the officers' professional standing, near monopoly of force, and political power.

If the military believes that a freely elected government is likely to challenge its corporate interests, but still prefers an open regime for reasons discussed below, the praetorians are usually able to exact certain guarantees before disengaging. Despite a desire to return to the barracks, the military is not about to do so without first obtaining satisfactory assurances when its corporate interests are thought to be threatened by the successor government.

In Ghana, for example, a military that intervened to fend off Nkrumah's concerted attempts to penetrate the officer corps took the unusual step of having certain guarantees written into the constitution of the Second Republic prior to the transfer of power. The constitution, which served as the democratic blueprint for the successor regime, also guaranteed the military's autonomy by establishing an Armed Forces Council made up solely

---

[5] See the following section of this chapter.

[6] Here it should also be recalled that the penetration model of civilian control has only been applied in regimes with a single locus of power—a condition that is not satisfied in open regimes, whereas it is often found in authoritarian and mobilization regimes. See p. 18.

of officers, with exclusive responsibility for managing all aspects of the military's internal affairs. The Turkish military did not allow the legislature to convene after the 1965 elections until it had been assured that its past actions would not be publicly criticized, and that those officers who were forced to retire for opposing the military government would not be permitted to return to active duty, since this would adversely affect military unity (Yalman, p. 140). The military government of Guatemala did not allow the president-elect to assume office after the 1966 election until he had agreed that the officers would be given a free hand in all military matters, including powers normally exercised by the civilian president—the selection of the minister of defense and the chief of staff (Weaver, p. 6).

The establishment of open regimes is generally compatible with the economic and political interests of the middle class. Its leaders can quite confidently expect to attain a prominent and probably a predominant position within the governments of most open regimes. This is especially so in the least economically modernized countries. For not only does the negligible politicization of workers and peasants obviate a threat from below, while in power the military have probably weakened if not neutralized the power of the traditional oligarchy in pursuit of corporate and middle-class interests. Although the situation is quite different in societies featuring a politicized lower class, capable of translating numbers into political power within the context of an open regime, the middle-class minority is not without advantages and resources which can be used to attain considerable political leverage. Compared with their lower-class rivals, middle-class leaders are often more experienced politically. Its wealthier members occupy economically strategic positions which can be translated into political coin, its members are more highly politicized, and its parties are frequently better financed and more cohesive. These factors provide middle-class parties and candidates with decided if not decisive advantages in the competition for legislative and executive offices.

The military governors may be less than enthusiastic about ushering in an open regime, given their inordinate concern for political order and bias against mass political activity. Yet it turns out that these attitudinal preferences are *more* likely to be realized by the establishment of an open regime. There may well be a good deal of governmental instability, political turmoil, severe conflict, and perhaps violence within such a regime, but to try to usher in an authoritarian or mobilization regime would markedly increase the probabilities of such undesired outcomes. For in attempting to do so the praetorians would be acting contrary to more or less widespread popular preferences.

In the post-1945 period the rational-legal principles of constitutionalism, regularized competition for governmental officers, and popular participation in choosing the "winners" have emerged as a widely preferred legitimizing formula. The praetorians themselves helped turn such preferences into expectations and demands by justifying military government as a temporary expedient to prepare the country for democratic rule.[7] In addition, both the middle class and the politicized lower classes generally prefer an open regime in which they have the opportunity to flex their political muscles. They and their political leaders do not want to be bound by the heavy-handed restrictions of authoritarian or mobilization regimes.[8] And to this should be added a simple but basic fact: while particular classes or communal segments may very well prefer something other than an open regime, they are not about to reach an agreement with their rivals as to who shall control it. An authoritarian or a mobilization regime would consequently have to be imposed by one section of the population upon the other, which is likely to eventuate in just those disorderly and violent outcomes that the praetorians want to avoid. The soldiers might then also be left with the unpalatable task of restoring order as "unprofessional" policemen.

Those military governors who are particularly concerned about the unhappy consequences of mass participation and competition sometimes impose certain restrictions upon their successors prior to disengagement. Just as they have obtained guarantees regarding their corporate interests, they have exacted other kinds of assurances when anxious about the realization of their attitudinal preferences and middle-class interests. These include restrictions upon the kinds of political appeals that may be made by the competing parties; the exclusion of "objectionable" parties and leaders from the electoral process; and the promulgation of electoral laws and arrangements that are advantageous to the "acceptable" political parties. By imposing such restrictions the praetorians are, of course, turning the successor regimes into less than fully open ones. In some instances the restrictions are so fundamental that it becomes difficult to classify the new regime as open or closed, as in the Guatemalan case where only a single candidate was allowed to "compete" in the 1966 presidential election.

---

[7] This statement also applies to the time when ruler-type praetorians disengage. For they too have portrayed their rule as a temporary expedient, although adding the crucial caveat that the changes that have to be made are so fundamental that it will be a long time before the country is prepared for democracy. For a discussion of the current "debate" about disengagement within Brazil's ruler-type regime, see Sanders (1975A).

[8] Of sixty-four Nigerian politicians who were asked whether "a one-party state [is] desirable or feasible" after the military disengaged, only one said yes (Bienen, forthcoming, Chapter 7).

SOME GENERAL CONSEQUENCES OF MILITARY GOVERNMENT

This then is the inheritance that military governments have purposefully bestowed upon their successors—the establishment of open regimes, with possibly some restrictions upon mass participation and competition. We now turn to the second part of the legacy—the general impact that military governments have had upon the problems confronting the successor regimes and their capabilities for dealing with them. Although we cannot generalize about the operating features and performance characterictics of these regimes, it is possible to identify some of the ways in which they are affected by the actions and inactions of the previous military governments.

To begin with, how have the democratic features of the successor regimes been affected by the former military governments? To what extent have the praetorians made good their claim to be serving as the midwife of democracy, justifying military government as necessary for the regeneration of the polity to allow for stable and effective democratic rule? The praetorians have been called "iron surgeons" because of their intention of restoring the body politic to good health, combined with a reliance upon force and determination in doing so. Witness the statement of South Korea's General Park upon taking power in 1961: "The military revolution is not the destruction of democracy in Korea. Rather, it is a way of saving it; it is a surgical operation intended to excise a malignant social, political and economic tumor. The revolution was staged with the compassion of a benevolent surgeon who sometimes must cause pain in order to preserve life and restore health" (Se-Jin Kim, 1971, p. 108).

Surgery is needed in many instances. But the "iron surgeons" regularly cut in the wrong places. The performance of democratic governments —particularly their legitimacy and popular responsiveness—very much depends upon the existence of fairly well organized political parties with significant grass-roots support. Yet this is exactly what has been weakened or "cut out" with the closure of military regimes. The scores of objectionable political leaders and activists that some military governments have eliminated obviously cannot be revived or quickly replaced. The political parties and organizations that have been emasculated, banned, or destroyed cannot be easily reconstituted, especially where the rapid withdrawal of the military has not allowed civilian politicians sufficient time to regroup and reorganize themselves. Nor is the regeneration of a meaningful party politics abetted by the praetorians' public disparagement of politics, politicians, and political parties, which may well have made the civilians more reluctant to participate in the competitive political process that constitutes the linchpin of democratic regimes.

In attempting to restore the polity to good health, the praetorians not only claim to be "iron surgeons." Some military governments also portray their role in a positive fashion as "democratic tutors," as governors who aim to engender appropriate democratic attitudes and behaviors. But even those who make this kind of claim rarely act upon it. The praetorians are quick to cut, but disinterested or negligent in replacing that which has been excised from the body politic. To continue with the rhetoric of the South Korean governors, the structures that were purportedly designed to prepare the country for democracy were labeled "Administrative Democracy." Yet it is hard to see how the substitution of "administration" for "politics" can help form democratic attitudes and behavior that relate to participation, competition, and partisanship.

If it is to occur, political learning requires the appropriate opportunities and lessons, which are hardly forthcoming within the context of authoritarian regimes where decisions are made and orders issued from above. The fact of regime closure, under whatever democratic, participatory, or populist facade, does not, in fact, allow the governors to act as "democratic tutors." As Be'eri has pointed out, the Middle Eastern praetorians say that the people have "not yet matured for a democratic life, they should be educated for it. [Yet] there is no worse educational system than beatings and orders. You can only learn to swim in water. Dictators regard their people with contempt and suspicion; independent forces are regarded as factors leading to destruction and anarchy." Rather than encourage the seedlings of democracy—the country's independent and creative elements—the praetorians "pulverized them with the regimentation of dictatorship" (Be'eri, p. 471). [9]

What then of the effects that military governments have had upon the problems confronting the civilian governors and their capabilities for dealing with them? The soldiers have sometimes mitigated some of the "sores" on the body politic: blatant corruption, extreme partisanship, inordinately coercive rule, and turmoil. On occasion the praetorians have also neutralized the political and economic power of narrowly based traditional oligarchies. But except for the latter kind of change, the others are usually shallow or temporary. Recall that guardian-type praetorians, with their limited objectives, are far more common than ruler types. The goals of most military governments thus relate solely to the tips of the political and economic ice-

[9] However, the repressive aspects of military regimes may help instill a greater appreciation of democratic structures, leading civilian rivals to be more cooperative in maintaining them after the soldiers disengage. The leaders of the major parties in Venezuela learned this lesson while the military were in power between 1948 and 1958, and applied it successfully after 1958 by reducing the intensity of partisan conflict and accepting the rules of democratic competition (Levine, pp. 42–43).

bergs which constitute the country's most pressing problems. And due to the short duration of most military regimes there is insufficient time for the consolidation of whatever beneficial changes may have been implemented. It takes more than a few years for new attitudinal, behavioral, and institutional patterns to take root.

In addition, the relatively poor performance of military governments means that the successor governments are usually faced with problems that are at least as severe as those that confronted their civilian predecessors before the takeover. Not having markedly improved the rate of economic growth, and having rarely brought about major economic changes of a modernizing and progressive variety, the praetorians have not eased the problems of material scarcities and inequities. Nor have the politically inflammable offshoots of these problems been mitigated. The inadequate responsiveness of military governments to large sections, if not the majority, of the population has probably intensified conflicts with which the civilian successors are now confronted. Given their poor record in preventing the violent eruption of class and communally based conflicts, the praetorians have sometimes endowed the civilians with the ravishes and revengeful memories of past violence. In fact, the level of violence in one decade is strongly related to the number of deaths from domestic political conflict in the previous decade (Hibbs, p. 181). Somewhat paradoxically, the poor performance of military governments in relying upon coercive measures is of some benefit to the successor governments. For there is a significant association between the application of coercive measures in one decade and a lower level of violence in the following one (Hibbs, p. 181). [10]

How then evaluate the legacy of military governments? Upon their withdrawal they have almost invariably sponsored the establishment of open regimes. But in some cases these have been encumbered with restrictions which make them less than fully open to mass participation and competition. Furthermore, during their tenure in office the soldiers have done virtually nothing to strengthen the democratic institutions they have sponsored, simultaneously acting in ways that significantly undercut their potential legitimacy and popular responsiveness. And due to their inadequate performance, military governments have not eased and often exacerbated, the problems confronting the successor governments, without having enhanced their capabilities for dealing with them.

We can now offer an *overall* assessment of praetorianism. With regard to the coup itself, the positive and negative sides of the ledger tend to balance each other. But the performance of military governments, which is the single most important basis for evaluating praetorianism, was seen to be dis-

---

[10] Both of Hibbs's findings are almost identcal for the non-Western states alone.

tinctly and consistently negative relative to that of civilian governments. And we have just seen that the inheritance that the soldiers have bequeathed to the civilians is not a beneficial one; in some important respects it is markedly negative. Although there are of course exceptions, this analysis leads us to place a distinctly negative evaluative stamp on the actions and consequences of military governments. On the whole, military intervention turns out to be less than desirable.

THE AFTERMATH: MORE OF THE SAME   In this, the final selection of the book, we will be looking at the behavior of the officers after they have relinquished power to the civilians. In doing so we shall be coming full circle in the study of praetorianism. For the most frequent sequel to military coups and government is more of the same. After disengaging, the officers almost invariably play an important political role as moderator-type praetorians. Some successor regimes may be more accurately described as mixed civilian-military regimes. And then sooner or later—usually sooner— the soldiers regularly return to the center of the political stage by overthrowing the civilian incumbents and taking up the mantle of government once again. Where the soldiers have once assumed the highest offices, the most common subsequent pattern is an alternation between civilian and military regimes, with the officers almost always remaining within the political elite as moderator types when the government is headed by civilians. The aftermath of military intervention is military intervention.

The recurring pattern of military coups and governments is strikingly evidenced among the Latin American countries. These have been classified according to the level of intervention for each year between 1951 and 1965 (Putnam, p. 109). In eleven countries the military that occupied the seats of government had disengaged prior to 1965; in eight of these eleven cases the soldiers had already taken up the reins of government again by 1965. Fully 70 percent of the Latin American praetorians who turned power over to the civilians subsequently took it back within a short time. On the average, they did so within six years after disengaging. The recurring pattern of military takeovers is also suggested by a quantitative study showing that the single most important "determinant" of the coups that occurred between 1958 and 1967 is the incidence of coups during the previous ten-year period (Hibbs, pp. 109, 189–90).[11] Although the data refer to coups rather than military governments, it is fairly safe to surmise that the statistical association largely represents a pattern of coups, military governments, and disen-

---

[11] The same conclusion emerged from a reanalysis of the data for the non-Western states alone.

gagement during one decade, followed by coups and military governments in the next decade.

The most important explanations for the recurring pattern of military intervention have already been set out in Chapter 3. For the motivations and facilitating conditions that account for the first coup are not markedly different from those that explain subsequent takeovers. However, there are several considerations that pertain specifically to the second and third coups. These additional factors not only help account for the recurring pattern of intervention. They also suggest that the probability of military government is somewhat greater in those countries that have already experienced a hearty dose of praetorianism. Whatever the likelihood of a takeover in countries that have not experienced military government, the probability is somewhat higher in those that have already done so.

In Chapter 1 it was said that the officers' internalization of the civilian ethic provides something of a barrier to intervention. Soldiers who subscribe to the normative belief in civilian supremacy are less likely to intervene; a decidedly consequential challenge to their corporate interests is required for them to overcome the attitudinal disposition to accept civilian control. The recurring pattern of intervention, as well as the heightened probability of takeovers after the military has already done so, is partly explained by the weakening of the civilian ethic after the first coup. No matter how strongly internalized the principle of civilian control may have been prior to the first takeover, it will be a long time before it is strongly reasserted. To the extent that soldiers accept the principle of civilian control in the aftermath of military government, they do so in a diluted, conditional manner. Future takeovers are a "thinkable" possibility, depending upon the actions of the civilian governors.

Having come full circle in our study, it would be well to illustrate this generalization by returning to the Ghanaian case discussed in Chapter 1. It was only with the greatest difficulty that a small group of Ghanaian officers overcame their commitment to the principle of civilian supremacy in overthrowing Nkrumah. Yet while the military was still in power, one of the leading conspirators behind the first coup was already writing about the possibility of overthrowing the next civilian government. When General Ocran stated that the military would not remain "politically indifferent" under a future civilian regime, he explicitly set aside the previously unquestioned assumption of civilian supremacy. The acceptance of civilian rule became conditional. Whether the Ghanaian army would "take up arms again . . . depends very much on the showing of the next civilian government. In the final analysis it is the future government's performance that will either keep the soldiers in the barracks or bring them out again, rifle in hand, to seize power" (Ocran, p. 94). They did just that in 1972, after three years of civilian rule.

This quotation also illustrates other changes that have occurred since the original takeover. Having successfully carried out one coup, the officer corps is now more confident of its ability to carry out another. What was done before can be done again. And whereas the officer corps may or may not have been acting as moderator-type praetorians prior to the first coup, after relinquishing power the officer corps almost invariably plays a moderator-type role. In the post-1945 period there have been only two Latin American officer corps (those of Venezuela and Colombia) that accepted civilian supremacy after returning to the barracks. None are found in Asia, Africa, and the Middle East. It is much easier to move from a moderator-type practorianism to the seizure of power than to do so after serving as a politically neutral or "politically indifferent" officer corps.

Subsequent takeovers also become more likely due to the less than valuable inheritance that military governments have commonly bequeathed to the successor governments. These are faced with problems and conflicts which are at least as severe as those that indirectly contributed to the overthrow of their civilian predecessors. With the military governors not having made it any easier for their successors to govern effectively, and in some ways having made it harder, civilian performance failures and legitimacy deflations that helped bring about the first coup are likely to be at least as frequent and serious.

On the other hand, there are two factors that might help reduce the frequency of successive takeovers. The civilian incumbents may have learned that challenges to the military's corporate interests are bound to engender strong interventionist motives. The successor governments may thus be more alert and wary about treading upon this dangerous terrain. Yet political learning—like any other kind—requires more than a single lesson. Civilian elites may have to "go to school" more than once before becoming fully sensitive to the military's abiding concern for its interests. Moreover, even if the lesson has been learned, civilian governments may infringe upon military interests in the belief that circumstances have changed sufficiently since the original coup to allow them to do so with impunity. Alterations in the distribution of political power may have prompted the belief that the civilian incumbents can say no to the soldiers without their acting upon their interventionist motives. The incumbents might also be so strongly prodded by their own political supporters to act contrary to military interests that they are left with little choice but to do just that.

With regard to the soldiers, their inclinations to take up the reins of government again have probably been weakened by their first experience in office. The governing of states turned out to be far more difficult than originally thought, the preferred governing style was seen to be inappropriate, the officers saw themselves becoming like the less than respectable politicians, the cohesiveness of the officer corps was threatened—these and other considerations prompted the praetorians to return to the barracks. The recollection and acceptance of the lasting reality of these factors may then make for a greater reluctance to undertake subsequent interventions. On the other hand, there is no reason to suppose that military officers are quicker to learn their lessons than are civilian elites. They too may forget the past or believe that circumstances have changed sufficiently to make for a quite different governing experience in the future. Those senior officers who have learned their lessons may soon be replaced by a new group of commanders. But even if more reluctant to take up the reins of government the second or third time around, the soldiers will certainly be motivated to do just that if their corporate interests are jeopardized.

Thus both the evidence and the underlying reasoning clearly suggest that the most common aftermath of military government is military government. Whatever else the foreseeable future may bring, two fundamental aspects of political life will surely not change: the soldiers will frequently wield their guns as praetorian soldiers, and they will do so on behalf of their corporate interests.

SELECTED BIBLIOGRAPHY

ABDEL-MALEK, ANOUAR, *Egypt: Military Society*. New York: Random House, 1968.

ABRAHAMSSON, BENGT, *Military Professionalism and Political Power*. Beverly Hills: Sage Publications, 1972.

ADAMS, RICHARD N., "The Development of the Guatemalan Military," *Studies in Comparative International Development*, No. 5, 1968–69.

ADELMAN, IRMA, AND CYNTHIA TAFT MORRIS, *Society, Politics and Economic Development: A Quantitative Approach*. Baltimore: Johns Hopkins, 1967.

AFRIFA, A. A., *The Ghana Coup*. London: Frank Cass, 1966.

ANDRESKI, STANISLAV, *Military Organization and Society*. Berkeley: University of California Press, 1968.

ASTIZ, CARLOS ALBERTO, *Pressure Groups and Power Elites in Peruvian Politics*. Ithaca: Cornell University Press, 1969A.

——, "The Argentine Armed Forces: Their Role and Political Involvement," *Western Political Quarterly*, December 1969B.

ASTIZ, CARLOS ALBERTO AND JOSÉ Z. GARCÍA, "The Peruvian Military: Achievement Orientation, Training and Political Tendencies," *Western Political Quarterly*, December 1972.

BADGLEY, JOHN H., "Two Styles of Military Rule: Thailand and Burma," *Government and Opposition*, Winter 1969.

BARBER, WILLARD F., AND RONNING C. NEALE, *Internal Security and Military Power: Counterinsurgency and Civic Action in Latin America*. Columbus: Ohio State University Press, 1966.

BEBLER, ANTON, *Military Rule in Africa: Dahomey, Ghana, Sierra Leone, and Mali*. New York: Praeger, 1973.

BE'ERI, ELIEZER, *Army Officers in Arab Politics and Society*. New York: Praeger, 1970.

BELL, M. J. V., "The Military in the New States of Africa," in Jacques van Doorn, ed., *Armed Forces and Society: Sociological Essays*. The Hague: Mouton, 1968.

BELTRÁN, VIRGILIO RAFAEL, "The Army and Structural Changes in 20th Century Argentina: An Initial Approach," in Jacques van Doorn, ed., *Armed Forces and Society*. The Hague: Mouton, 1968.

BEN-DOR, GABRIEL, "Civilianization of Military Regimes in the Arab World," *Armed Forces and Society,* Spring 1975.

BERNSTEIN, HARRY, *Venezuela and Colombia.* Englewood Cliffs, N.J.: Prentice-Hall, 1964.

BESHIR, MOHAMMED OMER, *The Southern Sudan: Background to Conflict.* New York: Praeger, 1968.

BIENEN, HENRY, *Tanzania: Party Transformation and Economic Development.* Princeton: Princeton University Press, 1970.

——, "Transition from Military Rule: The Case of Western State Nigeria," *Armed Forces and Society,* Spring 1975.

——, *Politics and Politicians in a Military Regime: The Western State Nigeria,* forthcoming.

BIENEN, HENRY, AND DAVID MORELL, "Transition from Military Rule: Thailand's Experience," in Catherine McArdle Kelleher, ed., *Political-Military Systems: Comparative Perspectives.* Beverly Hills: Sage Publications, 1974.

BRETTON, HENRY L., *Power and Politics in Africa.* Chicago: Aldine, 1973.

BRILL, WILLIAM H., *Military Intervention in Bolivia: The Overthrow of Paz Estenssoro and the MNR.* Washington, D.C.: Institute for the Comparative Study of Political Systems, 1967.

CHICK, J. D., AND A. A. MAZRUI, "The Nigerian Army and African Images of the Military," in Morris Janowitz and Jacques van Doorn, eds., *On Military Intervention.* Rotterdam: Rotterdam University Press, 1971.

COHEN, STEPHEN B., *The Indian Army: Its Contribution to the Development of a Nation.* Berkeley: University of California Press, 1971.

COLLINS, ROBERT O., "The Sudan: Link to the North," in Stanley Diamond and Fred G. Burke, eds., *The Transformation of East Africa.* New York: Basic Books, 1966.

COX, THOMAS S., *Civil-Military Relations in Sierra-Leone: A Case Study of African Soldiers in Politics.* Cambridge, Mass.: Harvard University Press, 1976.

CROUCH, HAROLD, "Generals and Business in Indonesia," *Pacific Affairs,* No. 4, 1975–76.

DAHL, ROBERT A., *Polyarchy: Participation and Opposition.* New Haven: Yale University Press, 1971.

DANN, URIEL, *Iraq under Qassem: A Political History, 1958–1963.* New York: Praeger, 1969.

DECALO, SAMUEL, *Coups and Army Rule in Africa: Studies in Military Style.* New Haven: Yale University Press, 1976.

DE IMAZ, JOSÉ LUIS, *Los que mandan.* Buenos Aires: Editorial Universitaria de Buenos Aires, 1964.

DENT, M. J., "The Military and Politics: A Study of the Relation between the Army and the Political Process in Nigeria," in Robert Melson and Howard Wolpe, eds., *Nigeria: Modernization and the Politics of Communalism.* Lansing: Michigan State University Press, 1971.

DI TELLA, TORCUATO, *El sistema político argentina y la clase obrera.* Buenos Aires: Editorial Universitaria de Buenos Aires, 1964.

DIX, ROBERT H., *Colombia: The Political Dimensions of Change.* New Haven: Yale University Press, 1967.

DOMÍNGUEZ, JORGE I., "The Civic Soldier in Cuba," in Catherine McArdle Kelleher, ed., *Political-Military Systems: Comparative Perspectives.* Beverly Hills: Sage Publications, 1974.

DONNISON, F. S. V., *Burma*. New York: Praeger, 1970.

DOWSE, ROBERT E., "The Military and Political Development," in Colin Leys, ed., *Politics and Change in Developing Countries*. Cambridge: Cambridge University Press, 1969.

DUBOIS, VICTOR, "Zaire under President Sese Seko Mobutu: The Return to Authenticity," American Universities Fieldstaff Reports, Central and Southern Africa Series, XVII, No. 1, 1973.

DUDLEY, B. J., "The Military and Politics in Nigeria: Some Reflections," in Jacques van Doorn, ed., *Military Profession and Military Regimes*. The Hague: Mouton, 1969.

DUPREE, LOUIS, "The Military is Dead! Long Live the Military," American Universities Fieldstaff Reports, South Asia Series, XIII, No. 3, 1969.

ECKSTEIN, HARRY, "On the Etiology of Internal Wars," *History and Theory*, No. 4, 1965.

EINAUDI, LUIGI, "Revolution from Within? Military Rule in Peru since 1968," *Studies in Comparative International Development*, Spring 1973.

EINAUDI, LUIGI, AND ALFRED STEPAN, *Latin American Institutional Development: Changing Military Perspectives in Peru and Brazil*. Santa Monica: Rand Corporation, 1971.

FEIT, EDWARD, *The Armed Bureaucrats: Military-Administrative Regimes and Political Development*. Boston: Houghton Mifflin, 1973.

FINER, S. E., *The Man on Horseback: The Role of the Military in Politics*. New York: Praeger, 1962.

FIRST, RUTH, *Power in Africa*. New York: Pantheon, 1970.

FOSSUM, EGON, "Factors Influencing the Occurrence of Military Coups d'Etat in Latin America," *Journal of Peace Research*, No. 3, 1967.

FRANDA, MARCUS F., "The Bangladesh Coup," American Universities Fieldstaff Reports, South Asia Series, XIX, No. 15, 1975.

GIBBON, EDWARD, *The Decline and Fall of the Roman Empire*, 2 vols. New York: Modern Library, 1957.

GRIFFITH, SAMUEL B., *The Chinese People's Liberation Army*. New York: McGraw-Hill, 1967.

GUTTERIDGE, WILLIAM F., *The Military in African Politics*. London: Methuen, 1969.

——, "Military Elites in Nigeria and Ghana," *African Forum*, No. 2, 1966.

GUYOT, JAMES F., "Political Involution in Burma," *Journal of Comparative Administration*, November 1970.

HALPERN, MANFRED, *The Politics of Social Change in the Middle East and North Africa*. Princeton: Princeton University Press, 1963.

HANNA, WILLARD A., "A Primer of Korupsi," American Universities Fieldstaff Reports, Southeast Asia Series, XIX, No. 8, 1971.

HEITOWEIT, HENRY, "Regionalism and Public Policy Making in Pakistan: The Failure of Development from Above," paper presented at the 1972 Annual Meeting of the American Political Science Association, Washington, D.C.

HENDERSON, GREGORY, *Korea: The Politics of the Vortex*. Cambridge, Mass.: Harvard University Press, 1968.

HIBBS, DOUGLAS A., *Mass Political Violence: A Cross-National Causal Analysis*. New York: John Wiley, 1973.

HIGGOTT, RICHARD, AND FINN FUGLESTAD, "The 1974 Coup d'Etat in Niger: Towards an Explanation," *Journal of Modern African Studies*, September 1975.

HOADLEY, J. STEPHEN, *Soldiers and Politics in Southeast Asia: Civil-Military Relations in Comparative Perspective*. Cambridge, Mass.: Schenkman, 1975.

HUNTINGTON, SAMUEL P., *The Soldier and the State: The Theory and Politics of Civil-Military Relations*. New York: Random House, 1957.

———, *Political Order in Changing Societies*. New Haven: Yale University Press, 1968.

HUREWITZ, J. C., *Middle East Politics: The Military Dimension*. New York: Praeger, 1969.

ISSAWI, CHARLES, *Egypt in Revolution*. London: Methuen, 1963.

JAHAN, ROUNAQ, "Ten Years of Ayub Khan and the Problem of National Integration," *Journal of Comparative Administration*, November 1970.

JANOWITZ, MORRIS, *The Military in the Political Development of New Nations*. Chicago: University of Chicago Press, 1964.

———, "The Comparative Analysis of Middle Eastern Military Institutions," in Morris Janowitz and Jacques van Doorn, eds., *On Military Intervention*. Rotterdam: Rottterdam University Press, 1971.

JAQUETTE, JANE S., "Revolution by Fiat: The Context of Policy-Making in Peru," *Western Political Quarterly*, December 1972.

JOFFE, ELLIS, *Party and Army: Professionalism and Political Control in the Chinese Officer Corps, 1949–1964*. Cambridge, Mass.: East Asian Research Center, Harvard University, 1965.

JOHNSON, JOHN J., *The Military and Society in Latin America*. Stanford: Stanford University Press, 1964.

KAU, YING-MAO, *The People's Liberation Army and China's Nation-Building*. White Plains, N.Y.: International Arts and Sciences Press, 1973.

KENNEDY, GAVIN, *The Military in the Third World*. New York: Scribner's, 1974.

KIM, C. I. EUGENE, "The South Korean Military Coup of May 1961: Its Causes and the Social Characteristics of Its Leaders," in Jacques van Doorn, ed., *Armed Forces and Society: Sociological Essays*. The Hague: Mouton, 1968.

———, "The Military in the Politics of South Korea: Creating Political Order," in Morris Janowitz and Jacques van Doorn, eds., *On Military Intervention*. Rotterdam: Rotterdam University Press, 1971.

———, "Transition from Military Rule: The Case of South Korea," *Armed Forces and Society*, Spring 1975.

KIM, SE-JIN, *The Politics of Military Revolution in Korea*. Chapel Hill: University of North Carolina Press, 1971.

KRAUS, JON, "Arms and Politics in Ghana," in Claude E. Welch, ed., *Soldier and State in Africa*. Evanston: Northwestern University Press, 1970.

LAPORTE, ROBERT, "Pakistan in 1971: The Disintegration of a Nation," *Asian Survey*, February 1972.

LEE, J. M., *African Armies and Civil Order*. London: Chatto & Windus, 1969.

LEFEVER, ERNEST W., *Spear and Scepter: Army, Police and Politics in Tropical Africa*. Washington, D.C.: Brookings Institution, 1970.

LERNER, DANIEL, AND RICHARD D. ROBINSON, "Swords and Ploughshares: The Turkish Army as a Modernizing Force," *World Politics*, January 1960.

LEVINE, DANIEL H., *Conflict and Political Change in Venezuela*. Princeton: Princeton University Press, 1973.

LEVY, MARION J., "Armed Force Organizations," in Henry Bienen, ed., *The Military and Modernization.* Chicago: Aldine and Atherton, 1971.

LIEUWEN, EDWIN, *Arms and Politics in Latin America,* rev. ed. New York: Praeger, 1961.

———, *Generals vs. Presidents: Neomilitarism in Latin America.* New York: Praeger, 1964.

LINZ, JUAN J., "The Future of an Authoritarian Situation or the Institutionalization of an Authoritarian Regime: The Case of Brazil," in Alfred Stepan, ed., *Authoritarian Brazil: Origins, Policies and Future.* New Haven: Yale University Press, 1973.

LOFCHIE, MICHAEL F., "The Uganda Coup: Class Action by the Military," *Journal of Modern African Studies,* No. 1, 1972.

LOWENTHAL, ABRAHAM F., "Peru's 'Revolutionary Government of the Armed Forces': Background and Context," in Catherine McArdle Kelleher, ed., *Political-Military Systems.* Beverly Hills: Sage Publications, 1974.

LUCKHAM, ROBIN, *The Nigerian Military: A Sociological Analysis of Authority and Revolt.* Cambridge: Cambridge University Press, 1971.

LUTTWAK, EDWARD, *Coup d'Etat: A Practical Handbook.* New York: Knopf, 1969.

MAUNG, MYA, "The Burmese Way to Socialism: Beyond the Welfare State," *Asian Survey,* June 1970.

MAYFIELD, JAMES B., *Rural Politics in Nasser's Egypt.* Austin: University of Texas Press, 1971.

McALISTER, LYLE M., "Recent Research and Writings on the Role of the Military in Latin America," *Latin America Research Review,* No. 1, 1966.

McALISTER, LYLE M., et al., *The Military in Latin American Sociopolitical Evolution: Four Case Studies.* Washington, D.C.: Center for Research in Social Systems, 1970.

McKINLAY, R. D., AND A. S. COHAN, "Military Coups, Military Regimes, and Social Change," paper presented at the 1974 Meeting of the American Political Science Association, Chicago.

———, "A Comparative Analysis of the Political and Economic Performance of Military and Civilian Regimes: A Cross-National Aggregate Study," *Comparative Politics,* October 1975.

MICHAELS, ALBERT L., "Background to a Coup: Civil-Military Relations in Twentieth Century Chile and the Overthrow of Salvadore Allende," paper presented at the Inter-University Seminar on Armed Forces and Society, Buffalo, 1974.

MINERS, N. J., *The Nigerian Army: 1956–1966.* London: Methuen, 1971.

MITTELMAN, JAMES H., "Dependency and Civil-Military Relations," paper presented at the Inter-University Seminar on Armed Forces and Society, Buffalo, 1974.

MORELL, DAVID, "Alternatives to Military Rule in Thailand," *Armed Forces and Society,* Spring 1975.

MORRISON, DONALD G., et al., *Black Africa: A Comparative Handbook.* New York: Free Press, 1972.

NASSER, GAMAL ABDEL, *Egypt's Liberation: The Philosophy of the Revolution.* Washington, D.C.: Public Affairs Press, 1955.

NEEDLER, MARTIN C., *Anatomy of a Coup d'Etat: Ecuador 1963.* Washington, D.C.: Institute for the Comparative Study of Political Systems, 1964.

———, *Political Development in Latin America: Instability, Violence, and Evolutionary Change.* New York: Random House, 1968.

———, "The Latin American Military: Predatory Reactionaries or Modernizing Patriots?" *Journal of Inter-American Studies,* April 1969.

NORDLINGER, ERIC A., "Soldiers in Mufti: The Impact of Military Rule upon Economic and Social Change in the Non-Western States," *American Political Science Review,* December 1970.

———, *Conflict Regulation in Divided Societies.* Cambridge, Mass.: Center for International Affairs, Harvard University, 1972.

NUN, JOSÉ, "The Middle-Class Military Coup," in Claudio Veliz, ed., *The Politics of Conformity in Latin America.* New York: Oxford University Press, 1967.

OCRAN, A. K., *A Myth is Broken.* London: Longmans, 1969.

O'DONNELL, GUILLERMO A., *Modernization and Bureaucratic-Authoritarianism: Studies in South American Politics.* Berkeley: Institute of International Studies, University of California, 1973.

OZBUDUN, ERGUN, *The Role of the Military in Recent Turkish Politics.* Cambridge, Mass.: Center for International Affairs, Harvard University, 1966.

PACKENHAM, ROBERT A., *Liberal America and the Third World.* Princeton: Princeton University Press, 1973.

PAUKER, GUY J., "The Role of the Military in Indonesia," in John J. Johnson, ed., *The Role of the Military in Underdeveloped Countries.* Princeton: Princeton University Press, 1962.

PERLMUTTER, AMOS, "From Obscurity to Rule: the Syrian Army and the Ba'th Party," *Western Political Quarterly,* December 1969.

———, "The Arab Military Elite," *World Politics,* January 1970.

———, *Egypt: The Praetorian State.* New Brunswick, N.J.: Transaction Books, 1974.

PINKNEY, ROBERT, *Ghana under Military Rule: 1966–1969.* London: Methuen, 1972.

PRICE, ROBERT M., "Military Officers and Political Leadership: The Ghanaian Case," *Comparative Politics,* April 1971A.

———, "A Theoretical Approach to Military Rule in New States: Reference-Group Theory and the Ghanaian Case," *World Politics,* January 1971B.

PUTNAM, ROBERT D., "Toward Explaining Military Intervention in Latin American Politics," *World Politics,* October 1967.

PYE, LUCIAN W., "Armies in the Process of Political Modernization," in John J. Johnson, ed., *The Role of the Military in Underdeveloped Countries.* Princeton: Princeton University Press, 1962A.

———, "The Army in Burmese Politics," in John J. Johnson, ed., *The Role of the Military in Underdeveloped Countries.* Princeton: Princeton University Press, 1962B.

QUIJANO, ANÍBAL, "Nationalism and Capitalism in Peru: A Study in Neo-Imperialism," *Monthly Review,* July–August 1971.

RONFELDT, DAVID, "Patterns of Civil-Military Rule," in Luigi Einaudi, ed., *Beyond Cuba: Latin America Takes Charge of its Future.* New York: Random House, 1973.

ROWE, JAMES W., "The 'Revolution' and the 'System': Notes on Brazilian Politics, Generals and Technocrats," *American Universities Fieldstaff Reports, East Coast South America Series,* XII, No. 5, 1966.

RUDOLPH, LLOYD I., AND SUSANNE HOEBER RUDOLPH, "Generals and Politicians in India," *Pacific Affairs,* No. 1, 1964.

RUSTOW, DANKWART A., *A World of Nations: Problems of Political Modernization.* Washington, D.C.: Brookings Institution, 1967.

SANDERS, THOMAS G., "The Process of Partisanship in Chile," American Universities Fieldstaff Reports, West Coast South American Series, XX, No. 1, 1973A.

———, "The Brazilian Model," American Universities Fieldstaff Reports, East Coast South American Series, XVII, No. 8, 1973B.

———, "Military Government in Chile: The Coup," American Universities Fieldstaff Reports, West Coast South American Series, XXII, No. 1, 1975A.

———, "Decompression in Brazil," American Universities Fieldstaff Reports, East Coast South American Series, XIX, No. 1, 1975B.

———, "Military Government in Chile: The New Regime," American Universities Fieldstaff Reports, West Coast South American Series, XXII, No. 2, 1975C.

SAYEED, KHALIL B., "The Role of the Military in Pakistan," in Jacques van Doorn, ed., Armed Forces and Society: Sociological Essays. The Hague: Mouton, 1968.

SCHMITTER, PHILIPPE C., "Military Intervention, Political Competitiveness and Public Policy in Latin America: 1950–1967," in Morris Janowitz and Jacques van Doorn, eds., On Military Intervention. Rotterdam: Rotterdam University Press, 1971.

SCHNEIDER, RONALD M., The Political System of Brazil: The Emergence of a "Modernizing" Authoritarian Regime, 1964–1970. New York: Columbia University Press, 1971.

SHABTAI, SABI, "The Role of the Military in the Process of National Integration in the New States of Tropical Africa," doctoral dissertation, University of Chicago, 1972.

SHILS, EDWARD, "The Military in the Political Development of New States," in John J. Johnson, ed., The Role of the Military in Underdeveloped Countries. Princeton: Princeton University Press, 1962.

SILVERSTEIN, JOSEF, "Burma: Ne Win's Revolution Considered," Asian Survey, No. 2, 1966.

SKIDMORE, THOMAS E., "Politics and Economic Policy Making in Authoritarian Brazil, 1937–1971," in Alfred Stepan, ed., Authoritarian Brazil: Origins, Policies and Future. New Haven: Yale University Press, 1973.

SKURNIK, W. A. E., "The Military and Politics: Dahomey and Upper Volta," in Claude E. Welch, ed., Soldier and State in Africa. Evanston: Northwestern University Press, 1970.

SOLAÚN, MAURICIO, AND MICHAEL A. QUINN, Sinners and Heretics: The Politics of Military Intervention in Latin America. Urbana: University of Illinois Press, 1975.

STEPAN, ALFRED, The Military in Politics: Changing Pattterns in Brazil. Princeton: Princeton University Press, 1971.

———, "The New Professionalism of Internal Warfare and Military Role Expansion," in Alfred Stepan, ed., Authoritarian Brazil: Origins, Policies and Future. New Haven: Yale University Press, 1973.

———, The State and Society: Peru in Comparative Perspective. Princeton: Princeton University Press, forthcoming.

TAYLOR, CHARLES LEWIS, AND MICHAEL C. HUDSON, World Handbook of Political and Social Indicators, 2nd ed. New Haven: Yale University Press, 1972.

TAYLOR, PHILIP B., The Venezuelan Golpe de Estado of 1958. Washington, D.C.: Public Affairs Press, 1968.

THOMPSON, WILLIAM R., The Grievances of Military Coup-Makers. Beverly Hills: Sage Publications, 1973.

TRAGER, FRANK N., Burma: From Kingdom to Republic. New York: Praeger, 1966.

VATIOKITIS, P. J., *The Egyptian Army in Politics*. Bloomington: Indiana University Press, 1961.

VILLANUEVA, VICTOR, *El Militarismo en el Perú*. Lima: Editorial Juan Mejía Baca, 1962.

——, *¿Nueva Mentalidad Militar en el Perú?* Lima: Editorial Juan Mejía Baca, 1969.

——, *El CAEM y la Revolución de la Fuerza Armada*. Lima: Instituto de Estudios Peruanos, 1972.

VON DER MEHDEN, FRED R., *Comparative Political Violence*. Englewood Cliffs: Prentice-Hall, 1973.

VON VORYS, KARL, *Political Development in Pakistan*. Princeton: Princeton University Press, 1965.

WAI, DUNSTAN M., ed., *The Southern Sudan: The Problem of National Integration*. London: Frank Cass, 1973.

WATERBURY, JOHN, "The Opening: De-Nasserization?" American Universities Fieldstaff Reports, Northeast Africa Series, XX, No. 4, 1975.

WEAVER, JERRY L., "Political Style of the Guatemalan Military Elite," *Studies in Comparative International Development*, No. 4, 1969–70.

WELCH, CLAUDE E., "The Roots and Implications of Military Intervention," in Claude E. Welch, ed., *Soldier and State in Africa*. Evanston: Northwestern University Press, 1970.

——, "Cincinnatus in Africa: The Possibility of Military Withdrawal from Politics," in Michael F. Lofchie, *The State of the Nations: Constraints on Development in Independent Africa*. Berkeley: University of California Press, 1971.

——, "Praetorianism in Commonwealth West Africa," *Journal of Modern African Studies*, July 1972.

WELCH, CLAUDE E., AND ARTHUR K. SMITH, *Military Role and Rule: Perspectives on Civil-Military Relations*. North Scituate, Mass.: Duxbury Press, 1974.

WILLAME, JEAN-CLAUDE, "Congo-Kinshasa: General Mobutu and Two Political Generations," in Claude E. Welch, ed., *Soldier and State in Africa*. Evanston: Northwestern University Press, 1970.

WILLNER, ANN RUTH, "Perspectives on Military Elites as Rulers and Wielders of Power," *Journal of Comparative Administration*, November 1970.

YALMAN, NUR, "Intervention and Extrication: The Officer Corps in the Turkish Crisis," in Henry Bienen, ed., *The Military Intervenes: Case Studies in Political Development*. New York: Russell Sage Foundation, 1968.

ZARTMAN, I. WILLIAM, "The Algerian Army in Politics," in Claude E. Welch, ed., *Soldier and State in Africa*. Evanston: Northwestern University Press, 1970.

ZOLBERG, ARISTIDE R., "Military Intervention in the New States of Tropical Africa: Elements of Comparative Analysis," in Henry Bienen, ed., *The Military Intervenes: Case Studies in Political Development*. New York: Russell Sage Foundation, 1968.

——, "Military Rule and Political Development in Tropical Africa: A Preliminary Report," in Jacques van Doorn, ed., *Military Profession and Military Regimes*. The Hague: Mouton, 1969.

——, "The Military Decade in Africa," *World Politics*, January 1973.

INDEX

Abboud, Ibrahim, 128, 156
Acheampong, Ignatius K., 69
African countries, 6, 38, 39, 42, 79, 122, 127, 130, 209
Afrifa, A.A., 14, 69–70, 74
Algeria, 6, 75–76, 178n
Allende Gossens, Salvador, 10, 24, 28, 71, 76–77, 86n, 89–90
Amin, Idi, 66, 142n
Ankrah, J.A., 128
Arévalo, Juan, 82
Argentina, 19, 23–24, 33, 44n, 51n, 83–85, 102, 117n, 129n, 139, 140, 146, 178n
Arosemena, Julio Carlos, 77
Asian countries, 6, 38, 42, 79, 89, 130, 209
Authoritarian regimes. See Regime structure
Ayub Khan, Muhammed, 56, 134, 158–159

Bangladesh, 39, 158, 160
Batista, Fulgencio, 81
Ben Bella, Ahmad, 75
Benin. See Dahomey
Betancourt, Rómulo, 70
Biafra, 160, 164
Bolivia, 77
Bosch, Juan, 81
Boumédienne, Hawari, 75–76
Branco, Castello, 96, 119n
Brazil, 9, 19n, 24, 33, 51–52, 61n, 72–74, 86n, 89, 95–99, 119n, 120, 135, 139, 144n, 145n, 174, 203n
Bureaucratic characteristics of the military, 43–47, 48n, 120–121, 129

Bureaucrats. See Civilian bureaucrats
Burma, 33n, 118–119, 139, 143–145, 151, 182–186
Busia, Kofi A., 69

Castro, Fidel, 18, 80
Central African Republic, 6
Charismatic leadership, 129
Chile, 10, 24, 26, 33, 64n, 71, 76–77, 86n, 89–90, 174
Civilian bureaucrats and military governments, 28, 53n, 121–122
Civilian chief executives. See Civilian control of the military; Coups, and corporate interests of the military; Coups, and civilian governments' legitimacy deflations; Coups, and civilian governments' performance failures
Civilian control of the military, 6, 10–19, 28, 49n, 71n, 194–195, 209. See also Civilian ethic of officers
Civilian ethic of the officers, 13–14, 88, 95, 98–99, 208
Civilian successor regimes, 200–206
Class and class conflict
    the officers' class backgrounds and positions, 32–34, 172–173
    and the officers' political and economic objectives, 34–37, 79–85, 89–90, 95–96, 146, 170–171, 172–174, 178–189 passim, 200, 202–203
    structure of, 36–37, 79, 81, 82–83, 170–171, 173–174, 178–180 passim

Cohesiveness of the officer corps, 32, 37–42, 44, 46, 56–57, 61–62, 71, 74, 95, 97–98, 105–107, 141, 145–147, 155, 158, 202, 209
Colombia, 88, 91, 140, 209
Colonial armies, 14, 34, 39n, 132, 158
Communal conflict
  communal identities of the officers, 37–42, 175
  impact of military governments upon, 37–42, 59–60, 119, 121, 124, 149–165, 184n
  and military cohesiveness, 37–42
Communism, 9–10, 23, 77–78, 81, 82, 96, 124, 181, 182, 184
Communist China (People's Republic of China), 16–17, 18n, 28
Congo/Brazzaville, 6, 42, 61n, 71n
Corporate interests of the military, 46, 49, 65, 66–67, 68–70, 75
  and coups, 13–14, 17–18, 45–46, 49, 63–82, 84, 85, 95–96, 194–195, 209–210
  and economic policies of military governments, 166–167, 172, 181–182, 189
  and structure of civilian successor regimes, 200–201
Corruption
  among civilian governments, 85–88, 92–93
  among military governments, 88, 127–128
Costa e Silva, Arthur da, 144n
Coups
  and civilian governments' legitimacy deflations, 64, 86, 92–99, 193–194
  and civilian governments' performance failures, 64, 85–92, 193
  and class conflict, 79, 82–85, 89–90, 95–96
  and communal conflict, 40–42
  and corporate interests of the military, 13–14, 17–18, 45–46, 49, 63–82, 84, 85, 95–96, 194–195, 209–210
  displacement coups, 22–23
  frequency of, 5–6, 207–208.
  importance of, 6–7
  planning and executing of, 46–47, 95, 99–107
  and political attitudes of the officers, 55, 57, 79–80, 88, 92
  and professionalism of the officers, 9, 49–53, 54–55, 90, 94, 98n
  public rationale of, 19–21, 65–66, 85–86
  second and third coups, 143, 207–210
  and self-image of the officers, 55, 65–66, 90–91, 94, 195–196

Coups (Cont.)
  and weaknesses of civilian control of the military, 10–19
  assessment of, 192–196
  countercoups (against military governments), 139–141, 145n, 164, 165n, 178
Cuba, 17–18, 28, 80–81

Dahomey, 6, 42, 61n, 91, 120, 122, 140, 145n
Democratic regimes. See Regime structure
Disengagement of military governments. See Instability of military regimes; Restoration of civilian government
Divisions within the military. See Cohesiveness of the officer corps
Dominican Republic, 81

Economic policies and performance
  of civilian governments, 88–90, 93, 166, 169, 177, 199
  of military governments, 22, 25–27, 34–37, 55–56, 113–114, 145–146, 165–189, 199
Ecuador, 45n, 77–78
Egypt, 3–4, 6, 28, 33, 38, 52, 71–72, 100–101, 115–117, 129n, 131–132, 134n
Europe, 6, 11–12, 111n

Farouk, King, 71–72, 101, 116, 186
France, 6n
Frondizi, Arturo, 23, 84, 146

Ghana, 6, 12–14, 38, 53n, 68–70, 74, 75n, 87, 88, 89n, 106, 120, 122, 127–128
Goulart, João, 9, 72–74, 89, 95–99, 135
Governing style of the officers, 45, 49, 59, 117–124, 143, 152, 156–165 passim, 168–169, 185, 209
Governmental legitimacy
  of civilian governments, 64, 78n, 86, 88, 89, 92–99, 133, 197–198
  defined, 92, 124
  of military governments, 124–137, 141n, 197–198
Governmental performance
  of civilian governments, 20, 64, 78n, 85–92, 112, 125, 166, 169, 177, 193, 197–200, 206, 208, 209
  defined, 7–8, 196
  of military governments, 124–137, 149–189, 197–200, 206
Gowon, Yakubu, 164, 165n
Greece, 6n

Guardian-type praetorians, 21–26, 28, 52, 113–114, 142–143, 205
Guatemala, 45n, 64n, 82, 202, 203
Guinea, 17

Hierarchical structure of the military, 43–45
  and instability of military regimes, 145–147
  and military's corporate interests, 45–46, 72–73, 74
  and planning and executing the coup, 46–47, 102–103
  and political attitudes of the officers, 54, 56–57, 59, 94
Honduras, 76

Illía, Arturo, 102
India, 3, 33, 38, 160
Indonesia, 9, 33n, 88, 128, 139, 151
Instability of military regimes, 60, 138–147, 197n, 206, 209–210
Iraq, 6, 29n, 33, 123–124, 151, 178n, 188n
Ironsi, J.T.A. Aguiyi, 104, 119, 120, 161, 164

Jiménez, Perez, 127, 140, 145n

Keita, Modibo, 76, 120

Latin American countries, 2n, 6, 19n, 23, 29n, 33, 34, 44n, 47n, 64, 67, 77, 79–85, 89, 90, 102n, 118n, 121n, 125n, 127, 130, 150n, 172, 173, 178, 179
Lebanon, 40
Libya, 6, 172, 178n
Lin Piao, 18n

Mali, 76, 120, 122
Mao Tse-tung, 5, 16
Mexico, 3, 6
Middle class. See Class and class conflict
Middle Eastern countries, 6, 33, 34–35, 42, 79, 101, 103, 126, 130, 205, 209
Military expertise. See Military professionalism
Military governments, structure of, 109. See also Governing style of the officers; Governmental performance, of military governments; Military in-

Military governments (Cont.)
  tervention, types of
Military intervention. See also Coups
  aftermath of, 191–192, 200–210
  assessment of, 191–207
  defined, 3–4, 28–29
  frequency, 6–7
  public rationale of, 19–21, 65-66, 85–86
  types of, 21–27
Military professionalism,
  dimensions of, 47–49, 54n
  and duration of military regimes, 142
  and intervention, 9, 49–53, 54–55, 90, 94, 98n
Military virtues, 125–128
Mobilization regimes. See Regime structure
Mobutu, Sese Seko, 127n, 132
Moderator-type praetorians, 22–24, 26, 28, 52, 81, 142, 146, 198, 201, 207, 209
Mutinies, 2n, 73, 96, 98, 156

Naguib, Muhammed, 101
Nasser, Gamal Abdel, 4, 52, 56, 72, 115–116, 129, 131, 134n, 177, 186, 187, 189
Nationalism of officers, 58–59, 65–66
National integration. See Communal conflict, impact of military governments upon
Ne Win, 143, 177, 182-185
Nicaragua, 138n
Niger, 76
Nigeria, 6, 33, 38, 40, 41–42, 46–47, 52, 57, 87, 88, 90, 104, 119, 120, 121n, 139, 142, 151, 160–165, 203n
Nkrumah, Kwame, 12–14, 53n, 68–69, 74, 75n, 127, 201
North Korea, 17
North Vietnam, 17
Nyerere, Julius, 17–18

Ocran, A.K., 14, 68–70, 208
Ojukwu, O., 164
Onganía, Juan, 19–20

Pakistan, 39, 88, 125, 134, 139, 151, 157–160, 165, 173n
Paraguay, 138
Park, Chung-hee, 106, 136–137, 204
Paz Estensorro, Victor, 77
Peasantry. See Class and class conflict
P'eng Te-huai, 16
Perón, Isabela, 85

Perón, Juan, 84–85, 117n, 127, 129, 140
Peru, 9, 33, 36n, 51, 52, 67 85n, 177–182
Pinochet Ugarte, Augusto, 26
Political attitudes of the officers, 53–61, 63n, 79–80, 92, 94, 113, 114–119, 122, 152–154, 161, 183–184, 202–203. See also Civilian ethic of the officers
Portugal, 6n
Praetorian Guards of the Roman Empire, 2, 192–194, 196

Qaddafi, Muamar, 172
Qassem, 'Abd al-Salam, 123–124

Regime structure
of civilian regimes, 56, 112, 199, 200, 203
of military regimes, 7, 25–27, 28–29, 55, 57–58, 112–117, 133, 136–137, 176–177, 199, 200–201
typology of, 110–112
Restoration of civilian government, 21, 26, 60. See also Instability of military regimes; Military intervention, aftermath of
Rojas Pinilla, Gustavo, 140
Ruler-type praetorians, 21–23, 26–27, 28, 52, 113–117, 143, 183, 187, 203n, 205

Sadat, Anwar, 4, 28, 116, 196
Self-image of the officers, 45, 54–55, 57, 59, 65–66, 69–70, 74, 75, 90, 94, 96–97, 118, 120, 122, 123, 143, 195–196
Sierra Leone, 3n, 61n, 102n, 120, 122
Soglo, Christophe, 140, 145n

South Korea, 52, 57, 95n, 106–107, 135–137, 139, 204–205
South Vietnam, 9n, 64n, 88
Stroessner, Alfredo, 138
Sudan, 6, 39, 88, 128, 139, 151, 156–157, 165
Suharto, 128
Syria, 6, 29, 91–92, 139, 178n, 188n

Tanzania, 17–18
Thailand, 29, 88, 128n, 131n, 138, 139
Togo, 42
Traditional elite. See Class and class conflict
Turkey, 33, 91, 145n, 202

Uganda, 42, 66, 88
United States reactions to military intervention, 9–10
Upper class. See Class and class conflict
Upper Volta, 6, 91

Velasco, Alvarado Juan, 177–179
Velasco Ibarra, José María, 78
Venezuela, 70, 85, 88, 140, 145n, 205n, 209
Villeda, Morales, 76

Working class. See Class and class conflict

Yahya Khan, Agah Muhammed, 159–160

Za'im, Husni, 92
Zaire, 6, 127n, 132, 139